Fast Cars and Bad Girls

TRAVEL WRITING ACROSS THE DISCIPLINES

THEORY AND PEDAGOGY

Kristi E. Siegel
General Editor

Vol. 9

PETER LANG
New York • Washington, D.C./Baltimore • Bern
Frankfurt am Main • Berlin • Brussels • Vienna • Oxford

Deborah Paes de Barros

Fast Cars and Bad Girls

Nomadic Subjects and Women's Road Stories

PETER LANG
New York • Washington, D.C./Baltimore • Bern
Frankfurt am Main • Berlin • Brussels • Vienna • Oxford

Library of Congress Cataloging-in-Publication Data

Paes de Barros, Deborah.
Fast cars and bad girls: nomadic subjects and women's road stories /
Deborah Paes de Barros.
p.   cm. — (Travel writing across the disciplines; v. 9)
Includes bibliographical references and index.
1. Travelers' writings, American—History and criticism. 2. Austin, Mary Hunter,
1868–1934—Criticism and interpretation. 3. American fiction—Women
authors—History and criticism. 4. Frontier and pioneer life in literature.
5. Women and literature—United States. 6. Automobile travel in literature.
7. Women travelers in literature. 8. Women pioneers in literature.
9. Travel in literature. I. Title. II. Series.
PS366.T73P34   810.9'32—dc22   2004006662
ISBN 0-8204-7087-2
ISSN 1525-9722

Bibliographic information published by **Die Deutsche Bibliothek.**
Die Deutsche Bibliothek lists this publication in the "Deutsche
Nationalbibliografie"; detailed bibliographic data is available
on the Internet at http://dnb.ddb.de/.

Cover art by Trish Cornez

© 2004 Peter Lang Publishing, Inc., New York
275 Seventh Avenue, 28th Floor, New York, NY 10001
www.peterlangusa.com

Printed in the United States of America

To Samantha and Ben, who rode in that car.

And to Carlton, around the next slim bend in the road
    always, yes…

TABLE OF CONTENTS

ACKNOWLEDGMENTS

I want to thank: Emory Elliott (who refused to let this project languish), Katherine Kinney (for love, direction and endless conversation), Geoff Cohen (who kindly led me to Mary Hallock Foote), Myron Simon (who told me to go to school), Michael Clark (who taught me about theory, clarity and work), Sterling Stuckey (who shared his enthusiasm about Paule Marshall), and Heidi Burns (the most discerning, patient and supportive of editors). I am grateful too for the help of Scott Miller (be here now) and Trish Cornez (who is able to describe these women). Trish Cornez created the cover art. Palomar College contributed to this undertaking by funding sabbatical projects while my colleagues and friends in the English Department provided continual support. John Goldsworthy assisted me with my endless questions about technology.

Ann Maioroff remains unwaveringly helpful and kind, and my fellow "bad girls"—you know who you are—continue to create discursive space. Thank you too to Barbara Neault Kelber, my indispensable friend and moral compass on this road and to Paul Rohrer, who resists limitations. Without the insights and unwavering commitment of Carlton Smith I would never have completed this manuscript. Cindi Spencer lent her editing and technological genius, and, once again, without her insistence I'm quite certain that nothing would ever have been finished. Finally, I need to acknowledge Robert and Maria Thereza Rohrer, real and unknowing nomads.

CHAPTER ONE

Points of Departure

On the Road

In narrative, as in travel, all points of origination are contrived and artificial. There are no fixed points of departure, and no one ever really arrives. The linear movement of history is interrupted by the momentary incident; progress is effaced by the immediacy of the present. It is not the conclusion of the narrative that intrigues us; rather, we are enraptured by the details of the story. In this sense at least, travel resembles writing. For as Joan Didion reminds us in her essay "The White Album," writing consists of the fictive imposition of a narrative line upon the inexplicable and "shifting phantasmagoria" of experience (11). The experience that occurs between the borders, between the points of departure and arrival, that space between legitimate and well-defined locales is the subject of this text.

*   *   *

When I was a little girl, my father took me on road trips. An engineer, he loaded the car methodically, stacking suitcases and boxes as he checked off items from a list. No unsecured or unsorted paraphernalia was permitted. We would leave in the predawn hours, planning like Steinbeck's Joads to cross the desert before the heat. We drove in our Nash Rambler on old Route 66 and on thousands of miles of other highways. For me, arrival at a destination was always a letdown, a small disappointment. I liked the worn car seats, the dust, the heat, and the sense of motion. On the road, anything was possible.

Today, I like to say I am tired of driving, but I am not certain this is true. I argue I am not nomadic out of choice, that it is an aspect of contemporary academic life. Yet, the odometer on my dashboard whirls continuously. On my key chain are multiple keys: one for the house, one for the apartment kept near the college, one for the home of a friend and colleague who offers me a ready room, another key for an old bedroom in my parents' house. I play with the idea of keeping a house trailer—a mobile home—out by the beach. When I complain too much and tell my mother I seem to belong nowhere, she reminds me of her own resident alien status and tells me I at least had the good fortune to be born with dual citizenship.

But, of course, in Southern California, I am not the only person who daily navigates the freeways that run like clotted rivers over the landscape. Commuters in imported sports-cars, mini-vans, trucks and the omnipresent sport utility vehicles pour over the highways. Students speak tersely on cell phones, apparently too busy for languid private chats. Jets leave their white tracks in the sky. The average American family moves with alarming frequency. Our adult parents are typically several states away—we talk with them long-distance on Sundays. More land is devoted to cars than to housing. Popular songs and films celebrate the road and the car far more than they sing the praises of domesticity. We are a culture in love with distance. This rabid mobility marks our literature as well.

Road Literature: Traditional Trajectories

The literature of the road is one of the most preeminent American literary tropes. From early frontier narratives to late postmodern literature, the road story has figured significantly. In a sense, to be "on the road," is concurrent with notions of Manifest Destiny and the Puritan "errand into the wilderness." The road is resonant within the concept of nation building; it concerns evolution and becoming and is consequently compatible with the Enlightenment idea of progress. Historically, "going where you wanted, when you wanted was an idea that evolved from our romantic notions of the cowboy and the West" (Boyle 19). The road story, then, is almost a manifesto of American cultural consciousness; it is the mythic representation of history and ideology. American road narratives enact our national drama and examine the very mythology of freedom. In his *Romance of the Road: The Literature of the American Highway*, Ronald Primeau contends road narratives explore the "sacred" space of the American road through the consistent reapplication of dominant literary tropes. Using Bakhtin's notion of "genre memory," Primeau suggests repetition of the literary traditions, associated with the road, allow for a certain credibility and a willingness to provide license to the hero and his *Bildungsroman*.

> Central to the pattern is the journey of the hero who sets out on a quest, experiences ordeals and ultimately returns triumphant… A recurring hero deed in modern America is the automobile journey with its call to adventure on the open road, its initiation ties of trials, threshold crossings, conflict, return, and resurrection. (Primeau 7)

The road becomes a linear space, across which heroes proceed with fixed purpose and endless innocence and optimism, an optimism and a rewarded faith that is finally shared with the readers of the narrative.

But this mythic and optimistic road is a space generally accorded to white males. In accounts of the American road narrative, women and people of color occupy only a liminal periphery. Women and minority authors have historically been largely dismissed from discussions of road literature. But, in the few cases where their presence is considered, women alter the very geography of the road. Even in texts that offer little space to women's narratives, there is at least a grudging admission that the presence of women necessarily offers some modification to the largely masculine terrain of the road novel. Contends Primeau in his masculinized treatment of the narrative road trip,

> American road narratives by women slow the pace, rechart the itineraries and reassess the goals within the conventions of the typical road quest…. Women bring a calming influence to the American road. With not as many highs to seek and maintain, the accompanying lows are modulated. The quest is not so manic…. (Primeau 115–116)

For Primeau, despite laudable scholarly attempts to construct a more inclusive road, a more domesticated, gentle and feminized road, women are ultimately situated—as authors and characters—within the same traditional and sacred space of the heroic and picaresque road. Women are constructed within generic expectations. They function as diversion, scenery and romantic support for the hero's larger quest. In this traditional analysis of the road narrative, women exist typically as objects rather than subjects.

Some critics argue that even as writers attempt to feminize the road with their subject matter, such attention only makes obvious women's textual marginality. Writing about travel and narrative in *Gender, Identity and Place: Understanding Feminist Geographies*, Linda McDowell argues travel has become an increasingly popular and finally consistently masculine endeavor (at least in the popular mind). Insists McDowell:

> Some of the texts are "academic" in nature, but the increase is especially evident in the last few years in popular writing, in the main, but not only by men.... These authors tend to construct themselves as popular heroes, struggling, resisting and overcoming hardships and temptations.... (207–08)

For McDowell, the hero's road leads to selfhood, autonomy and celebrated deeds. By definition, continues McDowell, such accomplishments are masculine. The road of travel narratives is the road of the colonizer rather than the colonized.

Recent works, however, demonstrate a renewed and remarkable interest in women's travel narratives. Frances Bartkowski's *Travelers, Immigrants, Inmates: Essays in Estrangement*, Sidonie Smith's *Moving Lives: Twentieth Century Women's Travel Writing*, Bonnie Frederick and Susan McLeod's *Women and the Journey: The Female Travel Experience*, Marilyn C. Wesley's *Secret Journeys: The Trope of Women's Travel in American Literature*, and Minrose C. Gwin's *The Woman in the Red Dress: Gender, Space and Reading* all address the emergent trope of women's road narratives. Travel always reflects notions regarding the construction of space, borders and liminality; and, as Gwin notes "space is always tied to power relations, that are clearly a subject of crucial interest for feminism and feminist theory" (20). Such studies suggest, not only do women travel, but they also negotiate the road in ways that differ dramatically from traditionally masculine strategies of momentum.

Women's road literature has often been nearly invisible. Within the context of American fiction, the road has been a space and a genre associated primarily with men. As Eric Leed remarks in *The Mind of the Traveler: From Gilgamesh to Global Tourism*, travel is often a "spermatic journey" wherein the dynamism of movement is defined against the more static position of women (221). Jack Kerouac's *On the Road* provides a most dramatic example; it is a narrative written by a man about men for whom women provide only transitory pleasures. On the road traveled by Dean Moriarty and Sal, men pursue adventure and autonomy. Women do not figure significantly into the tale. But Kerouac's book simply operates within a larger tradition. The American road novel, as it is generally conceived, draws upon classical models and the road is, as a result, typically viewed as male terrain. Patterned on the tropes of the heroic quest and earlier picaresque novels, the conventional road story replicates its origins.

Rooted in the frontier experience, the American road novel is history in narrative form. Here, the classically constructed hero confronts a dangerous land and its hostile occupants. Lonely, often homesick, but committed to their particular goals, these heroes persevere. Kerouac's mythic *On the Road* and its narrator Sal are clearly impelled by this impulse. Indeed, the quest for "IT"—meaning in life, purpose, understanding, dharma, salvation—is concurrent with the hero's quest. Says Sal:

> [A] western kinsman of the sun, Dean. Although my aunt warned me that he would get me in trouble, I could hear a new call, and see a new horizon.... Somewhere along the line I knew there'd be girls, visions, everything; somewhere along the line the pearl would be handed to me. (Kerouac 8)

For Sal, Dean functions as a frontier guide, a proverbial Daniel Boone, who will lead him away from shallow domesticity and into the territory of a hardy manhood. Sal and the protagonists like him follow a migratory pattern. They are in pursuit of a particular goal; they travel in search of "the pearl." Dean ushers Sal down a road that offers experience and freedom, and at least the possibility of sex, romance and meaning.

While the American "westering" experience offered potential freedom and riches to its heroes, it also placed them in a kind of exile.

At times dangerous, the road was a space that celebrated individuation but also cursed the hero with an attenuated loneliness. Often alone and in unfamiliar territory, the hero traveled a road that was both glorified and feared. The road was both the space of the lost Garden and a devilish landscape. Even *On the Road*, the very bible of road narratives is marked by this duality. In the closing pages of the novel, Dean drops in upon a newly disillusioned Sal. "As in a dream I saw him tiptoe in from the dark hall in his stocking feet. He couldn't talk anymore" (Kerouac 304). Too many adventures, train rides, rides in "cabooses—old hard bench coaches" have undone Dean. Unable to persuade others, Dean emerges as pathetic, "sorrowful," foolish, and above all, alone. Riding off to a concert, Sal watches Dean disappear through the rear-view mirror. Like his frontier counterparts, Dean Moriarty, the romantic king of the road is also an exile.[1]

The same pattern, wherein the road is portrayed as both the space of sacred adventure and, alternately, as the empty place of exile, is seen repeatedly in American literature. This attitude reflects both the complexity of the wilderness experience, and a growing intuition that to journey into the perfect, natural world inevitably destroys that Edenic space. As has been noted extensively elsewhere, and in particular by Henry Nash Smith in his classic text *Virgin Land: The American West as Symbol and Myth*, the American road hero emerges as a kind of young Adam—both a naïve host of the Garden and a doomed wanderer. Thus, James Fenimore Cooper's Natty Bumppo is at once enraptured by the natural world, repelled by the artifice of "civilization," and yet aware the natural Eden of his youth is lost to him. Cooper's hero is both hopeful and nostalgic; the end he seeks is both the literal completion of his task and a return to a better world.

> Chingachgook and his friend left the spot [the lake] with melancholy feelings. It had been the region of their First Warpath and it carried the minds of both to scenes of tenderness as well as to hours of triumph... Time and circumstance have drawn an impenetrable mystery...[for] We live in a world of transgressions and selfishness.... (Cooper 508)

For Cooper, the road is both a pre- and a postlapsarian space, a place between a vanished past and a possibly redemptive future. Like

Kerouac's Sal, the traditional road hero dreams of finding "IT," and journeys forward in hope of arriving at some destination. But, there are other roads.

Woman as Nomadic Subject

Unlike the masculine hero who wants to get "somewhere" in particular, there are characters who move, oblivious of destination. These figures, blind to nostalgia and any sense of arrival, are nomadic—they are going, but going nowhere or, perhaps, anywhere. From this dramatically different figuration comes an oppositional aesthetic and narrative purpose. Born outside heroic consciousness, the nomad moves only for the purpose of moving and creates a narrative that resists the linear mobility of the conventional road.

Rosi Braidotti suggests in her text, *Nomadic Subjects: Embodiment and Sexual Difference in Contemporary Feminist Theory*, that the nomad is a conceptual figuration, a way of understanding movement through categories and the blurring of boundaries. The nomadic figure emerges as an emblem of hybridity, an expression of "polyglot practices" and aesthetics (Braidotti 8). Homeless (and thus always and never at home), the nomad responds to situational needs, and reads

> ...invisible maps, or maps written in the wind, on the sand and stones, in the flora... The desert is a gigantic map of signs for those who know how to read them, for those who can sing their way through the wilderness. (Braidotti17)

The nomad operates in opposition to the migrant who moves from one clearly defined destination to another, who retains nostalgia for his "origins," as he pursues a purposeful progress. For the nomad, just as there can be no arrival there is no fixed point of departure and no point of origin. Indeed, the nomad resists this very sense of fixed territory, her consciousness emerging as a site of political and epistemological resistance. Argues Braidotti:

> They [nomads] enact a rebellion of subjugated knowledges. The nomadic

> tense is the imperfect: it is active, continuous; the nomadic trajectory is
> controlled speed. The nomadic style is about transitions and passages
> without predetermined destinations or lost homelands. The nomad's
> relationship to the earth is one of transitory attachment.... (25)

Nomadic consciousness is the exploration of movement between borders; the nomad can never really arrive.

Just as there is no final point or destination, the nomad (unlike the wandering road hero) has no space of origin. This lack of origination or destination is significant because these missing finite determinants place the nomad outside of the system of capital—a system that must culminate with the finality of production—and apart from the legitimacy conferred by clear origination. Roaming outside of genealogy, the nomad operates as Deleuze and Guattari's "schizophrenic," producing nothing, lacking obvious objective relations, desiring only desire. "[T]he desiring-production subjugates social production...we are claiming the famous right to laziness, to nonproductivity, to dream and fantasy production..." (*Anti-Oedipus* 380). Deleuze and Guattari term the "nomad subject a residuum," someone born in the space between "the act of producing and the product" (*Anti-Oedipus* 26). The nomad then functions as a kind of terrorist, undermining the familial course of capital.

The nomadic women, who are the subject of this text, resist the structuring of desire. They refuse to become "desiring machines" (Deleuze and Guattari, *Anti-Oedipus* 5). Typically, they live lives outside of conventional coupling. Their histories are dotted with fractured romantic relationships. In the literature examined here, nomadic road women frequently experience heterosexual connection but find these relationships impossible to sustain. Often, their closest associates are children or other women. Outside the "desiring machine," these nomadic women fail to produce "surplus value"—typically expressed as inheritance, citizenship and the reproduction of bourgeois culture (Deleuze and Guattari, *Anti-Oedipus* 35–39). Instead, women nomads ignore the regulating effect of masculinity and reject the definition offered by the phallic signifier. Disorderly and disjunctive, nomadic women are dangerous to the patriarchal landscape of capital.

This danger is not only theoretical. As Deleuze and Guattari maintain in *Nomadology: The War Machine*, it is the function of "the State" to "striate the space," "not only to vanquish nomadism, but to control migrations...to establish a zone of rights over an entire 'exterior'" (59). The nomad's erasure of borders necessarily results in despotism, violence and subversion, for culture cannot allow resistance to boundaries and property. The nomad will always transgress such "despotic formations" because:

> [N]omad space lies between two striated spaces: that of the forest, with its gravitational verticals, and that of agriculture, with its grids and generalized parallels...being "between" also means that smooth space is controlled by these two flanks, which limit it, oppose its development...it turns against them, gnawing away at the forest on one side, on the other side gaining ground on the cultivated lands...the nomads turn first upon the forest and the mountain dwellers, then descend upon the farmers.... (Deleuze and Guattari, *Nomadology* 57)

The nomad's resistance, however lyrical, will always prove problematic for the more conventional and settled establishment.

In *America*, the late Jean Baudrillard considers the destructive and powerful capacity of obsessive travel, and the guerilla quality claimed by a nomadic culture. The culture of perpetual motion erases ideas of history and "exterminates" fixed meanings. Reading the United States as a nomadic state, Baudrillard suggests nomadic space is a "seismic form: a fractal, interstitial culture born of a rift...you have to follow its own rules..." (10). Such "seismic" spaces threaten established order as they threaten western notions of law, progress and time. Nomadic space undermines the legitimizing force of history and replaces it with the "immoral" moment. Civic authority is replaced with situational rules. Contends Baudrillard:

> Driving is a spectacular form of amnesia. Everything is to be discovered, everything is to be obliterated...the secondary brilliance of the journey begins, that of the excessive, pitiless distance, the infinity of anonymous faces and distances of certain miraculous geological formations, which ultimately testify to no human will, while keeping intact an image of upheaval.... The only question in this journey is: how far can we go in the extermination of meanings, how far can we go in the non-referential

desert…without cracking up? (9–10)

Ceaseless and undefined motion possesses an inherent violence toward fixed signification and traditional concepts of culture, and must inevitably undermine the familiar and the legitimate.

The theory of the nomad and the deterritorialization that accompanies this figure have obvious reverberations within the larger discourses of postmodernism and feminism. Clearly, postmodernism's claim of de-centeredness and play are not incompatible with nomadism.

More significant for this discussion however, are the ways deterritorialization and nomadic consciousness reverberate within contemporary discussions of feminism and, finally, women's literature. Resistance to hegemonic and patriarchal discourse marks both feminist and nomadic consciousness. Nomadism reflects a kind of constructed subjectivity—a subjectivity that is consistent with certain aspects of feminist discourse(s). But, if women are often affiliated with the nomadic sensibility through a certain shared subjectivity, the woman traveler—the literal woman nomad who ventures into the reality of the road—frequently forms a profound relationship with the notion of the nomad. That is to say, not only are women illustrations of a more vague nomadic theory, they function in the most literal sense as nomadic wanderers. Freed from the static domesticity that has often defined their identities, women travelers come to exist outside their cultural definitions. Their places and their identities become fluid. As Linda McDowell notes, geography and space are often experienced and thus understood in gendered terms.

> Travel, even the idea of traveling, challenges the spatial association between home and women that has been so important in structuring the social construction of femininity in the 'West', in Western social theories… Because it was taken for granted for so long that a woman's place was in the home, the history of her movement was ignored. (206)

Invisible, and inhabiting space in a radically different way, women became associated not with the heroic travel between borders, but with the silent navigation of the borders themselves. This is the terrain of the nomad.

In particular, women's road literature and travel narratives illustrate the nomadic subject position, each text situated within the specificity of historical contexts. It is the purpose—a merely situated purpose since the nomad can have no final objective—of this book to examine certain examples of women's road narrative and to understand these experiences as the voices of the invisible outsiders. These travel texts offer the audible erasure of borders as a kind of polyglot reconfiguration of both genre and geography.

*   *   *

Let us briefly contrast the roads experienced by Mark Twain's fictive Huck Finn and Harriet Beecher Stowe's Eliza. Huck is borne up by the slow-moving wide waters of the Mississippi River as he moves toward the liberation of Jim, his own autonomy and eventual maturity. Interrupted by missteps and miscalculation, he nevertheless moves toward a fixed purpose. Consider now the figure of Eliza, as she hops helter-skelter across the treacherous, fragmenting ice of the Ohio River.

> [W]ith one wild cry she vaulted sheer over the turbid current by the shore, on to the raft of the ice beyond. It was a desperate leap.... The huge green fragment of ice on which she alighted pitched and creaked as her weight came on it, but she stayed there not a moment. With wild cries and desperate energy she leaped to another and still another cake: — stumbling,—leaping,—slipping,—springing upwards again! Her shoes are gone,—her stockings cut from her feet,—while blood marked every step; but she saw nothing, felt nothing, till dimly, as in a dream, she saw the Ohio side. (Stowe 72)

For Eliza, the river/road is treacherous. It will not bear her weight. She has no permanent geographic destination. Her trip is not about individuation or the autonomy of the self. Eliza has no fixed goal. Her comprehension and embrace of unoccupied space is radically different from Huck's. Eliza's purpose is bound with her child; she will go where she must to protect her son.

Similarly, Frederick Douglass' *Narrative* and Harriet Jacobs' *Incidents in the Life of a Slave Girl* also exemplify the contrast between the roads traveled by male and female narrators. The very titles of the works delineate these distinctions. *Narrative of the Life of Frederick Douglass* proclaims a structure that is linear and progressive, and a straight if difficult path toward a noble goal. *Incidents* suggests something different, pages written by the author's account at "irregular intervals, whenever I could snatch an hour from my housekeeping duties" (Gates 335). And, in fact, Jacob's life and movement are fragmented and circular. She escapes from a master only to spend seven years in a tiny airless attic from which she can peer at her children. Her freedom is finite; she has housekeeping tasks and her duties to her "benefactor" Mrs. Bruce. "The dream of my life is not yet realized," writes Jacobs near the end of her work (Gates 513). She is "free," but that rhetorical and social designation has only a limited meaning for Jacobs; freedom provides no final, purposeful goal. Unlike Douglass, Jacobs has not completed the quest motif. Her accomplishment and freedom are limited. "We are as free from the power of slaveholders as are the white people of the north; and though that, according to my ideas, is not saying a great deal" (Gates 513). Unlike Douglass who perceives and celebrates a nearly infinite future as a free man, Jacobs, and her narrative and her travels are constructed by a different sense of narrative space. For Jacobs, space and direction are always delimited by familial and historic circumstance. As surely as she is confined by the walls that make up her attic chamber for seven years, Jacobs is confined by the cultural impositions of motherhood, by the "feminine" compunction to give service, and by the implication that it is the space between boundaries —the incidents and not the arrival—wherein the story occurs.

Bad Girls on the Road: Women's Stories

As Stowe and Jacobs' narratives make clear, there is a pervasive presence of children in nearly all of the women's texts discussed here. But this is not to say that the women constructed through these texts reify some essentialist notion of women and maternity. In fact, I venture to say quite the opposite is true. To a certain extent, of course, women's close involvement with their children is an aspect of very apparent specific historic conditions, conditions so obvious they do not need to be belabored here. But these texts address a more important issue. Within these stories, maternity is largely independent of patriarchy. Fathers are left, or unknown, or simply insignificant within the larger tale of the text. Thus, in her famous captivity narrative Mary Rowlandson makes relatively little mention of her husband, but sheds tears for her dead sister and her own dead baby. Mary Hallock Foote and Mary Austin create fictional masculine figurations that are deluded, alcoholic and unable to cope. In *Play It As It Lays*, Joan Didion's Carter is at once autocratic and limited, controlling and finally duplicitous, while Braverman's seldom-mentioned father figure in *Wonders of the West* is a weak man who makes the mother of the protagonist ill. "I'm thinking I wish Ernie were dead," mutters Braverman's Roxanne (26). And in Mona Simpson's similarly structured *Anywhere But Here*, all of the father figures are elusive and powerless. "Will Ted come?" wonders Simpson's Ann about her stepfather, as she and her mother prepare to leave for California. "He couldn't pass," says Adele. "Not in a million years" (Simpson 109). These narratives leave little space for the conventional masculine hero.

The texts under discussion here construct an alternative vision of familial life. Mothers and their children, most particularly their daughters, emerge as one another's primary love objects. This has the effect of destabilizing patriarchy. Heterosexual romance is consequently mostly transitory. The elaborate network of women, their children and friends creates a kind of viable social alternative and new way of being in the world. Within this new space, the women follow different rules. We can see this most vividly, perhaps, in Paula Sharp's *Crows Over a Wheatfield*, where the women in the text operate a new and illegal version of the Underground Railroad, a mobile system dedicated to freeing women and children from abusive men. Legitimated, patriarchal law has little sway within this confine. The effect of these maternal relations is tremendous. Rather than supporting myths and stereotypes of the maternal body and self, women's travel texts construct maternity as a point of resistance to patriarchal power. Necessarily matriarchal, these texts and their characters exist outside of conventional patriarchal rules. In consequence, nomadic women automatically appear as subversive. The road of the nomad, the road traveled in women's road narratives, is not simply traversed in a different manner and marked with various subtle sensitivities. It is a new space, a space between borders, a site outside compliance, a place often outside linear narrative and memory.

*   *   *

"Resistance and Revisions in the Wilderness: Women's Road Narratives and the Mythologies of Frontier Space" deals with the famous narrative of Mary Rowlandson, the often obscure writings of pioneer women and the "frontier" novels of Mary Hallock Foote. These writings provide an alternative canon, one that stands in opposition to the popular depiction of the frontier woman as an image of Rebecca Boone—the happy helpmate to her husband in his errand into the wilderness. In these texts women narrators resist the national impulse and narrative that has carried them westward. Some of these authors who, like Mary Rowlandson, wrote under the watchful eye of some male authority were forced to codify their resistance. Others, writing in the safe anonymity of their diaries were more forthright. Most of these women knew their audience and wrote essentially two texts, one text that kept in tune with the popular lexicon and the other secret and encoded. In decoding these frontier messages and in understanding the ways depression and even subversion are manifest in the language, Freud and Kristeva's works on melancholy figure prominently. The near erasure of the work of Mary Hallock Foote from the western canon and the very appropriation of her voice suggests to what degree alternative voices have been silenced.

Part of the road narrative has classically included the genre of the nature writer. The romantic tradition celebrated the euphoria of difficult expeditions. In the American West, naturalists and explorers like John Muir, Clarence King and John Wesley Powell sang of the delights of the country's untrammeled spaces. These spaces were perceived as beautiful, godly, and assuredly male. "Reclaiming the Territory: Mary Austin and Other (Un)Natural Girls" examines the decidedly different space inhabited by women (un)naturalists, women who do not necessarily celebrate the land and who undermine women's traditional frontier posture. Nomads, these women are subversive in the sense they occupy an entirely different "natural" West. The Eden of the romanticists and the American transcendentalists erodes in the work of women nature writers. The natural world, while sometimes beautiful, is often far from nurturing.

One of the tropes of the traditional road narrative involves the need of a young man to find his own identity through an altercation and subsequent separation from an older man who stands as a kind of father figure. Perhaps the most classic depiction of this can be seen in the film *Red River*, where the young Montgomery Clift ultimately rejects John Wayne and drives the cows his own way into the city of Abilene. In contrast, many women writers/textual selves travel a path that leads not to autonomy and individual selfhood, but instead winds backward, seeking reconnection with a matriarchal community. "In Search of the Maternal: Mothers and Daughters on the Road" explores the ways Dorothy Allison, Chelsea Cain, Beverly Donofrio, Barbara Kingsolver and Mona Simpson construct the road as a space that permits women to return to the mother as the primary love object, revising the strictly heterosexual identity required within patriarchal territory. The road provides sufficient space for interrogation of this nexus.

Conventional linear history traces a familiar path. Innocence is lost. After the Garden comes the Fall. Postlapsarian literature mourns the past, lost, golden time in elegiac terms. But postmodern eulogy differs a bit in that it claims no belief in the reality of the lost golden moment. Rather, one afflicted with a postmodern sensibility mourns with exquisite irony, acknowledging finally no so-called golden era ever existed. This ironic eulogy is the subject of "The Horsewomen of the Postapocalypse: Where the Road Marks the End of the Modern World." Here, in the work of Kate Braverman, Joan Didion, and Marilynne Robinson, the road emerges as both the space where one mourns loss and the site simultaneously that marks the absence—the unreality—of any loss at all. The literature of this absence acts as what Jacques Derrida in "Of an Apocalyptic Tone Recently Adopted in Philosophy" terms "a sending"—an encoded message prophesying some vast societal change (86).

For the contemporary authors discussed here, as well as their characters, the apocalypse has already occurred. In this fractured landscape there are no wonders, and the lost ideal world is revealed to be only illusion. "I've seen the Wonders of the West and I'm through being nickled and dimed," proclaims Roxanne, the cynical and mythical mother in Kate Braverman's road story, *Wonders of the West* (251). As Roxanne tours a frontier museum she muses on the fraudulent qualities of the exhibits and the celebration of fictionalized heritage. As she and her daughter observe a small town Fourth of July, Roxanne remarks, "this stuff is for hayseeds" and the naively credulous (Braverman 235).

The nomad rejects cultural nostalgia, easy sentimentality and the illusions and clichés offered by mainstream society. "Nomadic feminism ...argues that political agency has to do with the capacity to expose the illusion of ontological foundations," insists Braidotti (35). The nomadic sensibility reads through constructed cultural "truths." In their drives along the highways the women in travel narratives subvert the cultural status quo, exposing its epistemological weaknesses and eroding its claim to presence. These women's narratives are thus no ordinary literature; they mark what Julia Kristeva in *Black Sun: Depression and Melancholia* calls our "apocalyptic" epoch (223). In such eras, contends Kristeva, rumors reach the world regarding the end of the accepted and understood universe. And, the literature that records these rumors speaks of revelation.

If an older world must necessarily deconstruct itself, a new and better world can be constructed outside of society's parameters. On the road, it is possible to envision another way to live. While formal utopias tend to be rigid, a nomadic vision constantly shifts to incorporate a variety of perspectives and needs. "A New World Made: (Re)Envisioning Utopia from the Road" investigates the very idea of utopia and suggests it is possible to build a fluid, changeable community. Paula Sharp's *Crows Over a Wheatfield*, Sandra Cisneros' "Woman Hollering Creek," Paule Marshall's *Praisesong for the Widow* and Zora Neale Hurston's *Their Eyes Were Watching God* each offer the possibility of a new and better terrain. Only between arrival and departure is any utopian vision possible. Outside patriarchy, outside compulsory heterosexuality, the road and the process of the negotiation of borders allow for a new (and finite) world. Beyond the boundaries of what Lauren Berlant has called the "National Symbolic" exist other options (20). "New models of political and everyday life are always being produced...seeing out of the corner of her eye the hymen, like an asterisk, pointing her in another direction" (Berlant 56). The road to this new world is not linear. It is a space outside boundaries, a state of mind rather than a destination.

*   *   *

So much for the protagonists of this tale. Some years ago a bumper sticker became popular in Southern California. It read "Good Girls Go to Heaven. Bad Girls Go Everywhere Else." This book deals with the "bad" girls and their whereabouts. As characters and authors they are nonconforming, transients in the territory they traverse. If they need to "pass" in the world of "good" girls, they do. If conventional feminine wiles will help them, the gestures appear. They understand identity is always a temporary construct. Because they move outside origin and destination, road women's actions are constructed by their situation and by the momentary historic contingency within which they must operate. The nomadic woman walks outside of conventional ideas of "woman" and outside of contemporary political definitions of "feminist." In "What is Ethical Feminism?" Drucilla Cornell reminds us of debates regarding "good" and "bad" feminism, arguing for the need to make the term inclusive. The author bell hooks reiterates that the classical "trappings" of feminism and womanhood suggesting "prettiness, serenity, understanding, undemanding care and reliability" are tropes associated with the cultural psychical fantasy of womanhood (Nicholson 83). The road woman rejects all universal rules and categories. Her actions are specific to her place and situation. She is at turns pretty, serene, caring, and rabid and schizophrenic and free. She paints her nails red or refuses to comb her hair. She disavows all behavioral codes; she looks at the road and "plays it as it lays." She "blurs boundaries without burning bridges" (Braidotti 4). Whatever her appearance, the

road woman, the nomad is a subversive. This book, *Fast Cars and Bad
Girls*, is about the creation of nomadic consciousness, as it is
expressed in women's road literature.

It is also the task of the nomadic road woman to create
community. Unlike the hero, the nomad does not adopt an ethic of
rugged individualism. Nor does she seek to make new terrain safe for
future domesticity. She simply forges connections. Unlike the rugged
male hero who often travels alone, the nomadic woman is typically
accompanied by children, lovers of either gender, by sisters and by
friends. When she is alone, she seeks out others to hear her story. Her
tale is most often communal, even though the community must
constantly break and reform. The final closing recollections of Harriet
Jacobs' slave narrative concern not the glories of being free, but her
attachment to her grandmother. This attachment is not about
legalisms or bloodlines; it is about love.

The nomadic subject then does not claim origin or destination.
She belongs nowhere and heads no place. She resists the claims of
patriarchy that provide name, family and national identity. She is at
once an outlaw and a citizen of each tiny place wherein she locates
herself, however momentarily. She possesses multiple identities and
no identity. "She has no passport and too many of them" (Braidotti
33). She ignores boundaries. These chapters deal with the nomadic
woman's erasure of borders, her transgressive literary movements
and the fictive space between the countries she transitorily inhabits.

Resistance and Revisions in the Wilderness: Women's Road Narratives and the Mythologies of Frontier Space

The Burning Cabin

Consider Disney's Frontierland. Women in ruffles and exaggerated sunbonnets offer refreshments. Near the docks for the river boat cruise, dance hall girls flip their skirts and kick up their heels in an eternal gesture of innocent coquetry. But around a bend in the river a darker scene emerges. A settler's cabin burns perpetually. The scene is horrific, if barely visible, glimpsed only from the train windows or the forward decks of surrogate steamships. From the island woods come cries that even small children can identify as the terrifying war whoops of Native American warriors. At regular intervals the cavalry sounds its bugle call. No carnage is evident—this is Disneyland after all—but everyone understands what has occurred. Whether the cabin is viewed from the boat or only registered upon some inner screen of the mind, a clear image marks the side of the riverbank. The cabin in the woods burns. Flames dance from its windows. Inside, unseen tragedy unfolds. The burning cabin bespeaks death and ruin.

Strangely, although no figures are evident, the viewer knows the space is female. We picture the thin, haunted face, the dead babies. Sequestered in that cabin lived a woman, brave and alone. That continuously burning celluloid cabin constitutes the eternal flame for American frontier women. And, if we are to believe the lessons of our elementary school history classes and heed the larger popular narrative of American westward experience, these frontier women were stronger than contemporary females, more faithful, more willing to risk death and martyrdom so their partners might tame the West. Claimed by the traditional tale of the frontier, the pioneer woman stands framed, celebrated by the burning cabin.

The role of women in the drama of the road west is enshrined in our national memory. The image of the frontier woman, her face hidden in the recesses of a vast sunbonnet, remains familiar to all of us. Annie Oakley, Calamity Jane, Steinbeck's Ma Joad and the countless women making their way across the prairie find representation within our collective consciousness. The woman framed in the door of the log cabin is as much a part of frontier and road history as the man setting out for new territory. These historic road women are at once pragmatic heroines—sharp shooters and good cooks—and selfless females moving along the road at great personal cost for the benefit of family and nation. Steinbeck's *Grapes of Wrath* provides a poignant picture; abandoned by her husband, her child dead, her family broken and impoverished, Rose of Sharon follows her mother's urgings and takes a starving migrant man to her full breast. Whether they follow the faint wagon tracks of western Pennsylvania, the deep ruts of the Oregon Trail, or escape the Dust Bowl on Route 66, these women nurture a country of anonymous men at their collective breast. Exploited and ignored, the virtuous woman nonetheless finds reverence in masculine road chronicles.

But not all women share the desire to become a national icon. Another kind of woman rejects such celebration as simple and childlike illusion. Not recognizing or caring for the concepts of country or destiny, such women care little for nation building. In motion or standing still, the nomadic woman is not compelled by any vision of Manifest Destiny or familial glory. While our culture ennobles the woman in the burning cabin, women's road narratives often register a surprising resistance to the linear road story. Consciously or unconsciously, they subvert the role they are accorded within the masculinized road narrative, and seek to construct an alternate space. Within this alternative space, a nomadic consciousness develops, a consciousness no longer dominated by a single and fixed point of view. While we are inclined to accept the larger cultural narrative that insists women welcomed their assigned supportive roles, a variety of women's texts undermine this supposition. We think of the fiery cabin as the static space for women, a constant in the ever-roaming, masculine trajectory. But many women writers reject this confinement. As early as the seventeenth century, the road narratives of American women reflect the creation of another social economy, a counterpoised economy that resists the traditional parameters and conventional discourse of the masculine picaresque narrative.

It is not surprising that the creation of alternative forms of frontier consciousness and narrative are often ignored; women play a significant if relatively quiet and stationary role in the traditional canon of frontier literature. Women provide the wandering hero with diversion on lonely nights, a reason for his mission of Manifest Destiny and the domestication of the West, and become finally emblematic of the tamed land itself. Women—good women—are helpmates to their heroes.

Road narratives have long explored the mystique of the feminine. Homer's Odysseus is wed to the faithful Penelope, who waits for her husband for ten long years. Chaucer's Knight tells a tale dedicated to the praise of the fair and virginal Emily, suggesting men take to the road in search of honor, excitement and achievement, and that these elements are represented in the perfect woman. But in the American road novel, the importance of the woman as domestic partner becomes much more central. In part this was because Anglo-Americans brought women and children into the frontier to legitimate their enterprise. Unlike many other explorers, they perceived their endeavor in moral terms. The Anglo-Americans were in search not only of riches and national pride; they came to domesticate a tiny portion of a savage wilderness. As Sacvan Bercovitch notes in his seminal *The Puritan Origins of the American Self*, the Puritans sought to rebuild God's Jerusalem in the New World (97, 98). The New England settlers constructed churches, homes and schools with religious conquest in mind. "They moved from one crisis to the next—physical, institutional, ideological, generational—with their eyes fixed on that prospect" (Bercovitch 98). Thus, Governor John Winthrop was another biblical David and the New England settlements became the New Jerusalem where the Puritans waited for new halcyon days to commence. Continues Bercovitch:

[B]iographically, the New Englander and the Israelites were the correlative

types of Christ; historically, the struggles of the New England saints at the
times...were "chronicled before they happened."... (36)

Within the American enterprise the road west equaled more than a
simple avenue toward adventure; the final destination defined travel
and such an endpoint required the creation of a godly civilization.

Women were an integral part of this project, and the good
woman, patterned upon Rebecca Boone found herself configured into
the masculine text of the frontier. As historian and critic Annette
Kolodny writes in *The Lay of the Land*, the very presence of women
justified the conquest of the territory and women became, in time,
conflated with the idea of the land. Women were the land; like the
land they required a firm hand and willingness for domestication,
and like the land women were the very reason for westward travel.

[T]he European discovery of an unblemished and fertile continent allowed
the projection upon it of a residue of infantile experience in which all
needs—physical, erotic, spiritual and emotional—had been met by an
entity imaged as quintessentially female.... The initial discovery of the
continent, combined with its apparently limitless terrain, provided
Americans with a space of almost three hundred years during which to
believe that infantile fantasies were about to become adult realities, and, as
such, allowed those contents to be "transformed, generalized and put to
use in American culture" through the metaphorical experience of "the
land-as-woman." (Kolodny 153–154)[1]

The land, the process of civilization and women joined together
within a single metaphor.

Rebecca Boone provides the prototype of the frontier woman. She
was, according to Boone historian John Filson, "the first white woman
to stand beside the Kentucky River" (Slotkin, *Regeneration* 286). In his
1794 account in *The Adventures of Colonel Daniel Boone,* Filson refers to
Rebecca as "an Amiable Spouse," leaving her nearly nameless
(Slotkin, *Regeneration* 301). As a spouse, Rebecca consistently and
quietly supports Boone, embracing him publicly after his release from
Indian captivity. In his commentary on the Filson text, Richard
Slotkin notes the textual Rebecca was "subject to the conventional
weaknesses of the conventional sentimental heroine, suffering
deprivation and heartbreak without acquiring a personality of her

own" (*Regeneration* 301). Although she is passive and silent in Filson's narrative, Rebecca remains essential to the Boone mythology. It is her femininity that makes Boone masculine. Rebecca enables Daniel Boone to domesticate the wilderness. An historian subsequent to Filson, Timothy Flint further explores the Boone and Rebecca myth in his 1833 narrative, *Biographical Memoir of Daniel Boone: First Settler of Kentucky.* In Filson's tale, the young Boone follows a deer into the forest "and discovers it is not a deer at all, but a woman" (Slotkin, *Regeneration* 306). The final result of this encounter is Boone's marriage to Rebecca, a marriage that ushers in sexual consummation and the birth of Boone's heroic frontiersman career. In subjugating Rebecca, Boone subjugates nature and the land. The Boone legends suggest domination of the frontier requires Rebecca's acceptance of her role as "amiable spouse," along with the passive sexuality inherent in that role (Slotkin, *Regeneration* 306). The Boone legend and the larger masculine frontier narrative necessitate Rebecca Boone's small but defining presence.

The curious Fire-Hunt myth, an important part of the Boone legend, illustrates how Rebecca's silent sexuality represented the as yet unconquered wilderness. Through an act of symbiosis, Rebecca's body became the land. According to the story, Boone's legendary love of hunting frequently led him to search for prey in dangerous and isolated locations. On a particular night, Boone went hunting with a flaming torch in his hand in order to attract deer. In the darkness, the deer were invisible, only identifiable by the glitter of their two eyes in the torchlight. He was about to fire when he made a startling discovery. His actual target was a woman.

> After a long wait, Boone saw the double gleam and prepared to fire, but some intuition stayed him. He moved toward the gleams, pushed aside the brush, and discovered Rebecca who turned and fled home. ...soon after, Daniel came courting. (Slotkin, *Regeneration* 299)

Rebecca becomes the doe; their bodies merged into a single entity. She is both the reason for and the subject of domestication.

Yet, Rebecca Boone combined the metaphorical and lyrical with real frontier skills and virtues. She was faithful, patient and forgiving. She was also tall and physically strong. She was "a fair shot" and a skilled housekeeper.

> It was she who held the family [and the farm] together when he [Daniel
> Boone] vanished on long hunts, which might last only a season or a couple
> of years. When he was taken by the Shawnee and presumed dead, she
> packed up the family and [traveled]...by herself through Indian country at
> the height of the Indian wars. (Slotkin, *Regeneration* 300)

In short, Rebecca Boone was the ideal frontier woman; her seeming
alliance with nature allowed her to bond with the natural forces of the
land; she was willing to totally support Boone's endeavor, and she
was strong and pragmatic.

In fact, the idea of this idealized frontier woman finds visual as
well as literary representation in a variety of historical texts. Referred
to as the "Madonna of the Trail," this image celebrates the frontier
woman in art and poetry. Typically these images, like the statue in
Lamar, Colorado, depict the frontier woman as a kind of earth mother
in a sunbonnet, stalwart in her vision as a child clings to her long skirt
and a baby sleeps in her arms. An alternative vision appears in
W.H.D. Koener's oil painting of "The Madonna of the Prairie."
Framed by a halo of light created by the wagon top, this Madonna is
young, large eyed, and virginal and yet obviously fertile. Saint-like,
she stares from the wagon, ready to sacrifice herself to any necessity.
Like Rebecca Boone, these Madonna icons reflected what historian
Barbara Welter called "The Cult of True Womanhood," and an
insistence that the frontier woman demonstrate piety, purity,
domesticity and submissiveness (Armitage and Jameson 151–156).
This cult finds representation in numerous histories of the frontier
experience. Dee Brown's 1958 account of pioneer women records in
its very title, *The Gentle Tamers: Women of the Old Wild West*, the
persistent notion that women must "tame" the wild frontier.[2]

Not all frontier women struggling westward were a Rebecca
Boone or a Prairie Madonna. Rebecca Boone represents a social
fantasy of a subordinate feminine understood only in "binary
opposition of masculine/feminine" (Butler, *Gender* 36). As Judith
Butler maintains, masculinity by definition requires a passive
feminine presence and, thus, masculine narratives need the presence
of the Madonna. Yet, the desire to succor suffering heroes is not a

resonant theme in the road narratives composed by women. Many women were less than celebratory of their mission and resisted—sometimes overtly but often with covert action—the assigned role of women in the errand into the wilderness. The texts of these women suggest a different understanding of the confined frontier cabin. Nearly invisible, less compliant, women haunt the narrative of the road in an effort to remake it. Their texts are both mimetic and subversive, reminding us of Luce Irigaray's notion of mimesis. In women's road narratives, women share certain qualities with their mythic (more domesticated) and male-derived literary ancestors. Nomadic women are similar to their more conventional frontier sisters, but also utterly different. Such women use frontier lexicon in order to supplant the discourse. For as Irigaray notes, in *This Sex Which Is Not One*, mimesis constitutes both a recapitulation and a subversion of the original.

> To play with mimesis is thus, for a woman, to try to recover the place of her exploitation by discourse, without allowing her self to be simply reduced to it. It means to resubmit herself...but so as to make "visible" by an effort of playful repetition what was supposed to remain invisible: the cover up of a possible operation of the feminine in language. (Irigaray, *This* 76)

Women's travel narratives problematize and reconstruct the space of the road. Using a traditional masculine trope and strategy—the road and the hero's quest—women write entirely new and spectral frontier texts.[3]

Mary Rowlandson: Not Like Rebecca

Mary White Rowlandson's captivity narrative, *The Sovereignty and Goodness of God, Together With the Faithfulness of His Promises, Displayed; Being a Narrative of the Captivity and Restoration of Mrs. Mary Rowlandson*, constitutes what is perhaps the most famous of women's frontier road stories. Published in 1682, Rowlandson's text speaks of the atrocities of the Indian Other while it celebrates God and Increase Mather's plan for the colonies.[4] As Bercovitch notes, captivity narratives like Rowlandson's

> ...transform what elsewhere would be considered evidence of private
> regeneration into a testimonial for the colonial cause. Mary Rowlandson
> proves through her capture and long imprisonment that 'New England's
> present troubles are both justified and temporary.' (Bercovitch 116–117)

Encoded however, within its more apparent message, Rowlandson's text offers something of a cultural critique and an admission that Rowlandson's unsought travel experiences distanced her from the farm wife she once was.

Famously, Rowlandson's narrative describes the February 1676, morning massacre of most of the inhabitants of her Lancaster, Pennsylvania farm. Victims of King Philip's War (or Metacom's War, 1675–76), seventeen of Rowlandson's relatives and friends, including a sister, brother-in-law and nephew, died that morning, leaving Rowlandson's daughter Sarah fatally injured and Rowlandson hurt. The house and barns were burned, and Rowlandson, her wounded daughter, her son, Joseph, her older daughter, Mary, and twenty-four others were taken hostage by the attackers, Native Americans Rowlandson refers to as the Narragansett tribe. In fact, Rowlandson's captors included members from a variety of tribes, including the Narragansetts, the Nipmucks and the Wampanoags (Rowlandson 25). Rowlandson was separated from her son and older daughter, and her baby died soon after. For eleven weeks, Rowlandson traveled with the tribes until her husband, minister Joseph Rowlandson, who was in Boston at the time of the attack, ransomed her. The Rowlandsons subsequently settled in Wethersfield, Connecticut, and shortly thereafter, Joseph Rowlandson passed away. As Neal Salisbury (editor of the more recent 1997 edition of the frequently republished text) explains, "the circumstances under which Rowlandson began composing her narrative are not made explicit in any surviving evidence" (Rowlandson 40). Historical conjecture places the writing of the narrative in late 1677 and early 1678, since Rowlandson writes her book as if Joseph Rowlandson were still alive. Her words focus upon her attempt to deal with the trauma and loss experienced during her captivity.

Published in 1682 the text found a wide readership and it is popularly assumed "Increase Mather played a central role in getting the manuscript published." In fact, most historians suggest the preface—the "per Amicum"—was written by Mather (Rowlandson 44). The narrative was originally published by Samuel Green, a printer who was greatly aided in his work by the patronage of Mather and consequently in his debt (Breitwieser 7). Further, there seems little doubt Rowlandson and Increase Mather were acquainted. Rowlandson's own family (before her marriage) had been prominent and both Mather and the Rowlandson moved in religious circles. As Mitchell Breitwieser comments,

> Rowlandson probably knew Mather rather well. Her husband was a minister, which would have brought the family into Mather's sphere of acquaintance, an association that led Joseph to seek Mather's assistance in the negotiations for her release... Rowlandson could not have failed to perceive what Mather would have wanted from a narrative such as hers.... (Breitwieser 7)

Rowlandson's narrative quickly became one of the most frequently read works in both the colonies and in England. This popularity was augmented by the promotion and advertisements offered by its publisher, Samuel Green, Jr., who placed descriptions of the text within the pages of other popular books, citing details that would "whet a prospective reader's appetite" (Derounian 249).[5] Rowlandson's text gained repute as a popular statement concerning the correctness of the Puritan errand, and the heathen nature of the therefore expendable Indians. Rowlandson ultimately appears in the account as what Christopher Castiglia in his work on captivity and kidnapping terms "Our Lady of the Massacre" (19). In *Bound and Determined: Captivity, Culture-Crossing, and White Womanhood: From Mary Rowlandson to Patty Hearst*, Castiglia argues Rowlandson becomes the prototype for the white American captive female, emblematic of the sinister forces allied against domesticity, womanhood and American destiny. Traditional readings of captivity tales suggest both the need for militant vigilance against the peril of the Other and the moral superiority of domestic capitalism. Enshrined by narrative, only shortly after telling her tale, Rowlandson who had obtained the prestigious title of "Mistress" (instead of Goodwife) through her advantageous marriage to minister Joseph Rowlandson, remarries (Rowlandson 16). As Mistress Talcott, Rowlandson nearly disappears from history, contained forever within a seemingly conventional text.

Whatever the overt expressions of Puritan devotion that occur in Rowlandson's words, there is also much that suggests another possible reading. *A Narrative of the Captivity and Restoration* is filled with references to the "hell hounds," the butchering "bloody Heathen ready to knock us on the head if we stirred out," those "Barbarous Creatures," and to "the lively resemblance of hell" found in an Indian camp. Paired with this imagery are the depiction's of the settlers as "Christians lying in their blood," "Sheep torn by Wolves," and innocents shown the "wonderful power of God." But, in a narrative that was produced under the watchful eyes of Increase Mather and written to compel readers to "Stand still and see the Salvation of the Lord," there is some marked discomfort caused not only by Rowlandson's Native American captors, but also by her required role of pious frontier woman (Rowlandson 112). As Rowlandson ran from her burning cabin and entered the pages of a popular text, her actual experience was subjugated by a larger, popular representation. Indeed, if Rowlandson occupied the frontier log cabin that has become emblematic of the American western experience—that is to say if Rowlandson's self has become obscured by its representation as a sublime Puritan, frontier woman—her cabin and her narrative are haunted by Irigaray's specters. There is another more covert Rowlandson who lives in the text, a woman existing outside popular narrative.

As numerous historians have discussed, King Philip's War was a violent episode that imperiled the entire Puritan enterprise. Led by Metacom, who the English called King Philip, (and who is sometimes referred to as Metacomet) the War was a part of an ambitious project. Metacom successfully formed an intertribal coalition of the Wampanoag Indians with the Algonquian tribes (the Nipmucks, the Pocassets and the Narragansetts) and made alliances with other tribes that participated only in a limited fashion (Breitwieser 5). So sudden and violent was this War of 1675 that the tribes nearly annihilated the colonists dwelling outside of Boston or Plymouth. Commenting upon the war and its impact on the sparse colonial population, historian Richard Saunders Webb notes the "proportion of dead to living may have been higher than in any subsequent American war" (Breitwieser 6). Mitchell Breitwieser augments this description.

> Many of the settlements, including Providence, Rhode Island were destroyed, the accumulated capital of the previous generations consumed, and general prosperity was injured so severely that it would not regain its prewar level for a century...a few of the colonists...shared a view that the theocratic elite had both needlessly provoked and mismanaged the war. (6)

So painful and precarious were the general conditions it seemed natural for some of the colonists to question the direction and scope of the Puritan errand. It became essential that the theocracy solicit public support.[6]

Mary Rowlandson's husband Joseph was an associate and subordinate of Increase Mather's. Shortly after his wife's return, Joseph Rowlandson was appointed minister to a more desirable parish that lay well within Mather's sphere of influence (Breitwieser 9). It was at this time, under the tutelage and influence of Increase Mather, that Mary Rowlandson probably wrote her narrative. Quite clearly, Rowlandson crafted a book that supported Mather's larger aims. She represented the Indians as godless heathen that required elimination; she noted the supremacy of God's plan and the need of the devout to accept and submit, and implicitly urged good Christians to put down their grief and fear and to persevere in faith.[7] Her text proclaims all good Christians will be delivered by a just God and an equally virtuous colonial authority, just as Rowlandson is finally delivered from her own ordeal.

In particular, Rowlandson's narrative bears an admonition for women who might be even temporarily tempted to doubt either biblical or patriarchal injunction. Unwilling to acknowledge that her own misfortunes might be the result of mischance, bad planning or even divine neglect, Rowlandson indirectly blames herself for the raid upon her cabin. In the "Third Remove," the suffering Rowlandson while caring for her dying child remarks on her earlier life, confessing her enjoyment of the material world and need for God to chasten her spirit. She blames herself for her spiritual "carelessness," and assumes that a just god sought to punish her.

> I then remembered how careless I had been of Gods holy time, how many Sabbaths I had lost and mispent, and how evilly I had walked in Gods sight…it was easie for me to see how righteous it was with God to cut off the thread of my life and cast me out of his presence forever. (Rowlandson 74)

"I saw how in my walk with God," Rowlandson continues in a later Remove, "I had been a careless creature" (91). The punishment she suffers, Rowlandson maintains, is the rightful outcome of careless devotion and a lack of faith in God's plan.

Later, Rowlandson and her party are nearly rescued. The English Army pursues the Narragansetts, but is stopped by the natural barrier posed by the Baquag River. Mary Rowlandson can see her potential liberators, but cannot reach them.

> God did not give them courage or activity to go over [the river] after us; we were not ready for so great a mercy as victory and deliverance; if we had been, God would have out a way for the *English* to have passed this River…. (Rowlandson 80)

According to Rowlandson and the theology dominant at her time, God denied rescue and salvation to Rowlandson and her companions because of their own moral failings. It was not because of a political or military weakness that the mission failed. Again, the text illustrates the terrible cost exacted by God for moral weakness on the part of the colonists. Such an assumption would be entirely consistent with Mather's larger agenda; difficult times for the colonists were the result of their own folly. God would reward moral strength with victory.

Perhaps the most dramatic example of Rowlandson's propensity to attach blame to her fellow colonists for their suffering and captivity is found in her brief discussion of her sister. In the initial lines of the *Narrative*, as Rowlandson describes the morning attack, she accounts for the actions of her older sibling. As the women peer from the cabin door at the death and carnage in the yard, Rowlandson's sister learns her son has been killed. "And Lord, let me dy with them," she moans. "No sooner said," Rowlandson recounts, "then she was struck with a Bullet and fell down dead over the threshold" (Rowlandson 69–70). When Rowlandson comes to this point in her detailed depiction of the bloody disaster, she suddenly digresses and discusses instead her sister's moral history. This digression has a curious effect; the lines that chronicle her sister's earlier "trouble upon spiritual accounts," combined with the sister's momentary weakness of resolve, give the impression Rowlandson holds her sister potentially responsible, to at least some degree, for the tragedy. Even as Rowlandson hopes God will remember her sister's "faithful service" for the past twenty years, she makes the sister morally accountable (Rowlandson 70). Rowlandson interrupts her own fast-paced narrative to provide a homily to the reader. This lesson must have appealed to Increase Mather's own propaganda needs.

As Breitwieser elucidates, in his *American Puritanism and the Defense of Mourning: Religion, Grief, and Ethnology in Mary White Rowlandson's Captivity Narrative*, beneath such obvious attempts to support the Puritan theocracy's theological and political aims, Rowlandson's text makes a spectral protest. Despite Rowlandson's seeming eagerness to distance herself from any behavior that might remark upon a lack of godly devotion, despite her commentary on the fate of even marginally disobedient or impious women, she chooses to ally herself with one of the *Bible's* great figures of feminine impropriety. Rowlandson grieves for her dead baby and her losses, ignoring the Puritan pronouncement to accept the will of God. Strangely, she takes Lot's infamous wife as her model. "I understood something of Lot's wife's temptation," says Rowlandson, commenting upon her strange relationship with one of the more notorious women of the *Old Testament* (Rowlandson 80).[8] One might recall Lot's wife disobeyed her husband's and God's injunction: Lot's wife looked longingly backward and failed to share the forward vision of her husband. "Mourning and lamenting," Rowlandson disobeys the Puritan's insistence to accept the Lord's will. The unusual identification with Lot's wife alerts the reader that Rowlandson was not simply Mather's "good girl." There is no shortage of more submissive and laudable biblical models with whom

Rowlandson might have chosen to identify, making her choice particularly significant. Lot's wife, after all was guilty of disobedience, to her husband and to God, and of insisting upon a wider field of vision than that provided by the deity. Lot's wife could not keep her sight focused in one direction. She did not accept authority; indeed, she was eternally paralyzed for attempting to de-center authority and for claiming a more inclusive point of view. The identification with Lot's wife suggests Rowlandson could no longer see things solely from one dictated vantage point. In naming Lot's wife as her model, Rowlandson projects a counter-narrative that reveals an important ambivalence toward the patriarchal discourse that necessarily informs her own tale. Structurally and politically compelled to follow the generic conventions of the captivity narrative, Rowlandson introduces a spectral and undermining element into her text through the introduction of Lot's wife.

As the narrative continues, Rowlandson enters into another social economy. As the weeks of her captivity go by, Rowlandson procures food for herself by knitting items of clothing and trading with her captors. She knits a pair of socks for one man in return for a handful of "Ground-nuts" and also makes a shirt for King Philip's son.

> During my abode in this place, Philip spake to me to make a shirt for his boy, which I did, for which he gave me a shilling: I offered the money to my master, but he bade me keep it: and with it I bought a piece of Horse flesh. Afterwards he asked me to make a cap for his boy...there was a squaw who spake to me to make a shirt for Sannup for which she gave me a piece of Bear. Another asked me to knit a pair of stockins.... (Rowlandson 83)

In this newly constructed commerce, Rowlandson made dress goods and clothing, often being paid with some other item or commodity she could then trade for food or tobacco.

Away from her husband and Lancaster, Rowlandson created an alternative system of exchange, one in which she played a pivotal role. In these moments, Rowlandson inhabits an alternative space; her road narrative takes her outside conventional economy and social discourse. Unable to depend on her husband for support,

Rowlandson is thrown upon her own resources. In fact, Rowlandson participates in arranging her own ransom. When the tribes involved in the war meet to discuss the future of the captives, Rowlandson is consulted. Summoned by the "Council about the Captives," Rowlandson must bargain and negotiate her own release. Aware the Lancaster farm she once shared with her husband no longer exists, Rowlandson knows her spouse's available resources are limited. If she names too low a price, her redemption cannot take place. But, if Rowlandson in her desire to be free provides a recklessly high figure, it will be impossible to procure the necessary sum (Rowlandson 98). Like any auctioneer, Rowlandson needs to talk, guess and bluff, placing herself further into the world of commerce.

> They bid me speak what I thought he [Rowlandson's husband] would give. Now knowing that all we had was destroyed by the *Indians*, I was in great strait: I thought if I should speak of but a little, it would be slighted, and hinder the matter; if of a great sum, I knew not where it should be procured: yet as a venture, I said *Twentypounds*, yet desired them to take less.... (Rowlandson 98)

Finally, with community (and possibly Increase Mather's) assistance, Joseph Rowlandson succeeds in purchasing his wife's freedom. Returned to Puritan society, Mary Rowlandson also returns to her former cultural position. No longer a negotiator or entrepreneur, Rowlandson becomes once more a commodity, a property of her family and society. She belongs again to the colonists' economy, with little ability to manipulate that structure. Ironically, Rowlandson's longed for freedom in some certain ways limits Rowlandson's economic reach. Purchased by her husband, Rowlandson returns to the traditional masculine (white) economy.

The degree to which Rowlandson has slipped out of her usual place is revealed startlingly when Metacom (King Philip) interviews her. Sympathetically, he informs Rowlandson she should not grieve, as she will soon be returned to her "master"—that is to say her husband, Joseph Rowlandson. Metacom then inspects Rowlandson and asks her how long it has been since she has bathed. "I told him not this month, then he fetched some water himself and bid me wash" (Rowlandson 96). As if to illustrate to Rowlandson how far outside she was from conventional mores, Metacom holds up a mirror. Significant within the larger text, this mirror scene not only demonstrates Rowlandson's deterioration but also makes her the dirty "savage" in comparison to King Philip. Unlike the woman who accompanies Metacom, "A severe and proud Dame...bestowing everyday in dressing herself nearly as much time as any of the gentry," Rowlandson is uncombed and dirty (Rowlandson 96, 97). King Philip, who was killed before Rowlandson ever commenced writing her *Narrative*, is given a nearly heroic role in Rowlandson's story. Through Rowlandson's narrative, Metacom, the subaltern, emerges as both a sympathetic interlocutor and a business partner. His appearance is typically accompanied by fair treatment, and even the *Narrative's* rough approximations of his speech imply he is man of some eloquence. "I was wonderfully revived with this favor that he shewed me," says Rowlandson. Then, in another one of her curious turns of phrase, she follows this statement immediately with a biblical phrase, "He made them also to be pitied, of all of those that carried them Captives" (96). The two lines are in a single sentence, linked by a comma, and while "He" is obviously God, the phrasing of the statement also makes Metacom the grammatical antecedent of "He." The juxtaposition of the lines argues it is Metacom who engenders pity and religious feeling. The line from Psalm 106 implies too that Rowlandson's captors are seen as equal, "also pitied" in the eyes of God. The hitherto "savage" Indian is granted human status. Such an equation between the "godless heathen" and a good Puritan woman is radical, perhaps only possible because of Rowlandson's travel and consequently widening field of vision.

Rowlandson's words also raise some question regarding her response to the death of Metacom. The "demon King" was ambushed and shot a few months after Rowlandson's release (Rowlandson 35–37). He was drawn, quartered, and beheaded, and his wife and children (the children for whom Rowlandson had knitted clothing) were sold into slavery in the West Indies. Of this, Rowlandson makes no comment and her very silence on the subject, after her affectionate praise, might imply her feelings concerning Metacom were different from those of the other colonists.

It is not only Metacom who challenges Rowlandson's perception of the Indian as the alien Other. There are other individuals who refuse to conform to the colonist's conventional narrative that casts the Indians as bloodthirsty and cold killers. As she travels with the tribe, Rowlandson perceives a network of familial relations combined in ways she would previously have thought impossible with a nomadic movement. As the weeks go on, Rowlandson experiences emotion and social interaction within the space she is forced to inhabit. In the course of the "Eighth Remove" Rowlandson breaks down and weeps, overcome with exhaustion and despair. She has not, she tells us, wept before.

> One of them asked me why I wept, I could hardly tell what to say: yet I answered, they would kill me. No one said, none will hurt you. Then came one of them and gave me two spoon-fulls of Meal to comfort me…. (82)

The gentleness apparent in this passage contrasts dramatically with the traditional anti-Indian rhetoric that is found throughout the text. Against her will, Rowlandson is forced to see the Indians as emergent individuals with interests in common with her own. Even in anger, Rowlandson's identification with the Other continues. As her mistress mourns the death of her own baby, Rowlandson refuses to give her comfort, proclaiming now at least there will be more room in the wigwam. Rowlandson denies sympathy not on the grounds the woman's grief is dissimilar, but on the basis it is exactly the same as what she herself has endured. "I confess, I could not much condole with them. Many sorrowfull dayses I had in this place: often getting alone" (91). Rowlandson rejects the woman precisely because they are the same. Rowlandson knows and acknowledges her Indian mistress shares an identical pain. If Rowlandson's rejection seems callous, it also underscores her perceived connection to her captors. They are more alike than different. In the new social economy of Rowlandson's life, she has more in common with her nomadic captors and more in common with Lot's wife than with her former Lancaster neighbors. She has truly entered a new space.

While Rowlandson stresses in her book her happiness upon her recovery, and instructs the reader that her text is written for a didactic purpose, her reputed happiness remains unconvincing. Her text speaks continuously of the goodness and power of God, of Rowlandson's devotion and her return to contentment, and of her desire others pay attention to her moral tale. But her words fail to construct an image of a happy woman. At the conclusion of the *Narrative*, Rowlandson uses the words of the biblical David, writing "I watered my Couch with my tears" (Rowlandson 111). She speaks at length of her new understanding of affliction and of her new "low estate." Inexpressible grief and continued discomfort seem to affect Rowlandson even after she has been ransomed and returned to her husband.

> Oh! The wonderfull power of God that mine eyes have seen, affording matter enough for my thoughts to run in, that when others are sleeping mine eyes are weeping. I have seen the extreme vanity of this World: one hour I have been in health, and wealth, wanting nothing: But the next hour in sickness and wounds, and death, having nothing but sorrow and affliction. (111)

The text is marked with nearly perpetual weeping. The notion all is "but vanity" continues through Rowlandson's work; she sees little of value in the world that is restored to her.

A new restlessness now afflicts Rowlandson. Back within the constructed cabin, now in Connecticut, she suffers from insomnia and ponders over and over again what she has seen.

> I can remember the time when I used to sleep quietly without workings in my thoughts, whole nights together, but now it is other wayes with me. When all are fast about me, and no eye open, but his who ever waketh, my thoughts are upon things past. (111)

Rowlandson's travels have opened her eyes and enriched her experience; she sees more than she used to and is thus troubled by "the workings" in her thoughts. This disruption is the cost of exposure and change, all the more difficult because her return forces her to adopt again a more narrow and fixed point of view. She suffers, consequently, a kind of psychic disruption. Rowlandson is not altogether blind to this issue. She mentions in her youth she used to long for some "affliction." "Before I knew what affliction meant, I was ready sometimes to wish for it" (112). She wants these afflictions, she says, to change "the comforts of the World around me" (112). But there is nothing that suggests Rowlandson wanted to confront death and pain. Rather, it seems, affliction meant to her, in her youthful perspective, passion, surprise and a break from the careful conventions of the cabin in Lancaster. She wanted, simply, change. Her confessions regarding her youthful desires display a longing for variety and some altered world.

Restored to comfort, it is still affliction that occupies Rowlandson's mind. She cannot close out the visions of the wider world outside the Puritan garden. "It is hard work" Rowlandson remarks, "to persuade myself that I should ever be satisfied with bread again" (110). A vastly more complex world confronts her. And through the specter of Rowlandson's narrative the reader sees at once a comment on the way Rowlandson lived, and more importantly perhaps, a comment upon what her travels on the frontier road gave her. Despite the nearly propaganda-like quality of her text, Rowlandson ultimately evolves for the reader as a woman who has been forced to see a wider world, to create—however briefly—an alternate reality. Because she cannot erase that wider field of vision, Rowlandson can never really totally inhabit the cabin again. She is recast as a nomad. Whether she moves or stands still she recognizes the ephemeral quality of attachment.

"The nomad's relationship to the earth is one of transitory attachment and cyclical frequentation; the antithesis of the farmer," writes Rosa Braidotti. "Their memory is activated against the stream; they enact a rebellion of subjugated knowledges" (Braidotti 25). This activated memory and collection of denied and "subjugated knowledges" speaks through Rowlandson's text. In her narrative, she has ceased to be the object, a mere convention in frontier stories. Through a tremendously painful process, Rowlandson becomes a subject in her own tale. No longer only an object or a commodity, Rowlandson discovers a sense of self. The difficult progress of the road subverts stasis and creates change. This change permits new insights. Revolutionary knowledge is the product of the road; Rowlandson's displacement results in the construction of a new narrative space.

Pushing the Boundaries of the Cabin: Pioneer Diaries

Mary Rowlandson's *Narrative* was followed by innumerable other travel tales. Of these colonial documents, Sarah Kemble Knight's *The Journal of Madam Knight* may be the best known. Written as a journalistic account of Knight's journey from Boston to New York in 1704–1705, *The Journal* was initially published in 1825. Radically different from Rowlandson doleful account, Knight's story depicts a woman leaving the safety of her home to engage quite openly with an outside economy. The text's clear sense of its literary antecedents adds to its importance. The tale opens with the narrator speaking with her fellow guests in a tavern, in a clear reference to Chaucer's *Canterbury Tales*. Acutely aware of the genre within which she works, Knight self-consciously rewrites the travel narrative as a story in which women can play central roles.

Numerous feminine captivity narratives found publication, and the genre became immensely popular in the nineteenth century. As Jane Tompkins mentions in *Sensational Designs*, "Americans wrote seventy-three novels dealing with Indian-white relations" and the incarceration and eventual return of white heroes and heroines (110). As Manifest Destiny continued to require the expansion of western borders, women wrote increasingly about their own experiences on the frontier trek. Frontier correspondences and journals became a common genre. These journals, nearly Victorian in the sense they were written for both God and posterity, provide a continued commentary regarding how the experience of the road changed its female authors.

The diaries and letters from women traveling the Overland Trail are very frequently marked with regret or even resistance to the entire expedition. As Elizabeth Jameson discusses in *The Women's West*, the decision to move west was nearly always a male decision. Women's responses to this course of action are cryptic; like Mary Rowlandson they announce they are ruled by duty and like Mary Rowlandson's text, their words often hide a bitter denunciation of that task. Abby Fulkerath wrote from the Overland Trail that she was:

Agreeable to the wish of my husband, I left all my relatives in Ohio and

started on this long and somewhat perilous journey...it proved a hard task
to leave them but harder still to leave my children buried in graveyards.
(Armitage and Jameson 149)

Like Rowlandson, these women were affected by death and by an
inadequate space within which to mourn that death.[9]

The most difficult aspect of these women's journeys seemed to be
not only the endless work assigned them but also the rupture of the
communities they had established in their eastern homes. Their very
identities, settled in a particular way in their former homes, are
disrupted by the move. The daily work required by a pioneer woman
was typically vastly different than what they had previously
experienced. Society prized Victorian gentlewomen for their inability
to do much physical work, and when complete indolence was not
possible, a gendered division of the labor was essential. But on the
frontier, women frequently coupled domestic tasks and child rearing
with work that might be regarded as "masculine." Frontiersmen were
often gone for days and weeks and even months at a time.
Consequently, women had to attend to their own gendered tasks, but
also to be prepared to assume other duties. Like Rebecca Boone,
women were periodically responsible for all work. Yet, the literature
promoting continental crossings often suggested a very different
world. Writes Jameson,

> The public image of women's work, however, was often idealized. The
> public literature said, for instance, that 'the interior of the home of the
> average industrious miner of the Cripple Creek district...would be a
> revelation... Their homes are neatly furnished, carpets on the floor,
> kitchens furnished with all of the conveniences...' (Armitage and Jameson
> 151)

The disjunction between the idealized public self and the private
reality could only have been problematic. Women's growing litany of
tasks and their own often intense isolation must have led to silent
questions about identity and selfhood. The space between popular
narrative and the reality of their own lives was vast.

Within these idealized homes, all was not always wonderful. Far
from feminine support, the frontier home was often the site of

violence and alcoholism. Indeed, the specter of a drunken spouse too often haunts the pages composed by frontier women. (While in women's diary entries, this alcoholism is nearly always associated with men; historians suggest women were not all immune to this difficulty.)[10] Plains settler Martha Farnsworth writes very poignantly of her first husband's drunkenness.

> I've cried so bitterly all day. Johnny is getting over his drunken spree enough to be cross and has abused me shamefully all day, when I'm home, my tears will fall... Oh! God have mercy on me and let me die. I don't want to live. My Boy does not love me... God look down in pity and take me home to Thee. (Farnsworth 64)

These lines were not uncommon.

Drinking often led to violence. Mrs. Lee Whipple Haslam commented in her memoir, "Turbulence and Evil of Every Description," that "men wore guns and shot to kill" (Moynihan, Armitage and Dichamp 28–30). Haslam describes the implicit violence that shaped her girlhood in California mining towns. Melody Graulich develops this theme further in her "Violence Against Women: Power Dynamics in the Literature of the Western Family." She contends the very structure of pioneer life was patriarchal, and that this extreme and physically isolated patriarchy gave rise to domestic violence. "Violence against women is the result of patriarchal definitions of gender and marriage rather than individual pathology" (Armitage and Jameson 113). The emergent portrait of frontier life is somewhat at odds with the legend of Daniel Boone.

But, perhaps because of the very dark side of frontier life, women's lives and texts begin to whisper of alternative ways of being in the world. Increasingly, women entered into economic transactions, sometimes engaging in barter and sometimes earning actual money. They could grow and trade food and other goods, and when they lived in the vicinity of other pioneers they could sew and cook and wash for the many single men on the frontier. Elliot West borrows an ironic comment from one oral history; "[S]he was a wife of the right sort...she earn't her old man nine hundred dollars in nine weeks, clear of all expenses, by washing" (186). Like Rowlandson before her, the frontier washerwoman used her skills to barter for a place within a separate economy.

Inside frontier culture—often alone with their children for weeks at a time—women tended to forge strong bonds with other women. These friendships and groups frequently functioned as a smaller, even secret society, within a larger more public and male sphere. Here women's concerns could be addressed, and in a most subtle way these associations displaced the patriarchal West with a powerful alternative landscape. While religious institutions denounced birth control, and society's dictates against it would eventually find legal voice in the Comstock Laws of 1873, birth control, along with the practices of childbirth, became part of the arcane knowledge of women's discourse. Practically speaking, pregnancy and childbirth increased both women's vulnerability and their already difficult workloads. Elizabeth Jameson argues in "Women as Workers, Women as Civilizers: True Womanhood in the West" (Armitage and Jameson) that,

> A rich and largely private world of women sharing information about contraception, pregnancy, birth and menopause is beginning to be documented from a number of places…. Whether or not a woman's mother explained the facts of life to her, some older woman usually offered advice…. The variety of suggested contraceptives demonstrates women's determination to find something that worked. (151–152)

Through discussions about sexuality, birth control, pregnancy and death, women addressed forbidden or erased topics. In these increasingly documented exchanges, frontier women grasped control of their bodies. They took this control through the unauthorized exchange of language, thereby creating an alternate culture. Nomadic in both the traditional sense and in the sense they share the notion of a nomadic consciousness which refuses to recognize borders, these women persisted in seeking a lexicon "which cannot easily be fitted within the parameters of phallocentric language" (Braidotti 76). This polyglot language, a language "that has no vernacular but many lines of transit, of transgression. [A] site of symbolic exchange that links," a semiotic that creates house wherein "no one is master," is a whisper that ripples through the journals and oral histories of frontier women (Braidotti 76). These whispers find representation in literature.

"I Am Your Text": The Fiction of Mary Hallock Foote and the
Reclaimed Body of the Frontier Woman

In *Nostalgia and Sexual Difference: The Resistance to Contemporary Feminism*, authors Janice Doane and Devon Hodges argue the recent allegiance to "family values" reveals a fear that contemporary women will break free from the widely accepted "rhetorical practice" that assigns women the role of fulfilling the "domestic fantasies" of men. The legends of the Prairie Madonna and Rebecca Boone illustrate this rhetorical practice, and the popular sentimental nineteenth century stories of the frontier demonstrate an equally keen desire to keep this mythology in place. Indeed, the growing popularity of the sentimental western story parallels the discreet but growing whispers among women authors who elected to resist the canon of the good western woman. Mary Hallock Foote was one of those women whose texts offer a resistance, and, who, nomad-like, redraws the perimeters of the semiotic territory of the frontier.

Foote's story is doubly interesting, for not only do her fictive texts seek to reinterpret the West, but also the efforts to reinterpret and perhaps even suppress Foote's works suggest our continued devotion to the rhetoric of the Madonna. Interestingly enough, it is at the very site of Foote's body that male writers and literary critics seek to remake her; reconfiguring her bodily history allows the dismembrance of her representation of the West.

A little known artist today, Mary Hallock Foote (1847–1948) enjoyed popularity and a respectably large number of readers. A contemporary of Owen Wister, Foote quickly saw her own literary status diminish as the public showed its preference for Wister's *Virginian* (1902) and his masculinized vision of the frontier. Educated at Cooper Union's Art Institute, Foote was employed as a successful illustrator. She received commissions from such well-established writers as Howells, Harte, and Longfellow, and enjoyed inclusion within Boston's closed circle of intellectuals. At twenty-nine, a bit nervous about her spinster status, Mary Hallock married Arthur Foote. She followed her engineer husband into the West, and enlarged her artistic work to include the writing of essays and fiction. She entertained and corresponded with a number of prominent authors and western notables, including Helen Hunt Jackson, Clarence King and John Wesley Powell. But by the early twentieth century, Foote's work slipped into obscurity.

In the mid nineteen fifties, the then young western writer and historian Wallace Stegner became sufficiently impressed with Foote's work to include her short story "How the Pump Stopped at the Morning Watch" in his 1958 collection, *Selected American Prose*. Contending Foote illustrated "a woman's point of view," Stegner wrote, "she is too honest to be totally lost" as he insisted upon her brief inclusion in the anthology (Stegner, *Selected* xi). Credited with "discovering" Foote, Stegner noted Foote's life failed to offer a suitable subject for either literary biography or historical fiction. As a writer engaged in both of these genres, Stegner explained his position, writing "Foote's career [was] not important enough for a biography or...[for] an historical novel..." (*Literary History of the American West* 983). In the subsequent years Stegner's own literary reputation flourished. Scholar, historian, novelist, essayist, teacher, and editor, Stegner is widely regarded as one of the most distinguished of American western writers. A recipient of well-earned national acclaim, Stegner drew scholarly attention to the previously too often neglected field of western literature.

In 1971, Stegner published the work that secured his literary reputation and won him both the Pulitzer Prize and a staggering number of literary accolades. Stegner's award-winning novel, *The Angle of Repose* details the reputedly fictive life of Susan Burling Ward, frontier artist and writer. So successful was the work it was quickly rewritten as an opera, opening five years later in New York City. The flyleaf makes a cryptic thank you to "J.M. and her sister for the loan of their ancestors" and makes a standard disclaimer regarding the merging of truth and fiction. The novel constitutes, however, a very thinly veiled biography of the life of Mary Hallock Foote. While Foote and some of her immediate family and a number of her friends are given different names, the names and facts presented through much of the novel are entirely consistent with Foote's own life. Indeed, a great deal of the novel is taken word for word from Foote's correspondence with her close friend Helena Gilder and from her own memoir, *A Victorian Gentlewoman in the Far*

West: The Reminiscences of Mary Hallock Foote. Writes Foote wistfully at the close of her *Reminiscences* (posthumously published in 1972), "that angle of repose...which...one finds from time to time but is always seeking in one way or another" (309). *The Angle of Repose* is largely Mary Hallock Foote's story, a fact that becomes the source of some literary gossip.

But, Stegner's work differs from Foote's in at least two vastly significant ways. Stegner's account, while often sympathetic, is finally deeply critical of Foote's sensibility and her rejection of the masculine terrain of the West. Even more importantly, Stegner—who changes so few facts about Foote's life—dramatically changes those facts that have to do with Foote's sexuality. For Stegner, Foote's body becomes the final space upon which to enact both her rebellion and her punishment. Thus, Foote's life and work are appropriated and reconfigured to fit Stegner's larger narrative of the West.

Throughout his novel, Stegner chides his subject, Susan Burling Ward/Mary Hallock Foote for her effete eastern aesthetics and her refusal to accept her husband on his own terms. Like Susan Ward, Foote was married to a mining engineer who suffered from the recurrent alcoholism prevalent on the frontier. Stegner's novel reproves Ward/Foote, counseling, "[T]ake it easy. Don't act like a Victorian prude. Don't lose your sense of proportion. Ask yourself whether his unhappy drinking has really hurt you or your children" (Stegner, *Angle* 396). But Foote's interpretation of her life is different; she is "sick at heart" over the life[11] forced upon her.

Stegner's most dramatic alterations occur near the close of his novel. In his story, Ward/Foote is so disappointed by her husband's failures that she falls in love with the young mining engineer who is her husband's assistant. Foote's own letters suggest Harry Tompkins (the model for Stegner's luckless Frank Sargeant) did perhaps have a youthful "crush" on Foote, but her story is quite different from Stegner's. In Stegner's account, the love affair finally leads to a tryst, where Susan and Frank (Foote and Tompkins) lose sight of four-year-old Agnes Ward. As a result, Agnes is drowned in the nearby irrigation ditch. A few days later, in Stegner's novel, Frank shoots himself while lying on top of Ward/Foote's old bed. So persuasive is Stegner, so justified in depicting the punishment that must fall upon a recalcitrant woman, that even Foote's old neighbors and relatives believe his story. Stegner erased Foote's life and narrative and replaced it with a much more believable revision. Foote's granddaughter, Marian Conway writes that since the publication of *Angle of Repose* her late grandmother's friends and neighbors in Grass Valley have constantly approached her. These neighbors

> ...would stop me on the street and say, in essence, "I never knew your grandmother did **that**." Even though some of them listened politely to denials of all these evil doings, it was only a matter of time until a man in our local bookstore said to my brother-in-law, "Don't worry—there's one in every family." (Walsh 201)[12]

The word for the kind of "one" found in each family is clear, suggesting how the representation of narrative is, for women, inevitably perhaps, tied to sexuality.

In point of fact, Foote appears not to have had an affair with Tompkins, although she clearly found him both a friend and source of support. By all accounts, Harry Tompkins continued to have great affection for Foote. At the time of his engagement, he took his fiancée to visit the woman he still esteemed and "had loved in Idaho," much to Foote's delight.[13] Foote's youngest daughter Agnes, given the same name in Stegner's text, does die. But, unlike Stegner's four-year old Agnes, who drowns in an irrigation ditch while her mother dallies with her lover, the actual Agnes Foote died in late adolescence of appendicitis. "An ambush of fate," Foote called this tragedy.[14] Sad as this tale is, Agnes' death had no relation to her mother's sexuality. But for Stegner, Agnes' death was the just reward for "a woman who refused to submit," who "held myself above my chosen life with results that I must repent and grieve all my days" (Stegner, *Angle* 473).

Stegner's prose constitutes an amazing revision. *The Angle of Repose* is a novel about self-acknowledged guilt. But Foote's own writings suggest she felt no guilt about her assessment of her husband's alcoholism, nor does she blame herself over the unhappy state of their marriage. She sometimes lives apart from her husband—not as a punishment as Stegner's contends, but as a matter of necessity—and Foote routinely comments she provides the principal support for the family. In "discovering" and appropriating Foote's story, Stegner radically rewrites her narrative so it conforms to some larger mythic and masculine vision of the West. His fictional heroine suffers for her failure to match the stoicism and practical skills demonstrated by Rebecca Boone. Foote, on the other hand, has no desire to cast herself as a prairie Madonna. She writes of her own westward pilgrimage, in her largely autobiographical *Edith Bonham*, "I hated it."

The significance of Stegner's narrative revision cannot be overlooked. In much the same way Increase Mather appropriated Mary Rowlandson's captivity experience for his own use, as he "assisted" her with its completion and publication, Stegner "borrows" Foote's narrative. It seems critical that the epicenter of his text—and the place for its complete separation from the facts of Foote's life—lies within the confines of Susan Ward/Mary Hallock Foote's body. Stegner thus not only appropriates narrative and experience but he further understands this act of appropriation is made both possible and necessary by gender. The revision becomes a sort of textual cannibalism, in which one text is consumed for the larger "good" of the prevailing narrative. A great deal of discussion has been engendered in recent years regarding Stegner's consumption of Foote's texts. Much attention focuses upon Stegner's literary "borrowing," and upon the nearly word for word transcription of Foote's work. In 1982, in a larger volume of collected essays devoted to Stegner's work, Mary Ellen Williams Walsh noted in her essay "*Angle of Repose* and the Writings of Mary Hallock Foote: A Source Study" that large sections of Stegner's novel duplicated Foote's private letters as well as her autobiography. A resultant controversy ensued. As Christine Hill Smith states,

> The fallout from this event has yet to finish falling, with outraged Foote supporters and defiant Stegner defenders lining up to take pot shots to this day, but most of Walsh's scholarship has stood the test of time. (35)

Increasingly, critics agree vast sections of Stegner's work reproduce Foote's documents.

Apologists for Stegner insist that he took relatively staid material and gave it verve and psychological insight. Explains Christine Hill Smith:

> Still, one can hardly blame Wallace Stegner for wanting to liven up Foote's inner life as he did in *Angle of Repose*... He had read the source material...perhaps had been frustrated by a lack of inner life in it.... (38)

Other readers are not so charitable in their explanation, and some have hinted at plagiarism in their discussions. Sands Hall, an acquaintance of Stegner, contends the large sections of Stegner's work that come so directly from Foote's material constitute, perhaps, intellectual theft. Indeed, Hall continues, the sections of the novel that reproduce Foote's letters are the sections most praised by critics. She cites the commendations offered by the *Atlantic Monthly*, positive reviews that focused upon the "triumph of verisimilitude" evident in the fictional "Susan's letters" (Hall, "Fair Game" 3). Deeply offended at the "patriarchy" contained in Stegner's gesture, Sands Hall wrote the play *Fair Use*, a work that interrogates Stegner's choices through, interestingly, a fictionalized dialogue between Stegner and Foote. In March of 2003, the *Los Angeles Times* explored the controversy in Susan Salter Reynolds' "Tangle of Repose; Three Decades After Publication of Wallace Stegner's *Angle of Repose*, Messy Questions About His Use of Mary Hallock Foote's Writings Are Haunting the Famed Novelist." The article brought the debate into mainstream literary culture, focusing upon the question of what constitutes "fair use," and strangely, with the word "haunting" suggesting a spectral literary presence.

It seems to me however, that the more interesting question does not really concern the issue of plagiarism. Of greater concern (to all but the litigious) is the issue of appropriation. Foote's voice, her experiences, her narrative trajectory and her literary legacy were appropriated by the larger conventional and masculine narrative of the West. She was silenced. Her sexuality and familial relations were re-defined. Stegner's story requires the very claiming of Foote's maternal body. Real consequences stem from Stegner's text; Foote's experience of the road is marginalized. Stegner effectively rewrites Foote's tale so it conforms to some larger, more acceptable narrative territory. Like Rowlandson, Foote's work is used to justify the frontier mission and the power structure that supports it.

This sort of literary appropriation is not new or without explanation. Rosa Braidotti comments upon textual cannibalism and its necessity for the masculine tale.

> The problem is that the exclusion of women and the denigration of the feminine are not just a small omission that can be fixed with a little good will. Rather, they point to the underlying theme in the textual and historical continuity of masculine self-legitimation and ideal self-projection. It's on the woman's body—on her absence, her silence, her disqualification—that phallocentric discourse rests. This sort of "metaphysical cannibalism," which Ti-Grace Atkinson analyzed in terms of uterus envy, positions the woman as the silent groundwork of male subjectivity—the condition of possibility for his story. (139)

The popular and phallocentric story of the American road requires women's silent textual accommodation.

Gilles Deleuze and Felix Guattari consider the notion of "metaphysical cannibalism" in another context. In their *Anti-Oedipus*, the act of consumption becomes finally a kind of colonization, a reclamation of a territory already claimed by another, an idea with obvious relevance to any discussion of the American West and the road to Manifest Destiny. Deleuze and Guattari retell a myth discussed in a text of Marcel Griaule. In this story, the character Yourougou steals a placenta and breaks it into pieces.

> This individual went away into the distance carrying with him a part of the nourishing placenta, which is to say a part of his own mother. He saw this organ as his own and as forming a part of his own person, in such a way that he identified himself with the one who gave birth to him. (Deleuze and Guattari 157)[15]

The female body is consumed and displaced with masculine (and Oedipal) narrative; the uterus is replaced with phallo-logic representation. The texts of Mary Hallock Foote and the eclipse and revision of her work are clear examples of narrative consumption.

Foote recognizes the frontier road is a vexed space, a terrain not frequently given representation within women's narrative. Her 1903 novella, *The Maid's Progress*, examines ideas regarding discursive space and narrative autonomy. A parody of the traditional western (nearly postmodern in its comic funeral scenes), Foote's novel concerns love, death and inheritance in the West. In this tale, the conventional western hero is replaced with the figure of a woman. Daphne, the enigmatic heroine dressed perpetually in mourning, drifts off the plains to appear at a funeral. In the opening scenes the mourners are confused as they gather in a dry gulch; the wind blows around them ceaselessly and all the signposts face the wrong way. It is useless to seek directions. Muffled, anonymous figures begin a memorial service in the vicinity of an unmarked grave. A man officiates, although he is necessarily vague because of the circumstances. Suddenly one of the black-garbed figures throws back her veil and usurps the ceremony.

> "Uncle," cried Daphne in a smothered voice, "never mind the text! I am your text! Listen to me...." (Foote, *Touch* 95)

Daphne takes over the ceremony, making herself its subject. The men at the funeral, all taking a proprietary interest in Daphne, try and preempt her place. Like her mythological namesake, Daphne resists their advances as well as their efforts to remove her from the center of the ceremony and the story.

As *The Maid's Progress* continues, the tale reveals that Daphne is affianced to a nonexistent man. Her masculine companions seek to erase her name and call her, with obvious attention to paradox, "the Maiden Widow." Daphne has no direction; her task is to wander the West and endure constant and inexplicable loss. Her movements are purposeless, for the frontier is revealed as a landscape of empty signifiers. Even the funeral that opens the story was held at the wrong site and reflected a case of mistaken identity. Signposts point in the wrong direction and the maps mark towns that never existed. The story concludes with Daphne trying unsuccessfully to locate the mythical town of Bliss, while never finding her lost and nameless lover. It is a story, finally, about representation. The popular frontier road story should conclude with an arrival at a destination and the bliss that results from submission to national narrative. But Foote's

Daphne is assertive; she insists upon a nomadic narrative.

The resistance to patriarchy and the national "errand into the wilderness" mark much of Foote's fiction and correspondence. "There is little joy in it," she wrote to Helena Gilder in 1848. In her *A Victorian Gentlewoman in the Far West: The Reminiscences of Mary Hallock Foote*, Foote wrote travel and life on the frontier required a rupture with culture and feminine associations.

> This meant farewell music, art, gossip of the workshop, schools...old friends better loved than ever and harder to part from—all the old backgrounds receding hopelessly and forever.... I felt adrift, cast off on a raft with my babies, swept past these wild shores uninhabited for us. My husband steering us with a surveyor's rod or some such futile thing—and where were we going on this flood of uncertainties? If my dreamer had been Moses I should have tried to stay his hand. (Foote, *Victorian* 273)

Foote's reminiscence suggests an errand marked by loss and futility. She did not share her husband or Wallace Stegner's enthusiasm for the popularized vision of the frontier.

Like her memoir, Foote's fiction attempts to inscribe an alternate narrative of the West. Her 1889 short story, "The Fate of a Voice" relates the adventures of a professional singer who foolishly ventures into the West with her new husband. The protagonist of the story finds the desert terribly arid and the climate permanently damages her voice, leaving her unable to sing.

> Somewhere in that vague and rapidly lessening region known as the frontier, there disappeared a few years ago a woman's voice... She threw away a charming career, just at its outset, and went West with a husband—not anybody in particular. (Foote, "Voice" 274)

"The Fate of a Voice" constitutes a prescient and depressing story about narrative erasure. Foote warns her readers women who follow the road west will find themselves diminished and their words unheeded and finally altered. The vocabulary of feminism is at odds with the masculine lexicon of the frontier journey.

It is this very lexicon that Foote critiques in her fiction, as she tries to establish some alternative space. Foote's novel, *Coeur D'Alene*, revolves around the story of the ironically named Faith, a young woman who is brought to the West by her miner father. Almost immediately, Faith revolts against the "rugged masculinity" that surrounds her. She watches the phallic mineshaft destroy the landscape and notes the miners are often equipped with guns. Another miner named Darcy asks Faith to marry him. Horrified, she reads his penetration and violation of the landscape as a natural accompaniment of his masculinity, and as a metaphor for the way in which he must inevitably eradicate her own sense of self. Darcy's initial charms are mitigated by his associations with violence and ownership.

> "He [Darcy] is not what I thought him. I don't understand. We all seem to have gone back to barbarism. ...we shall never know each other anymore." ...she would not meet his eyes. She swerved slightly away from him, avoiding his touch....she uttered just two words, "Oh don't!" There was not mistaking the accent of repulsion, almost of horror, with which they were spoken. (Foote, *Coeur* 144–145)

Faith's father dies and Darcy is wounded. She is urged to take up a gun for protection, and to accept the vocabulary of the West. But Faith does not wish to occupy a position or to bear arms. Instead, she dresses herself as a grieving fiancée and wraps the wounded Darcy in a mock shroud. Stricken, she confronts a masculine audience. She carries the seemingly dead—and figuratively emasculated—Darcy eastward, thus escaping the narrative of westward expansion.

The same distaste for masculine discourse is recorded in Foote's novella, *The Harshaw Bride*. Here the affianced Kitty is brought west to become a bride. But as Kitty surveys the ruptured landscape littered with ugly equipment, polluted streams and broken hills she begins to equate her lover's romantic desire with his need to possess his mining claim. Kitty locks herself into a boarding house room and weeps over the sight of the land and the trajectory of her own travels. Large and looming mining materials block out any possible view of the horizon. Vision is obscured, just as Kitty's individuality will be obliterated by her marriage.

> "I can't give in," she said. ..."the sight of it belongs to me," she said. "I will not have the place all littered up with their pipes and power-plants.... Has

anyone the right to come and spoil such a lovely thing as that?" (Foote,
Touch 256–257)

But Kitty's tears and resistance are futile; her future husband has paid
for her passage west and cannot be denied. Kitty and her story are
consumed by the prevailing discourse of the West.

The struggle to maintain a female voice within the larger
narratives of marriage and the road west emerge as themes in Foote's
work. In her novel, *The Chosen Valley*, Foote once again depicts a
woman who is forced into the frontier. The heroine, Dolly, is the
daughter of an irascible homesteader who relentlessly destroys the
irrigation ditches of the local engineering syndicate. Phillip, a young
engineer, is committed to these irrigation pathways because he
believes through his skillful water control the barren terrain will
bloom into an Eden. Phillip tells Dolly the waters "will sing" down
their reconstituted banks, and he and Dolly will also find a way to
successfully blend their mutual voices. But Dolly learns Phillip's
project is merely a commercial and potentially destructive act, rather
than an idealistic reclamation. Dolly is moved by the desire to recover
some lost and promised land, but she grows disenchanted as she
realizes Phillip seeks only the commodification of Eden. She realizes
too her body is also a commodity with a corresponding value. Phillip
argues, "Dolly, don't forget what we are here for: this is the land we
are going to reclaim... Our waters shall do their singing and shouting
up in the mountains; they come down here on business..." (Foote,
Chosen 282–283). But the engineering project fails; the valley is
flooded and the water leaves in its wake filth, destruction and death.
Nature evades, momentarily, the power of American technology and
commerce. Dolly's father is swept away in the resulting devastation
and Dolly realizes she cannot wed a man responsible for his death.
Insisting upon her right to mourn and to withdraw from the
masculine enterprise, Dolly withdraws from both the frontier and the
text. The novel ends abruptly with a coda delivered through the
persona of an objective narrator.

The same dilemmas structure Foote's most famous and perhaps
most successful novel, *The Led-Horse Claim*. Masculine possessiveness
and feminine voice again constitute Foote's subject. The central

conflict of the text revolves around two rival mining interests: the Shoshone and the Led-Horse companies. These rival firms establish claim shaft-houses that share a wall and tap into the same vein of silver ore. An artificial boundary is marked deep within the mine, but given the slippage inherent in the mining process, the interior darkness, and the lack of codified records, definitive claims prove impossible to make. The two rival claims resort to force. Against the background of this conflict, Conrath, superintendent of the Shoshone Mine, brings his pretty orphan sister, Cecilia, to the West. Cast as a gingham-clad Juliet, Cecilia immediately meets Hilgard, the manager of the rival Led-Horse firm. Ignorant of the vendetta, Cecilia falls quickly in love with Hilgard. The feud then encompasses not only tension over ore possession, but the physical possession of Cecilia as well.

In a dramatic scene Cecilia goes on a tour of the Shoshone mine. Escorted by her brother, she is left alone in the dark at the site of the barricade that distinguishes the two claims. As her brother leaves, Cecilia's lover approaches. Her body marks the site of the intersection of the two claims. When the torches are lit, the sordid violence of the mine is revealed. Sickened, Cecilia faints and is carried from the mine.

Several days later, Cecilia's lover Hilgard kills Conrath in a "fair fight." Despite Hilgard's protestations of innocence, Cecilia ends the relationship. Outraged, Hilgard protests:

> Cecil, you cannot put me out of your life, like this without a word! You cannot mean to mock me with a love that denies our very humanity. It is nonsense to say that I am dead to you when every nerve in my body starts at your touch. Did we make that tie? It is the oldest, the strongest tie between a man and a woman. There is no duty that can break it! I am your duty... (Foote, *Led-Horse* 186)

Hilgard insists upon the primacy of his own narrative and the power of its tradition. But Cecilia answers her former fiancé's charge with a narrative code of her own.

> There is an instinct that forbids me!... You have done your duty in spite of the cost.... But you cannot judge for me. A woman's duty is different. (Foote, *Led-Horse* 186)

Cecilia maintains her right to her own decisions and lexicon, and leaves the mining town. In Foote's original text, Cecilia's departure concludes the novel.

But Foote's novel is reconfigured by a textual revision that parallels the later biographical revision of Foote's own life. Citing public demand for "romance" and happy endings, Foote's editor insisted *The Led-Horse Claim* must end with a marriage. Despite her own narrative inclinations, Foote adds a final chapter to the story (Johnson 50).[16] In this peculiarly revised chapter, Foote both accommodates her editor's suggestions and quietly subverts her now conventional conclusion. In this final entry, the spurned Hilgard contrives to re-encounter Cecilia in the East. Despite her inner revulsion, Cecilia is persuaded it is her duty to marry Hilgard. The two are wed. But the final paragraph of the story severely undermines Foote's new happy ending. The sentence that follows Cecilia's acceptance of Hilgard's suit is followed by a line informing the reader of Cecilia's death and the location of her final resting place. Nowhere in the pages of the novel does Cecilia allow Hilgard access to her body, and Foote kills off her heroine before we can see her depicted as a wife. The marriage bed becomes Cecilia's grave and the final protection of her autonomous self. Foote's "happy ending" deconstructs the popular narrative, leaving Cecilia with an alternative, if morbid, discourse. Like Foote's other heroines, Cecilia claims no citizenship in the territory she occupies; instead, she moves across boundaries—geographical and textual—in search of space that will permit her autonomy and voice.

"No girl ever wanted to 'go west' less," writes Foote in her *Reminiscences* (114). Yet, she traveled west with her engineer husband who bears an uncanny resemblance to Hilgard in *The Led-Horse Claim*. Subsumed in the larger national tale concerning the glories of westward expansion, Foote and her work nearly disappeared. The editorial struggles surrounding the text suggest the tremendous pressure to rewrite women's narrative of the road west. Braidotti's notion of the "metaphysical cannibalism" that surrounds women's texts finds illustration in the lives and works of Mary Hallock Foote and Mary Rowlandson. Dominant discourse is necessarily driven to possess and reconfigure the language of nomadic women; the nomad resists this appropriation.

Masculine possession of the land and male ownership of women's bodies are celebrated with some frequency in traditional road narratives, and Annette Kolodny notes the difficulty in establishing women's voices within a narrative framed by masculine vocabulary. She comments upon this phenomenon when she contends in her *Lay of the Land* that the urge for "mastery and possession" can be blamed for "thwarting pastoral possibility" in both its narrative and environmental senses. Continues Kolodny:

> [W]e still are [bound] by the vocabulary of a feminine landscape and the psychological patterns of regression and violation that it implies. Fortunately, however, that same language that now appalls us with its implications of regression or willful violation also supplies a framework, open to examination within which the kinds of symbolic functioning we have examined here get maximum exposure. It gives us, to begin with, at least some indication of how these peculiar intersections of human psychology, historical accident and New World geography combined to create the vocabulary for the experience of the land-as-woman.... Our continuing fascination with the lone male in the wilderness, and our literary heritage of essentially adolescent, presexual pastoral heroes, suggest that we have yet to come up with a satisfying model for mature masculinity on this continent. (146–147)

Yet, bound as we might be by culture and literary history, voices continue to challenge the traditional configuration of the frontier.

A veritable mother (paternal) lode of historic road texts provides history and context for twentieth century writers seeking to recapitulate and reinterpret the masculine narrative of the American road. Similarly, despite attempts at erasure and revision and the frequent need for discretion, American frontier women offer another narrative tradition that explores an alternative discursive terrain. These frontier women, like Rowlandson and Foote, made the road not only a site of popular narrative, but also a resistant space between destinations wherein alternative lexicons might exist. Their specters haunt the traditional road west.

CHAPTER THREE

Reclaiming the Territory:
Mary Austin and Other (Un)Natural Girls

> *You of the house habit can hardly understand the*
> *sense of the hills. No doubt the labor of being*
> *comfortable gives you an exaggerated opinion of*
> *yourself....*
>> Mary Austin, *The Land of Little Rain*

> *Mind you, it is men who go mostly into the desert...*
>> Mary Austin, *Lost Borders*

Leaving Eden Behind

The association of nature with the feminine and the sublime remains
an abiding principle of romanticism. Goethe's notion of the "eternal
feminine" originates for him in a young woman's flower-surrounded
innocence and that same guileless womanhood becomes, finally, a
vehicle for masculine salvation. Wordsworth's "Highland Lass" went
"reaping and singing by herself...alone she cuts and binds the grain,"
as she sang her eternal and pastoral song.[1] Historically, untrammeled
spaces suggest innocence and purity, aspects of idealized
womanhood. Within a more familiar geography, American
romanticism also endowed the earth with qualities both sublime and
feminine.

For numerous American authors, the road necessarily led to a
new Eden. Within this Eden, the natural landscape became the means
toward the achievement of a transcendent self. Through the enormity
of American geography, the sublime and individual self merged with
a larger national identity. Natural space provided the screen for the
American imagination. Leo Marx begins his well-known text, *The
Machine in the Garden*, by commenting upon the significance of
pastoral imaginary in the formulation of an American self.

> The pastoral ideal has been used to define the meaning of America ever
> since the age of discovery, and it has not yet lost its hold upon the native
> imagination. The reason is clear enough. The ruling motive of the good
> shepherd, leading figure of the classic, Virgilian mode, was to withdraw
> from the great world and begin a new life in a fresh, green landscape. And
> now here was a virgin continent! (Marx 3)

From the consummated relationship between the westward-bound
man and the frequently gendered land, a new and idealized identity
would be born.

The creation of this new natural self was not altogether benign in
its consequence. As numerous authors have pointed out, American
identity—complete with its "rugged individualism" and "natural"
expansiveness—fostered very early an enduring belief in American
exceptionalism. This exceptionalism led, in turn, to an enlarged sense
of mission, entitlement, and a belief in the politics of Manifest
Destiny[2] The pastoral genre was wedded to the pragmatics of frontier
policy. Here, in a land of vast and lyrical natural resources, "a
dialogue between man and God within the discourse of the will-to-
power over the manifest landscape" took place. Through the resulting
sense of the sublime and its associations with power, the romantic
sense of "American exceptionalism" was created (Wilson 32). In his
American Sublime: The Genealogy of a Poetic Genre, Rob Wilson remarks
upon the relationship between the so-called natural and exceptional
American self and its necessary relation to the colonial impulse.

> The American sublime functions as a trope of empowerment, emanating,
> in part, from a will to reimagine the American ground.... As poets we
> invest the sublime object with the "aura" of our own greatness...such
> representational structures of the sublime allow individual American
> subjects to imagine, by means of such constructs as such self-dwarfing
> realities such as Niagara Falls, the Grand Canyon, the Mojave Desert, the
> euphoric prairies of Bryant.... In a negative sense, ideology comprises the
> collective fictions and poetic enchantments, which a culture tells its self as
> a way of sustaining its own interests and power over others.... (Wilson
> 34–36)

Nature, then, becomes a way through which the transcendental self
joins with the transcendent power of the nation.

American nature writers have been greatly influenced by the Emersonian tradition, a tradition that places nature in the service of a larger eternal self. In consideration of the spiritual properties associated with nature, Emerson famously writes, "[I]n the woods, we return to reason and faith. There I feel that nothing can befall me in life—no disgrace, no calamity...which nature cannot repair...all mean egotism vanishes. I become a transparent eyeball." Nature, as Donald Pease writes in his *Visionary Compacts*, occupies for Emerson, "the same place in the discourse of idealism as that of the spirit... the space of the sublime" (Pease 227). The wilderness, once the dark space of the infidel and savage, becomes in the romantic mind a clean space through which innocence and the divine can be apprehended.

The relation of nature to the larger cultural over-soul is more than evident in the work of western traveler, naturalist, and writer, John Muir. For Muir, again, the terrain of the West derives its power not only from each individual aspect but also from the unity of the total natural experience. Throughout his travels, recounted in *The Yosemite* and *The Mountains of California*, Muir makes clear, natural phenomenon manifests the words of a larger divine system of vocabulary. For Muir, nature is a way to be reborn and returned to God. Describing a dangerous near fall, Muir writes:

> When this final danger flashed upon me, I became nerve-shaken for the first time since setting foot on the mountains, and my mind seemed to fill with a stifling smoke. But this terrible eclipse lasted only a moment, when life blazed forth again with a prenatural clearness. I seemed suddenly to become possessed of a new sense. The other self, bygone experiences, Instinct of Guardian Angel—call it what you will—came forward and assumed control. Then my trembling muscles became firm again, every rift and flaw in the rock was seen as through a microscope, and my limbs moved with a positiveness and precision with which I seemed to have nothing at all to do. Had I been borne aloft upon wings, my deliverance could not be more complete. (Muir, *Mountains* 28)

For Muir, and his fellow romantics, the natural world corresponds to a larger and more divine realm. He finds "salvation in [the] surrender to landscape" (Wyatt 45).

Sometime associate of Muir, geologist Clarence King also

perceived individual geographical occurrences as signifiers of some larger cosmic meaning. For King, however, this vast natural narrative included a pragmatic commentary on the West's resources. Surveyor, mountaineer, fossil-hunter, director of the U.S. Geological Survey and (albeit largely unsuccessful) miner, Clarence King was named by his friend Henry Adams as "the most remarkable man of our time" (Wyatt 60). Educated with Wordsworth's sense of "the infinite," King found in his western travels both the qualities of the eternal and his own identity. He "invest[s] these great dominating peaks with consciousness" (Wyatt 60). But for King, geology marked not only the vastness of history and consciousness; geological signs indicated the possibility of wealth. A renowned geologist, and author of *Systematic Geology*, King left scholarship and government employment to seek the buried treasures of western mines. The clues left by rock and fossil could be interpreted in literal as well as transcendent ways. (King ultimately ran a number of mines in Mexico, but by 1893, he was bankrupt and unemployed.) Clarence King was not alone in suggesting transcendent vision could be wedded to concrete national and personal concerns.

Like Muir and King, John Wesley Powell read the frontier as a geography ripe with possibility. The creator of the U.S. Geological Survey and author of the 1878 *Report on the Lands of the Arid Region of the United States*, Powell saw the West as a vast garden ready for reclamation. He and his supporters wrote of the desert as a mythic territory, arguing for irrigation systems and the "reclamation" of the lost dry spaces. For Powell and those like him, the empty and nearly uninhabitable land was biblical and clearly mythic. With water and the careful application of a reclamation system, the lost wanderers of the West could once again live in a lush garden. The reclamation of land, and of Eden—a process that required finally the control of nature—would recreate a lost innocence. For the nineteenth century American mind, this attempted recovery of innocence inevitably resulted in a correspondent claim of national expansion, technology and wealth.[3] And indeed, this vision of the West as a natural, mythic garden persists.

Famed and iconoclastic naturalist and writer Edward Abbey, author of *Abbey's Road*, returns repeatedly to the idea that nature bespeaks the sublime. Like his predecessors, Abbey travels the westward roads to rise above the lonely and pedestrian limits of the urban self. Writes Abbey,

> Walking up the trail to my lookout tower last night, I saw the new moon emerge from a shoal of black clouds and hang for a time beyond the black silhouette of a shaggy, giant Douglas fir. I stopped to look. And what I saw was the moon—the moon itself, nothing else; and the tree alive and conscious in its own spiral of time; and my hands, palms upward, raised toward the sky. We were there. We are. That is what we know. This is all we can know. And each such moment holds more magic and miracle and mystery than we...shall ever be able to understand. Holds all that we could possibly need... (131)

The trail, the moon, and the Douglas fir transport Abbey to another self and to another, better world. They constitute romantic vehicles. Abbey's vision is incomplete, for like most of his fellow romantics, Abbey posits the presence of women as a necessary element in recaptured paradise. Women factored into this return to the garden, for they were seen as both a part of nature—perhaps the best part of nature—yet they also possessed the potential power to un-make that paradise. Contemplating the need for women, Abbey writes frequently that the westward experience is incomplete without a female companion. "A mistake to come to a perfect place...without a good woman" (75). He is forthright about his reasoning; perfection and romance, and women and landscape are bound together in Abbey's vision of the West.

> When I think of travel, I think of certain women I have known. So many of my own journeys have been made in pursuit of love. In pursuit of pain. And in flight from both, landscape and women. Whenever I discover a natural scene that pleases me, that I find beautiful, my first thought is: What a place to bring a girl! And our world is so rich in both—beautiful places, lovely women. We should all be as happy as birds. (181)

For Abbey, travel and the West are always about recreating Eden, a notion that requires both a transcendent garden and the body of a woman.

This romantic—in both its sublime and conjugal sense—reading of the West is shared by Abbey and generations of American naturalists and writers. David Wyatt concludes his work on California and the West, *The Fall Into Eden*, with a discussion of the interplay of travel and the western American landscape.

> Through their encounters with natural space, writers on the continent developed new ways of knowing. Unsponsored imaginations found in unfallen landscape a stage on which to reenact Milton's story: We have heard enough about American Eves and Adams.... In its responsiveness to projection, landscape evolved into a palimpsest on which Americans could revise Old-World ideas.... If landscape has meant one thing to Americans, it has meant innocence, and the ways in which we make use of it.... (Wyatt 206–207)

In the traditional canon of American literature, landscape functions as a representation of the sublime, the feminine spirit, and a return to both. The natural world functions as a cosmic signifier; traditionally women act as the muses of this transcendent territory.

In contrast to these historic masculine projections of nature as sublime and romantic, a significant number of women writers have read nature differently. For them, nature is not necessarily sublime nor is it feminine. For these women authors, nature can assume a predatory aspect. It can be masculine or it can simply exist without spiritual or sentimental associations. Mary Austin found the natural world to be not a place of reverence, but rather a space of escape. Her westward road is noticeably not transcendent; instead, it offers both a darker vision of loss and a critique of women's social position in the West. Other more contemporary accounts, offered by Pam Huston, Diane Smith, Annie Dillard, and Annie Proulix, parody and simply pre-empt the ways in which natural phenomenon has been traditionally and textually controlled by men. For these authors, nature is not necessarily divine, not gendered, and, indeed, not always benign. These writers reject the classic genre of the pastoral; sometimes they distort the genre, sometimes they occupy textual spaces previously considered masculine, and sometimes they simply refuse to read the road as a pathway toward the sublime. Writers about nature, they reject the "natural" place of women within romantic western terrain.

Mary Austin: Walking Away from Womanhood
in the West

In the arid land east of California's Sierra Nevada mountain range, south of Mammoth Mountain and Yosemite National Park, lies the small town of Independence. Composed largely of fishing-tackle shops, single-story motels, a few glass-fronted coffee shops, and several fast-food establishments, Independence is inhabited by tourists, hikers and fishermen, sun-worn retirees, a few aspiring ranchers and a tiny number of dispossessed teenagers. There are a few blocks of neat, wood-framed houses with well-kept yards that try and keep the desert at bay. But, a few blocks off of Highway 395, Independence also hosts the Mary Austin Museum. The museum is a celebration of the Owens River Valley, of a bygone era when the town prospered (before the water in the Owens River was re-routed south), and of the town's most illustrious former citizen—naturalist, writer, and schoolteacher, Mary Hunter Austin.

Housed in an old school building, the museum occupies the very space in which Austin once taught. Inside, visitors are instructed in the outlines of Austin's life, shown her papers and manuscripts, and are urged to buy her reissued texts or other books for sale in the small shop. Mostly, the museum contains the collected flotsam of another era. Splintering wooden wagon wheels, farmers' tools, and scuffed and dilapidated women's high top shoes abound. Closely examined, some of the displayed texts do quietly note Austin's divorce and her eventual disappearance from the town. Yet the narrative finally implies that Mary Austin was a forthright and respected "school marm" in Independence, that she loved the town, enjoyed small children, and adored the West—especially its landscapes and natural attributes. Her literary stature gives dignity to the town while her gender once again reminds tourists the West was "civilized" by its righteous women.

The Mary Austin Museum is not alone in its relatively sentimental interpretation of Austin. Often anthologized today, Austin is still regarded as a "nature writer" (although with increasing frequency since the 1980s that title is sometimes combined with "feminist").[4] She is sometimes described as an author associated with a resurgence of the local color movement, and regarded as a "new regionalist" remarking upon the connection between landscape and character (Malone and Etulain 176–177). Edward Abbey, in his introduction to Austin's reissued edition of *The Land of Little Rain*, contends Austin shared the tradition of "nature writing" with John Muir, John C. Van Dyke and John Burroughs.

For Abbey, Austin is a writer who is able to endow the seemingly natural world with rare feeling and even devotion. Her observations and emotions, felt Abbey, matched his own.

> When Mary Austin looked at the desert world, she saw it clearly and in detail.... She noticed things that most human desert dwellers never see or even know about..."none other than this long grown land" says our author, "lays such a hold on the affections." (Austin, *Land* xii–xiii)

While gently scolding Austin for her tendency to be "too fussy, even prissy at first," Abbey overlooks such evidence of female sentimentality because she is, finally, a genuine nature writer.

> Mary Austin has something special going for her...the world of Nature. The natural scene. The country out there, yonder, beyond the wall, beyond the interstate highways.... Beyond that wall lies the natural, nonhuman world. Nature. What's left of it...we save what we can of the original world that could have been our lordly inheritance. Mary Austin's *Land of Little Rain* is one of them, another nature book. That is, a book about earth, sky, weather, about some of the plants and animals that survive... (Austin, *Land* viii–ix)

A "tough" woman, schoolteacher and rancher, capable of "turning the water hose full blast onto a group of uninvited guests," Abbey casts Austin within the traditional narrative of the West (Austin, *Land* vi). She is the schoolteacher with the heart of a gold and strength enough to pull a wagon, the woman who failed at love but found solace in nature. In Austin, Abbey found a feminine reflection of his own sensibility.

Other critics too, most notably David Wyatt, have read Austin's work as commentary on "nature and nurturance," and on Austin's romantic desire to remake the Garden and to compensate for her own failed maternal projects. For Wyatt, Austin falls clearly within the romantic sensibility sketched in his *The Fall Into Eden*. Eve is Austin's "precursor," writes Wyatt. Considering the unpublished parable, "The Lost Garden," Wyatt argues Austin's work is "a kind of last judgment on the art of her life...a revision of the myth of paradise." This effort to reconstitute paradise stems from guilt and a sense of personal failure, a moral "fall" on the part of Austin. "Only by fastening their love on places rather than persons," continues Wyatt, "can natures such as Austin's, she seems to say, escape the limiting history of identification with their halved precursor, Eve..." (Wyatt 94). According to Wyatt, Austin's guilt and incompleteness arise from unresolved issues with her own mother—a sense of being unwanted—from her daughter's mental disabilities and eventual death, and from her failure to make her niece Mary Hunter into a surrogate and perfect child (72–75). Life within nature, coupled with a textual attempt to represent that natural world, becomes for Austin a kind of compensation. In Wyatt's well-researched view, Austin emerges as a tragic figure, her desire to reclaim Eden doomed, as are all romantic projects.

Viewed more closely, Austin proves a difficult and recalcitrant romantic. The landscape she evokes is often hellish and sinister. Austin ties her emotionally troubled infant daughter to a chair where she remains in her own feces until the neighbors, disturbed by her screams, intervene (Fink 109). While Austin may speak from time to time of the garden, her texts are finally more about movement and travel than they ever are about destination. Austin is a nomad, discontent and subversive, intent upon negotiating the dark aspects of both the landscape and human emotion.

Born in Carlinville, Illinois, in 1868, Austin endured a difficult childhood. Before her tenth birthday, both her father and her younger sister, Jennie, had passed away, and these deaths were followed by the family's immediate fall into penury. The Hunters moved to a "small and stuffy house" on an unpleasant street. Writing about herself in her autobiography, *Earth Horizon*, Austin uses a peculiar and inconsistent third person voice to tell her story of familial loss. In her memoir, Austin remarks that the dead Jennie "was the only one who ever unselfishly loved me" (Austin, *Earth* 124). She was "unwanted" by her mother, Mary Hunter, Austin tells the reader of her autobiography, although she obtains this information not from her mother but from her father's previous fiancée some forty years after the fact (Austin, *Earth* 316). A few years after the death of Austin's father, George Hunter, her maternal grandfather also died. The abbreviated family circle now included only Mary Hunter (Austin), her mother, and her brother. Mrs. Hunter determined the family should move west, and

> ...against all advice our home was dismantled, our goods sold or shipped, tenants found for the house. Within a week or two of Mary's graduation, we were on our way... The road for which we had set out was Camino Real. (Austin, *Earth* 184–85)

The road west proved arduous and slow, even by the standards of 1888. The Hunter's passage to California took over a year, slowed by a series of family visits. In Austin's later recollection of this trip, each recounted family visit is marked by a death. There was a "White Plague" that hung over the western territory, remarked Austin (184).

This so-called "White Plague" would eventually attach itself to Austin herself. Upon her arrival in California's San Joaquin Valley, newly armed with her teaching certificate, Austin fell into a "plague-like" malaise she would later call her "breakdown." In the rural San Joaquin, Austin and her mother settled into a shabby one-room cabin where they endeavored to become farmwomen. Still an adolescent with a taste for books and poetry, and used to the comforts of a long-settled Midwestern suburb, Austin found her new life appalling. The unremitting physical labor, the intense heat, and the complete lack of domestic space offered by the nineteenth century West made life claustrophobic and unbearable. Writes Austin, as she considers her frontier despair:

> All grief is dreadfully alike. For once Mary had nothing to say...there was livestock to be looked after and settlements to be made.... I have no instant of recovered recollection.... life was simply stripped of all imaginative excursions.... (*Earth* 48)

Contained by the furnace of the cage-like cabin, Austin found herself unable to sleep or to move. Her memory began to erode, a condition

Austin would later blame upon the ahistoric nature of the West. It was impossible, she felt, to remember anything in a land where time had seemingly passed without any written recollection. As her condition worsened, Austin found herself unable to remember the comforting familiarity of old habits, and finally even her ability to remember words themselves began to disappear. Without physical space or emotional breathing room, Austin's very identity unraveled (Austin, *Earth* 193–196).

The relationship between spatial containment, melancholia and linguistic/literary representation has been frequently discussed since Virginia Woolf's "A Room of One's Own." Sandra Gilbert and Susan Gubar address this topic in their now nearly canonical *The Madwoman in the Attic.* Using a word oddly relevant to the frontier since it was associated with both childbearing and the daily conditions of women's lives, Gilbert and Gubar suggest "confinement" and lack of space are central to the female experience. In *The Gendering of Melancholia*, Juliana Schiesari suggests female "hysteria," the classic "nervous breakdown," and "melancholia" are the result of containment, and a

> ...devalued status in a symbolic governed by a masculine economy of self-recuperation. Such a depression then may indeed be a way to re-inscribe women's losses through another type of representation. (Schiesari 77)

Luce Irigaray makes this same point in her *Speculum of the Other Woman,* for it is her contention melancholia occurs when women are excluded from the spatial and signifying economy of a culture. In this sense, women are constructed as "outsiders," occupying only a limited and liminal space, lacking any signifying capacity.

The notion of insufficient space has found new meaning in the literature of anorexia. As Jennifer Shute points out in her memoir, *Life Size*, women are historically concerned about "taking up space." The sense of self is eradicated by a diminished entitlement to "space" and territory for the self. Shute writes the real issue concerns "how much space a woman feels entitled to take up in the world" (17). Without self, there can be, finally, no history and no representation or real involvement in the symbolic economy of language. As Julia Kristeva writes in her account of female melancholia in *Black Sun: Depression and Melancholia,* "melancholia then ends up in asymbolia, in loss of meaning" (42). For Mary Hunter Austin, confined to a one-room cabin like generations of frontier women, confinement and asymbolia were more than theoretical constructions. Stripped of intellectual pursuits and converted only into a body inadequate to its tasks, deprived of space and signifying identity, Austin withdrew into illness.

Much later in her life, Austin would comment on both her early illness in the West and upon a recurrent mental and physical despair. Her words suggest to what degree confinement and resistance to confinement shaped her melancholia.

> Sometimes I think it is the frustration of that incomplete adventure that is the source of deep resentment I feel... I wake in the night convinced that there are still uncorrupted corners from which the Spirit of the Arroyos calls me... I resolve that next year or the next at farthest [I will go there]... I am never able to manage it. (Austin, *Earth* 189)

For Austin the nomad self would forever be in conflict with the cultural imposition of place, as well as the pragmatics imposed by travel itself. The cost of that conflict was frustration and illness.

If Austin's depression and physical sickness were caused by emotional and spatial confinement, her "cure" was found in a rejection of the confines of the cabin and travel. As she reveals in both her autobiography and in *Everyman's Genius,* her study of parapsychology and mysticism, Austin began to take excursions, both imaginative and physical. Denied access to her earlier intellectual pursuits, she turned to meditation and outward movement. "Marooned in the desert," meditation and walking "released Mary" from her mute melancholia (Austin, *Earth* 195). Austin recognized the transgressive nature of her "cure," for she comments in her autobiography her therapy is not "Christian;" indeed, she is uneasily aware she is walking away from respectable female identity.

Presumably "cured," and anxious to leave her mother's cabin, Mary Hunter (Austin) married Stafford Austin in 1891. While the marriage did have the advantage that it removed her from her San Joaquin home, the relationship offered little relief. Stafford Austin was a frustrated, failed visionary. He devised complex irrigation projects for use along the Owens River, only to encounter constant failure. He pursued a career as a vintner, but his grapes died on the vine and his wine business quickly became insolvent. Despondent, Stafford Austin sought release in alcohol, drinking so much his absences and deviations from polite behavior were common knowledge in the small town of Lone Pine. In need of financial support, Stafford and Mary Austin both sought employment by the school district. Stafford Austin was quickly promoted to district superintendent while his wife taught. But as Stafford's drinking problem worsened, Mary Austin was forced to assume her husband's professional obligations as well as her own. Then, in 1892, Austin gave birth to a severely disabled child.

Ruth Austin suffered from profound, if vaguely diagnosed, cognitive impairment. Some biographers (Abbey among them) term Ruth's disability "mental retardation." Others, like August Fink, author of *I-Mary*, describe a physically beautiful baby whose behavior was marked by terrible and inexplicable temper tantrums, implying the child suffered from autism. Regardless, Mary Austin's reaction to her child is both interesting and at odds with the convention of frontier maternity. Austin moved to nearby Bishop where she found a room at the rather squalid Drake Motel. While Austin taught at the Inyo Academy, her daughter was left alone, tied up in the room, until her screams and the smell of excrement drew the attention of the neighbors.

> They thought her handling of Ruth was shameful. Half the time the child was farmed out to strangers and when she was home, she was abused. Hearing Ruth's screams, neighbors would go to the house to find Mary pacing the floor, hair hanging down her back, apparently oblivious to her daughter who was strapped to a chair. (Fink 109)

Eventually, Austin found a farm couple willing to care for her daughter. This inaugurated a series of informal care-taking accommodations until Ruth was placed in an institution. When Ruth died in 1918, her remains were held until 1922, when Austin finally made arrangements to have her ashes stored in the First National Bank of Monterey. Austin evidently neglected to pay for this storage, and seven years later the bank wrote to Mary Austin, noting the unpaid bill and stating they had been trying "to get in touch with Mrs. Austin for the past few years" (Wyatt 75). During the intervening time, Austin had separated from and finally divorced Stafford Austin, permanently leaving the Owens River Valley after an abortive attempt to live in Independence. The troubled relationship between Mary Austin and her daughter was not the stuff of romantic imagery.[5]

Similar flaws marked Austin's relationship with the eastern California desert and its frontier communities. Alienated from her husband, scorned by her neighbors, forced by economic circumstances to teach uninterested youth in stuffy schoolhouses, Austin took little interest in the companionship of the town's citizens. She (like Edward Abbey) did, however, fight attempts to modernize the desert, and was particularly opposed to the Owens River Valley water projects (Wyatt 92). Austin's experience in the California desert was largely characterized by her desire to leave it. Despite the near canonization of Austin that takes place today in Independence (and in a variety of nature and western anthologies), she had little love for the desert terrain. It was a landscape, she said, "that had little in it to love," "a landscape out of hell...squeezed up out of chaos" (Austin, *Land* 5). Frequently regarded as a kind of "earth mother" for the eastern desert, Austin had more affinity for travel and escape than she had for western geography. She left the Owens River territory for Los Angeles, Carmel, San Francisco, England, Italy, and finally the Southwest. She escaped from the demonized landscape through motion.

Austin's texts detail her cultivation of a nomadic sensibility and her dark—even sinister vision—of the West. Just as she cured herself of the "White Plague" and her breakdown through walking, Austin's texts prescribe motion as a general and necessary curative for women.[6] In both her short story collection, aptly named *Lost Borders* and in her fantasy novel, *The Outland*, Austin evokes a bleak and even hostile portrait of the West, depicting a mysterious landscape of blurred borders and indistinguishable terrain. It is a geography populated by irresponsible and dominating men, and by nameless mobile women, women without fixed identity, who must negotiate this unmapped space. In this literature, "grief...is converted into the desire for option in space. Walking becomes a metaphor for grace under pressure, of imaginative gain despite natural loss" (Wyatt 79). Of all of Austin's many works, her story "The Walking Woman" is perhaps most emblematic of Austin's literature and her nomadic sensibility.

Contained within *Lost Borders*, "The Walking Woman" takes place in the black and lava-laden desert east of the Sierra Nevada, and concerns a "Mrs. Walker"—a woman who has walked and traveled so extensively motion has become her identity. As the story opens, Austin—as narrator—describes in somewhat morbid terms the east desert terrain, and the myth of Mrs. Walker.

> We had come all one day between blunt, whitish bluffs rising from mirage water, with a thick, pale wake of dust billowing from the wheels of the dead wall of the foothills sliding and shimmering with heat. (*Lost* 196)

The desert is hellishly hot, so hot it creates the illusion of water in the suffering observer's mind. Except for the black lava, the landscape is parched of color. It is a landscape without fixed signifiers, where the dust blurs vision and acts as a "wake" for the "dead" body of the nearby hills. The narrator mentions Mrs. Walker, for she is anxious to meet her, having heard from the desert cowboys and ranch hands of "the muse of the travel which this untrammeled space begets" (196). Some believe her to be young, while others describe her as old. She is both "comely" and "deformed," "straight" and "broken." She can appear and disappear at will.

A western "Everywoman," Mrs. Walker represents the condition of her frontier sisters and converses with them intermittently. By reputation, Mrs. Walker travels in "dust clouds," like the genies of middle-eastern legend; she embodies the nomadic spirit and her appearance varies according to the observer.

Traveling herself through the Owens River Valley, the narrator pauses at polluted pool, a pool that again suggests the uninhabitable and even malevolent nature of the desert terrain. Even the water is incapable of supplying salvation, for it is:

> [A] pool of waste full of weeds of a poisonous dark green, every reed

> ringed about the water-level with a muddy white incrustation... The grass
> is thick and brittle and bleached straw-color... (Austin, *Lost* 197)

In this dark vision of the brooding and "blue hot desert," Mrs. Walker
suddenly appears. The conversation of the narrator and Mrs. Walker
"flows as smoothly as the river of mirage"(197).

The narrator tries to document Mrs. Walker's real identity so she
can demystify and explain this nomadic apparition. Mrs. Walker's
memory has been largely erased and her mind remains as white and
encrusted as the country around her. She too suffers from the "White
Plague." Still, she does possess bits of disconnected recollection, and
she shares these memories with the narrator. For the most part
unaware of dates, towns, names and territories, Mrs. Walker confides
she too once suffered from a nervous breakdown. Unable to
authenticate her story, Mrs. Walker tells the narrator she believes she
once nursed a male invalid in the West; the strain of his continuous
care resulted in her own nervous collapse. Tired and isolated,
afflicted with a paralyzing melancholia and without any apparent
recourse, Mrs. Walker walks. Movement rehabilitates her.

> By her own account she had begun by walking off an illness. There had
> been an invalid to be taken care of...leaving her at last broken in body
> with no recourse but her own feet to carry her out of that
> predicament...that drove her into the open...it must have been about that
> time that she lost her name... (Austin, *Lost* 198)

Too strictly constrained by a repressive masculine economy, Mrs.
Walker becomes a nomad—a woman without a passport, community
citizenship, or fixed identity. She does not travel in order to reach a
destination; in fact, she does not even recognize the notion of
destination. Quite simply, Mrs. Walker walks for the sake of walking.

The narrator persistently continues with her questions. She wants
to know the particulars of why and how Mrs. Walker travels. Mrs.
Walker can provide no direct answers, but she does tell the narrator
another story. After many countless seasons of walking, Mrs. Walker
tired of her lonely existence. She met a shepherd named Filon
Geraud, a shepherd who watched his flocks on the eastern slopes of
the Sierra Nevada. Mrs. Walker recounts the impression made upon

her by this "red-blooded" male "with an indubitable spark for women," when an unexpected sandstorm occurred. "Sand-storms are incalculable disasters," explains Mrs. Walker, because they obscure the landscape and smother the ewes and lambs with their hot cloud of debris. But Geraud refused to be frightened or defeated by the storm; Boone-like he was able to discern the path and protect the livestock. Enraptured, Mrs. Walker now walked with her new companion, "running with the flock" and enchanted with her new pastoral life and her new identity as helpmate and lover (Austin, *Lost* 201).

But the pastoral garden proved to be an unstable and illusory paradise. By autumn Mrs. Walker could "no longer keep to the trail" (Austin, *Lost* 202). Geraud was leaving the Sierras and Mrs. Walker remarks, "it was a good time and longer than he could be expected to have loved one like me" (202). Left in the solitary garden as winter approaches, the now pregnant Mrs. Walker finds herself unable to travel or find help. Romance, community and the fellowship of men have failed her. Alone in the shadows of the Sierra, she delivers her child. Perhaps, Mrs. Walker postulates, she "would have given up walking to keep at home and tend him," but she never has the chance (202). The baby dies and she buries him beside the trial. The Eden of fixed community and permanent attachment proves to be a true mirage. Mrs. Walker returns to the road, propelled not only by her old losses and frustrations but by this new grief as well. Since her child could not stay long enough to "do his own walking," she must do it for him. "...`[W]henever the wind blows in the night,' said the Walking Woman, `I wake and wonder if he is well covered'" (Austin, *Lost* 202). She walks to negotiate a vast landscape of indeterminacy and terror, and to recover from the pain inflicted on her by culture. She walks to reclaim an identity far outside the fixed structures of society.

As Mrs. Walker finishes her tale, she suddenly picks up her bag and blanket and leaves. Dissatisfied with the terminated conversation, the narrator pursues Mrs. Walker, who was, after all, only a few steps ahead. But Mrs. Walker has vanished. Far in the distance, further away than it would be possible to walk in that brief time, the narrator spies a vague figure moving with a "queer sidelong gait." As the narrator scans the horizon, she wonders if perhaps, afflicted by heat and curiosity, she might have imagined the encounter. But as she looks down, she sees "...in the bare, hot sand the track of her two feet bore evenly and white" (203). No picture or documentable evidence of the nomadic Mrs. Walker exists; still, she has left her trace on the landscape.

Readers will recall that Defoe's Crusoe mistakes his own footprints for those of a possible savage and cannibal, and in the same manner Austin projects her own identity on to the elusive Mrs. Walker. Not a great deal of psychological insight is required in order to find Austin in her character.[7] The "Walking Woman" emerges as a textual artifact of Austin's own commitment to a nomadic sensibility. In the story are thematic elements that will emerge in much of her work: an evocation of a natural world that is blighted and nearly demonic, a general indictment of the traditional patriarchal culture, and an insistence women ought to inhabit a dynamic rather than static space. Women, as nomads, will find comfort not in arrival, but in the unmarked spaces in between destinations.

Austin continues to explore these same themes in her strange mythological text, *The Outland*. This novel unfolds in a large, nameless, thickly forested country that bears some overt resemblance to the woods of Artemis in Greek mythology but is also clearly referential of James Fennimore Cooper's American wilderness. Into these literary woods stumble the novel's narrator, Mona and her lover, Herman. Captured by the "wood people"—the frontiersmen, the couple is informed that ritual sacrifice defines this mysterious country. Every year, they are told, a young maiden is selected as a sacrifice, that the woods nation "may grow and prosper." Horrified, Mona and Herman watch the selection of the virginal Daria. Like "The Walking Woman," *Outland* emerges as a meta-commentary on the nature of women and the frontier space.

Outland once again reminds the reader to distrust nature and the pastoral genre. The people of the woods select Daria so the woodland gods might be appeased and thus allow the community an opportunity to discover "the King's Desire." This vast treasure of unsurpassed wealth exists, supposedly, in the far recesses of the woods and only a people endowed with grace will be able to find it.

The virgin must be sacrificed so the treasure can be found. Trained to comply with their tribal destiny, most maidens seemingly cooperate. But Daria refuses her sacrificial duties. She resists her role as the "Ward," and begs her father to intervene in her selection. Her father though is humiliated by Daria's lack of deference and informs her that through her selfishness she dishonors both the family and the community. Daria struggles, but her resistance proves useless. Societal need supersedes her personal desires. She is as necessary to the "wood people" as the "Madonna of the Prairie" is to the pioneers. Given a drug that produces amnesia, abandoned deep in the forest, Daria suffers for the good of her country.

Lonely, Daria walks through the "chaldean" and "primeval" forest. Because of the drug, she cannot remember who she is or where she is going. Stripped of memory, Daria no longer can claim an identity. She has no sense of purpose. She moves though woods that are suffocating, dark and demonic, while legendary in their beauty. Celebrated by the poets, nature proves to be a cage. Daria's mind cannot remember or discern choices, but her body, once loved by a young man, recollects vaguely that once there was something more. The drug is not fully effective. Stirred by a sense of something other than the frontier woods, Daria walks. Nature, mythology and community have failed her. Movement of her body is all that is left. Austin's *Outland* clearly references and implicates frontier culture and its romantic sacrifice of women. Like the masculinized frontier, the *Outland*'s woodlands constitute a space where the land is plundered and women are sacrificed in pursuit of expansion and wealth. Seemingly creatures of nature, the people of the woods are only interested in enhancing their own lives. But in this investigation, the text again creates a new heroine, a woman who ignores the vulgar signifiers of name, nation, destination, and community, and simply, disinterestedly walks.

Outland was published in 1919, and its style and subject indicate the influence of both Sarah Orne Jewett's *The Country of Pointed Firs* and Charlotte Perkins Gilman's work. Austin problematizes the mythical frontier woods in a way that is consonant with Jewett's work. Patriarchy and the burden of sexuality taint both conceptual forests. Like Gilman, Austin interrogates the place of women in culture. Such influence was more than unconscious. In 1899–1900, Austin worked in Los Angeles. As Lummis' protégé, she met the famed author of "The Yellow Wall Paper" (Fink 99–100). During this period, Gilman was at work on what would become her three feminist utopian novels, most famously, *Herland*. Given even the similarity of Austin's *Outland* title, it seems highly probable the two women discussed the place of women within a repressive culture. But unlike Jewett and Gilman, Austin does not become trapped within her failed conceptual utopias. She eschews ideology; she does not endow nature with the means to salvation. "Women hate," she writes, "with implicitness the life like the land, stretching interminably..." (Austin, *Lost* 10). Like the Walking Woman, Austin uses her feet to walk away from an unacceptable paradigmatic and natural West.

Re-Configuring the Natural World in a Contemporary Context: Diane Smith, Pam Huston and Annie Proulix

If, in the traditional literature of the West, the land is verdant and feminine, the man is quintessentially masculine, and the woman is a stalwart lady who wears a sunbonnet and follows her husband, then the works of contemporary writers Diane Smith, Pam Huston and Annie Proulix are at odds with tradition. "Nature writers" on their own, Smith, Huston and Proulix continue the tradition of counter-narrative, as they reinterpret the relationship of gender and the natural landscape. The result of the remaking of the naturalistic canon is that nature itself emerges in a new way, a way far removed from any romantic inclination.

Diane Smith's epistolary novel, *Letters from Yellowstone*, seems, on first reading, to be an unsurprising account of life during the early days of Yellowstone Park. Set in the nineteenth century, the novel traces the work, adventures and correspondence of a young botanist named A.E. Bartram. Dr. Bartram is hired by a distinguished naturalist to do survey work in the Yellowstone Park area, and after some comic mishaps is revealed to be a Miss Bartram—Alexandria Bartram. In typical fashion, Bartram's botanical enterprise is threatened by her supervisor's discovery of her gender. Outraged, the esteemed Dr. Merriam writes to his mother:

> She is quiet, understated and respectful, not at all the chatty old woman that the botanical field is wont to attract amongst the female sex. Even so, if she were to join us in the field, I fear the entire enterprise would be put at risk. Where would she sleep? With whom would she travel into the backcountry? How could she possibly endure...such primitive condition? I desperately need the manpower but...you see, even the language conspires against me. (D. Smith 27)

But, of course, Bartram prevails, and in the course of the novel wins over her own family's support, Dr. Merriam's loyalty and the affection of nearly all her associates. Alexandria Bartram is a true nineteenth century heroine—hardworking, virtuous, and deserving. Yet, as traditional as *Letters from Yellowstone* appears to be, several unusual points become evident in the text.

The most obvious disparity between the novel and the earlier works it clearly emulates is found in the character of Alexandra Bartram. Neither a spinster nor a girl looking for a husband, Bartram is a scientist. Despite the surprise of Merriam and the reader alike, no romance distracts Bartram from her field. She is a female character cast in a role usually accorded to a male. She has a "male" occupation, and her colleagues and family read her preoccupation with science as masculine. The feminine and romantic qualities associated with nature are absent from Bartram's personality. This usurping of masculine territory by a female protagonist is one of the primary elements introduced to the genre of "nature writing" by female authors. Smith, a "nature" and scientific writer on her own, with a prevailing interest in Yellowstone history, is well aware of the conventions that have historically constructed investigations of the landscape.

Perhaps more significantly, Smith offers a view of nature that is neither feminine nor gentle. In her text there is violence associated with the earth that violates the generative notion of "mother earth." For Smith and her heroine, the natural world is not ordered by a mythic, transcendent power. It is instead a mechanical universe, ruled by logical classification and the laws of physics. Early in the text, Bartram argues with Dr. Merriam, when he attempts to equate Native

American lore with the more "scientific" discipline of astronomy, and then goes so far as to suggest the position of the stars have some larger bearing on the world. Bartram is shocked, even horrified by such outright, unmediated romanticism.

> "You have no right to say that myth and science are the same.... I do not wish to be impertinent but are you saying that the constellations somehow affect the seasons?" As she said this she suppressed a laugh, but I could not tell if she was thinking the whole notion humorous or simply preposterous... (D. Smith 182)

The debate between Merriam and Bartram continues throughout the novel. Merriam reads nature finally as epic and mythic while Alexandra Bartram despises any thinking that is not strictly rational and scientific. Between them, the two characters have reversed the prevailing stereotype regarding women and science.

For Bertram, the natural forces that govern the land can be brutal and harsh. She associates the earth with the color red and the idea of blood. When she drinks a glass of wine, Bartram remarks it "tasted of the blood of the earth." Later in the text, as she watches Old Faithful geyser, Bartram equates the land to a large steam machine, "a large blast of water from a cone..."(D. Smith 201). In Bartram's view, nature is a mechanical system. In Bartram's nature, bears eat young women, the earth bursts unpredictably into flame, and even a gentle riding expedition in the rain can prove deadly. Despite her "slight build and demeanor," as she rides and walks through the Park, surveying its natural resources, Bartram moves away from conventional representations of women and nature.

The novel concludes with Miss Bartram resisting her family's efforts to bring her home and refusing the romance that seems inevitable in this quasi-Victorian, epistolary text. Instead, Bartram remains committed to her botanizing, and replaces devotion to husband or place with marriage to travel. "I cannot predict the future," she writes, but "I too will travel down that narrow, windy road out of the Park with a great sense of expectation.... You must travel west..." (D. Smith 226). Instead of a home, Bartram will have the "narrow windy road," and in the place of family she claims "my science clan" (226). Only on the road, outside of society, can Bartram find sufficient freedom from cultural restraints. She is committed to the life of a nomad.

*   *   *

River rafter, hunting guide and writer, Pam Huston provides an even more dramatic view of how women, as they travel down the rivers and roads of the West, must forge new relationships with nature. A gifted essayist, Huston herself is a traveler of western roads and a writer for a variety of nature and outdoor magazines. Like her predecessor, Mary Austin, Huston depicts a west that forces women to take to the road in order to escape the pain forced upon them by masculine narratives. The collected stories in *Cowboys Are My Weakness* delineate how the traditional narrative of the western road displaces and disadvantages women, and how women struggle to pre-empt men's "natural" frontier prerogatives, and how, once again, nature takes on a sinister and annihilating quality.

The title story of the collection, "Cowboys Are My Weakness," explores the allure of the traditional frontier narrative and exposes the impossibility and pain necessarily associated with the western mythology. The narrator begins by confessing she has an idealized image of modern "cowboy" life, but the story acts as a meditation on the failure of this dream. Writes Huston,

> I have a picture in my mind of a tiny ranch on the edge of pine trees with some horses in the yard. There's a woman standing in the doorway in cutoffs and a blue chambray work shirt and she's just kissed her tall, bearded, and soft-spoken husband goodbye.... If I were a painter, I'd paint that picture just to see if the girl in the doorway would turn out to be me...but I still don't know where that ranch is. (108)

Yet, the ranch where the narrator could kiss her husband, hang laundry, watch "the morning sun ...filtering through the tree branches like spiderwebs," and hike with her lover to count the whitetail deer is nonexistent. Instead, what the narrator discovers is "happy endings" are not possible with her cowboy lover, Homer, and by extension simply not possible in the West. Homer is silent, rude, unloving and unreliable. When the narrator tells him she might be pregnant, he urges to her to go quickly to "a state where abortion is still legal." The landscape is fraught with infidelity and loneliness. The narrator acknowledges what she looked for in the West was the product of "a made-for-TV movie mentality" (Huston 115). Although she spent her youth driving with her "sun-lover" parents, and her early adulthood looking for stability, the narrator is finally forced to drive away from the ranch, listening to country western music and repeating, "This is not my happy ending. This is not my story" (125).

A similar if more brutal theme is explored in the story "Dall." Here, the self-confessed non-violent heroine spends the hunting season as a guide so she can be with her hyper-masculine, abusive lover who is appropriately named Boone. Like his namesake, Boone is an expert marksman, shares a rare affinity with animals, and knows all the secret trails of Alaska. He also beats his lover, and throws her outside into the snow where she encounters a hostile mother grizzly bear. Boone attacks more than the physical body of the narrator; he psychologically assaults her identity. "Boone told me I would get used to watching the rams die," says the narrator, and eventually the narrator's code of nonviolence is corrupted (Huston 106). As "hours, maybe days" go by without speaking as the two characters hike for miles, the narrator realizes her relationship with Boone is doomed. Once again, Boone's masculine vocabulary precludes real intimacy or even hope.

"How To Talk to a Hunter" repeats the same now too familiar refrain. Huston contends frontier men inevitably corrupt women. "They lie to us, they cheat on us, and we love them for it" (19). Here, still again, the narrator's hopes for a vagabond and lasting love with a cowboy-hunter are smashed, turned into the clichéd lyrics of country music. Once again, the narrator is confined to a small cabin where at night she is covered with animal skins. Her lover is inarticulate, dishonest, and betrays her with a "coyote woman." Although the story concludes before the narrator is ready to take action, it is clear her only way to escape pain will be to take to the road.

In an effort to reconstitute the mythology, some of Huston's heroines remake themselves in the image of the men who have hurt them. These women become promiscuous, interested in the innocence of younger men. Like men, Huston's women collect suitors and amorous experiences.

> [T]he men want me again. I can see it in the way they follow my
> movements, not just with their eyes but with their whole bodies... And I'll
> admit this: I am collecting them like gold-plated sugar spoons, one from
> every state...there is something so sweet about the first kiss, the first
> surrender.... (Huston 152)

In this retelling of the frontier narrative, Huston's narrators turn into
the cowboys who have eluded them. They travel between lovers,
remarking on "the joyful and slightly disconcerting feeling of being
very much in love, but not knowing exactly who with" (153). In this
scenario, in a complete reversal of traditional narrative, men become
the hunted, the animal prey. "You fall in love with a man's animal
spirit," says the narrator of "Symphony," and she pictures her lovers
as impalas, giraffes, a "young bull elephant," and "the big African
cats." Clearly, the female narrator is the conductor of the
multifaceted, romantic "symphony;" in these western stories, the
narrator wakes in one state with one lover and spends the following
night in another region with another man. She has usurped the
phallus of the frontier hero.

If Huston's women narrators have assumed the role of the
hunter-aggressor, nature has been de-feminized. No longer a field for
romantic transcendence, nature becomes in Huston's work a space for
scavengers, rotted flesh, angry bears, threatening waterways and
mutant cells. In the story "Selway," the narrator goes white-water
river rafting with her irresponsible boyfriend, Jack. While some of the
initial rapids are named for women (Miranda Jane, for example), the
rapids themselves are masculinized and dangerous. "It's white
fucking water," says one of the river men, as the characters watch the
body of a dead woman being recovered. The woman's pelvis has been
smashed, and she bleeds to death in moments after slamming up
against a large protruding boulder. The unknown woman has been
violated and killed by the hard sharp stones of the uncontrollable
water. As the narrator contemplates the scene, she sees fifty-feet high
granite walls, sharp rocks, and a current that "grabs" and possesses
the women who enter it.

Water itself turns aberrant. In the story "Highwater" the natural salt lake of a western town begins to rise for inexplicable reasons. The water laps at the highway, producing in the wind large waves that flood the road and the natural landscape. Asleep and despondent in her car, Millie is nearly drowned by the encroaching and mysterious water. "Ten thousand years ago ...the lake was as big as three states back east," and Millie fantasizes that the water covers lost mountains, capitol buildings and lives. Near the lake is a turnout that becomes the site where men with sexual intent often take women—for sex or for self-justifying conversation. The water is both murky and reflective; "you can see all the way to Nevada in the water," muses Millie. But the water is mirage-like; it reflects past buildings and romantic aspirations but does not reflect the truth. The water provides a screen for the projection of masculine narrative and it rises and falls without reason.

In the end, Huston's work seems to suggest our very natural flesh is corrupt. Early in the collection, one of Huston's narrators encounters a dead elk, "[P]robably not dead a year, and still mostly covered with matted brown fur. The skull was picked clean by scavengers, polished white by the sun and grinning" (34). The elk's cellular decomposition parallels finally the human condition. "In My Next Life" relates the story of a western horse-trainer, Abby, who encounters a lump in her breast. She resorts to mythic Native American medicine, to prayer and meditation. But the lump proves immune to New Age romanticism. The lump grows and quickly engulfs Abby's whole system. "The doctor came in and started to say words like 'chemotherapy,' like 'bone scan' and 'brain scan,' procedures certain to involve soul loss of one kind or another" (Huston 167). Neither science nor romantic imagery can cure Abby. The cellular corrosion is too powerful. Nature is not awesome, it is destructive, cruel and utterly without reason. Against this landscape, Huston's heroines ride, drive, or float down a road in an effort to alter their blighted western destinies. Their romantic sensibilities flounder and perish amid the harsh realities of nature.

*   *   *

In Annie Proulix' collection *Close Range: Wyoming Stories*, the same "unnatural" capacity of nature is revealed. Like Austin, Proulix suggests the familiar space of the pioneer cabin oppresses and even twists the consciousness of its mostly female inhabitants. The result is a frontier landscape of repression, violence, and unrepresentable sexuality, from which the only recourse is death or travel. Proulix' stories are filled with castration scenes, murders, triangulated romances. For her, nature becomes "monstrous." In Proulix' West, "Friend, it's easier than you think to yield up to the dark impulse" (207). Perhaps the most paradigmatic of her tales is the very brief "55-Miles to the Gas Pump." Here, Rancher Croom—drunk and filthy, gallops wildly "over the dark plain" and in the dawn spreads his arms out and plunges to his death over the edge of a cliff. Liberated from the cabin where she has lived for twelve years, Mrs. Croom saws through the roof into the attic where she finds, "just as she thought, the corpses of Mr. Croom's paramours" (Proulix 252). She observes the old newspaper clippings that paper the walls, and examines the desiccated body parts. "When you live a long way out," observes the narrator, "you make your own fun" (252). For Proulix, the frontier cabin becomes the site of the parodic, the unthinkable, and the "unnatural." The cabin is the site of dismembered women.

Both hideous and interesting, the notion of dismemberment embodies the frontier experience. If, as Austin maintains, the road west functions as the river Lethe for women, obliterating their memory and their identity, then Proulix' nearly comic dismemberment becomes the literal representation of this cultural obliteration. The "White Plague" has already taken away their histories and identities. Proulix' dismemberment reminds us that these women cannot (re)member. Literally cut away from any concept of self, these women can possess no identity. The burning cabin from which Rowlandson ran and the oppressive cabin that Austin walked away from, become in Proulix' work a clear metaphor for the condition of women's lives. In fact, the space of the cabin is explored in Proulix' "A Lonely Coast." In this tale, the modern female narrator moves to the vicinity of Crazy Woman Creek and rents the modern version of the cabin—a tiny house trailer "you'd tow behind a car." Mourning the tensions in her marriage to Riley, the narrator finds work waitressing and bar tending, and makes friends with several other women who also work at the Wig-Wag Lodge. The women's lives are headed toward disaster, the narrator informs the reader, and she uses the image of the burning cabin to make her point.

> You ever see a house burning up in the night, way to hell and gone out there on the plains? Nothing but blackness and headlights cutting a little wedge into it...in that big dark a crown of flame the size of your thumbnail trembles. You'll drive for an hour seeing it until it burns out or you do.... And you might think about the people in the burning house, see them trying for the stairs, but mostly you don't give a damn.... The year that I lived in the junk trailer in the Crazy Woman Creek drainage I thought Josanna Skiles was like that, the house on fire in the night that you could only watch. (Proulix 189)

For Proulix, the demise of Josanna Skiles finds its expression in the depiction of the burning cabin.

Like Huston's female narrators, many of Proulix' women characters adopt the traditional posture of masculine figures as they survey the collapse of the romantic and fictive West. Josanna, Palma and Ruth engaged in fights, "drank, smoked, shouted to friends and they didn't so much dance as straddle a man's leg" (Proulix 191). Even their appearances become masculinized: Josanna smells like her brother—"musty and a little sour," Palma is extraordinarily tall and "slams" her big body into people, and "Ruth had the shadow of a mustache" (194). But this reconstituted masculinity leaves Josanna dead, shot by a .22 in the course of a fight. However masculinity is constructed and assumed, Proulix' texts contend the mythic and hyper masculinity of the West necessarily results in death.

In the short story, "People in Hell Just Want a Drink of Water," a tale that unfolds against the backdrop of a feud between the Dunmires and the Tinsleys, an attempt is made to reconstruct the sexuality of one of the story's male characters. The tale relates the road adventures of the "intensely modest, sensitive and abhorring of marital nakedness" Mrs. Tinsley, and her amorous son, Ras. Against her will, Mrs. Tinsley is brought west. As a child she had been enamored of the idea of nature and wrote a poem insisting, "[O]ur life is a beautiful Fairy Land." She seems well suited to the role of "Prairie Madonna." But the road west fails to measure up to Mrs.

Tinsley childhood ideal, and she is unnerved by the trip from Missouri to Wyoming. The vision of the Prairie Madonna proves false. She cannot bear "the infant howling intolerably, the wagon bungling along, stones sliding beneath the wheels" (Proulix 104). As the wagon crosses the Little Laramie River, Mrs. Tinsley throws her infant daughter into the river.

In the years following, attempting to compensate for her actions, Mrs. Tinsley engages in an exaggerated if clearly dysfunctional maternity, tying her children up to prevent them from going outside and making them spend much of their time in bed. Rebelling against such "feminine" treatment, her son Ras runs away. After some years, Ras is injured in a train wreck. He suffers from apparent brain damage and terrible disfigurement. He comes home, and all would be well except Ras keeps unveiling his huge phallus for the sight of the Dunmires' young daughters. He is castrated as punishment, and dies of a resulting gangrene. In Proulix' decidedly unromantic vision of the West, Ras is emasculated and Mrs. Tinsley repudiates the narrative of the kind and resourceful frontier mother. Clearly, there is little that is "naturally" maternal in her constitution. The text rejects the conventional notions of gender that are associated with the traditional frontier narrative.

Most disturbing in Proulix' stories is the vision of nature itself. Here, human flesh is vile and pestilent. Grasshoppers "hit against...the wall in their black and yellow thousands," and bits of prairie inexplicably ignite. The narrator of "A Lonely Coast" learns she and Riley can never have children, although no explanation for this problem is ever provided. In that same story, as the young heifers prepare to give birth in the spring, their bodies contort. "We figured twins," says the narrator. But when the cows are born, they are simply gigantic—over a third the size of the mother cows. The maternal cows are torn in half by the birth of the "monster" calves (Proulix 204). Similarly, women's bodies are inexplicably huge and deformed (as is Ottaline's in "The Bunchgrass Edge of the World"). But it is human nature that becomes the most unnatural and dysfunctional. Cruelty, a lack of acuity, and the complete erosion of anything resembling love become for Proulix the real natural world.

For Proulix' heroines—road girls and frontier women, the only solution is escape. Ottaline's sister, Shan, goes to Las Vegas knowing only a change of scenery will help. In "Pair a Spurs," the mud-encrusted Mrs. Freeze becomes a drifter. But escape offers only a temporary solution; every location suffers from some version of the same ills. The violence is terminal. In the West, all roads lead to the same bleak destination. The only solace is found, perhaps, between locales.

The West, the blissful land of primeval woods finally emerges as a monstrous and terrifying space. In *West of Everything: The Inner Life of Westerns*, Jane Tompkins contends this imaginative transformation is not surprising. For, she argues, the mystique of the frontier is always necessarily steeped in violence, a violence that ultimately must lead to death.

> The western is secular, materialist, and anti-feminist; it focuses on conflict in the public space, is obsessed by death, and worships the phallus.... it is a narrative of male violence.... (Tompkins 29)

Even when this masculinity is reconstructed, Proulix implies, the structural problems remain. The woman cannot assume the phallus without assuming its accompanying violence. The paths into the frontier occupy a macabre territory.

*   *   *

"There was a row of ancient trees," wrote Wordsworth, commenting upon the natural beauty he encountered in "The Prelude."

> They who dwelt in the neglected mansion house supplied Fresh butter, tea-kettle and earthenware, and chafing dish with smoking coals, and so and so beneath the trees we sat... (II/ll 150–154)

For the romantic, nature and her female inhabitants were nurturing, beautiful, and a vehicle whose "trailing clouds of glory" might take the viewer to God. For naturalist John Muir, nature comprises that "majestic domed pavilion."

> These blessed mountains are so compactly filled with God's beauty, no

> petty personal hope or experience has room to be…to feel beauty when
> exposed to it as it falls through the campfire or sunshine, entering not the
> eyes alone but the campfire through all one's flesh like radiant heat,
> making a passionate ecstatic pleasure-glow… (Muir, *Yosemite* 131)

In the work of any number of women western "nature" writers, the "mansion house" and the "majestic domed pavilion" are no longer shaped by romantic preconception. Mary Austin and the subsequent generations of women writers reinterpret nature in the West. Muir's divine "pleasure-glow" thus takes on darker and more sinister possibilities. Instead of being viewed as a mansion or pavilion, the West finally emerges as a kind of fun house, filled with freakish distorting mirrors and blind corridors. Such images reflect an alternative discourse and dark aesthetic that opposes the mythic, masculine West. These female writers mark their peril as they walk out of the romantics' house of nature and follow the paths of the frontier.

Postmodernity, and post-colonial and feminist notions in particular, make romantic theorizing of the subject similarly perilous and problematic. Like Mary Austin and the more contemporary women "nature writers," post-colonial theory critiques the larger narratives within which the construction of the sublime must exist. In her text, *The Psychic Life of Power*, Judith Butler meditates on the cultural construction of the transcendent "soul," arguing the search for the sublime self takes place within "an imprisoning frame." But, the psyche resists this cultural frame, argues Butler. Inevitably, the psyche recognizes the translation of the discursive identity into a romantic production that

> …imprison[s] the body within the soul, to animate and contain the body
> within that ideal frame…of an externally framing and normalizing ideal.
> The psyche is what resists the regularization. (Butler, *Psychic* 86)

Later in the text, Butler returns to the mechanisms that this resistance may utilize. She contends, finally, that melancholia, passivity and mania—the throwing off of attachments and insignificant objects and habits—are ways of resisting discursive regulation. Like Homi Bhabha, Butler reads these psychic "disruptions" as attempts at "disincorporation of the Master" (190).[8]

The "disincorporation of the Master" is precisely the topic of Proulix' dismembered fiction and the mission of the nameless, faceless, border-inhabiting Walking Woman. These are narratives that resist "the regularization" of conventional views of nature and the western frontier. The so-called "White Plague"—amnesia, restlessness and simultaneous paralysis, anger, identity disintegration and "maniacal" activity—are manifest at times in all of the texts discussed here and the "Plague" is a part of the larger vocabulary of resistance.

Indeed, it is finally the "mania" of the characters included in this "nature fiction" that provides escape and resolution. "No/mad women here," writes Rosa Braidotti, quoting a former student. To be a nomad is to escape a larger patriarchal madness. These women might be called mad by their culture, but their transgressive ways permit them to construct a free space outside of established discourse and its mythic (mis)conceptions. Resistance to the romantic investiture in nature and a refusal to countenance a sublime that must inevitably regulate feminine identity into a simple narrative subject mark the texts of Austin, Smith, Huston and Proulix. They are the unnatural nature girls of the frontier.

CHAPTER FOUR

In Search of the Maternal:
Mothers and Daughters on the Road

The dark continent of all dark continents is the
mother-daughter relationship...
Rosi Braidotti

Theorizing the Maternal

Even in the most arcane of spaces, surrounded by academic theoreticians, uncontainable bodily realities sometimes emerge. The maternal body strains the limits of the abstract. Pregnant, lactating, grasped by the sticky fingers of small children, the corporal form of the mother confounds philosophical discourse. Motherhood and maternity remain a vexed topic today within the larger venue of feminism. We are perhaps troubled by the proposed reality offered by maternity, and we are uncertain about how to theorize a body so interned by the unmediated discourses of everyday life. Theorized as an abstract and essentialized as an unchanging entity, the very terrain of the feminine body is contested. We endlessly debate whether we construct femininity and thus maternal subjectivity or if its particular nature is inherent. This debate cuts to the heart of feminist criticism. If we completely theorize the body and claim gender as a constructed entity, we run the risk of erasing that feminine subjectivity we seek to explore. And, if we claim for women some inherent, naturalized subjective self, we may simply recapitulate the old familiar and subordinate categories traditionally assigned to women. Examined too closely, this question is both irresolvable and politically threatening. It may be best to avert our eyes from the dilemma of the female body, a body continuously in a state of discernable, tangible, theoretical and disturbing flux. Pregnancy and maternity exacerbate the dilemma, for no other condition makes the physical body so resistant to both theoretical erasure and idealized platitudes and so very difficult to ignore. The reality of the maternal body—its biological contingencies, its vast capacity for radical change, its evident sexuality and utility—make it truly Lacan and Zizek's "Symptom." That maternal body harbors the inexpressible Real.

Resisting the identity formations required by patriarchal discourse, feminist theory questions the materiality of the body. Writes Judith Butler, "This 'irreducible' materiality is constructed through a problematic gendered matrix," a materiality constituted finally "through the exclusion and degradation of the feminine" (Butler, *Bodies* 29–30). But Drucilla Cornell suggests debates concerning the constructed-ness of the female body merely replicate patriarchy's reading of women. Good girls, in the old-fashioned vernacular, lived apart from their bodies; bad girls actively associated themselves with their physicality. Debates concerning the materiality of the body replace this conventional categorization with "good feminism" and "bad feminism" (Nicholson 83). So-called "good" feminists allow that their identity is utterly constructed; "bad" feminists persist in focusing upon the social reality of that bodily self. According to Cornell then, complete and overt theorizing of the body simply replays that old patriarchal mythology wherein, unlike men, (good) women abandon their physical selves. Despite controversy and derision, especially from American theorists, Luce Irigaray contends the "feminine" must lie outside the phallocentric and essentialist logic of traditional philosophical debate. Focus on the maternal body merely sharpens the schism within feminism. Writing a new preface to her road mark sociological text, *The Reproduction of Mothering*, Nancy Chodorow remarks in discussing the very notion of mothering, she felt

> ...forced to choose between one position that seemed biologically determinist and entrapping of women and another that claimed women's feelings about mothering and their potentially reproductive bodies were a product of social structure and cultural mandate. (xvii)

The polar extremes in this discussion revolve around a desire to theorize the maternal body away or to engage in heterosexual celebration of the production of the maternal body.

Motherhood is a focus of larger feminist inquiry. In her essay, "Women's Time," Julia Kristeva contends the changeable maternal body fractures women's prior identity, creating a sort of symbolic psychosis that is the source of female poetic language. Women's movement into the symbolic space of language is associated with a return to the repressed maternal instinct. Within Kristeva's vocabulary, pregnancy represents a return to the mother, a socially sanctioned return, unlike the parallel act of lesbianism.[1] Significantly, for Kristeva, maternity is an impulse that lies outside culture and the symbolic domain of masculine language. In her Freudian based work, Chodorow makes a somewhat similar claim. In Chodorow's reading of the maternal body, the woman who once saw her own mother as the primary love object, and who has only partially separated from this object finds rapprochement through the reproduction of motherhood.[2] But Judith Butler counters that such discursive formations place maternity squarely within the "obligatory frame of reproductive heterosexuality."[3]

> Hence, for Kristeva, poetry and maternity represent privileged practices within paternally sanctioned culture which permit a nonpsychotic experience of that heterogeneity and dependency characteristic of the maternal terrain.... Hence, the subversion of paternally sanctioned culture cannot come from another version of culture, but only from the repressed interior of culture itself, from the heterogeneity of drives that constitutes culture's concealed foundation.... Poetic language is thus, for women, both displaced maternal dependency and, because that dependency is libidinal, displaced homosexuality. (*Gender* 85-86)

In all of these texts, the maternal body is read as an aspect—even perhaps as a rebellious aspect—of patriarchal culture.

Although popular culture tends to view the maternal body as subordinate and even invisible, there are however, other ways to understand this bodily construct. Indeed, motherhood can be understood as "a pillar of patriarchal domination" or as "one of the strongholds of female identity" (Braidotti 181). It is precisely women's position in this larger debate between cultural constructivism and pre-discursive biology that permits women to define themselves as nomadic. For the maternal body lies between theories, negotiates that difficult space. In motherhood, the body becomes the road, only temporarily situated.

> The women's body can change shape in pregnancy and childbearing; it is therefore capable of defeating the notion of fixed bodily form, of visible, clear, and distinct shapes as that which mark the contour of the body. She is morphologically dubious. The fact that the female body can change shape so drastically is troublesome in the eyes of the logocentric economy. (Braidotti 80)

Far from simply reifying patriarchy, this nomadic female body subverts and reconstitutes the symbolic landscape. The nomadic maternal body is not one single thing; rather, it is one thing and then another, according to situation and need. Immersed in what Donna Haraway refers to in *Simians, Cyborgs, and Women* as "situated knowledges," the maternal body defies the universals and constants that comprise patriarchy. This body, caught between ideological constructs, finds definition simultaneously as monster and Madonna. Rather than mimicking dominant discourse, the maternal figuration migrates between the polarities of political identity that create an alternate sensibility and alternative (and quite separate) power structure.

Within this alternate aesthetic lies the dangerous and familiar dyad of the mother-daughter relationship. Complex as maternity might be, it is the relationship between the mother and her off-spring—most particularly her female off-spring—that becomes the most difficult nexus of all. Doubly constructed, doubly enmeshed in ideology, often contradictory, this relationship and dyad must be significant in feminist discourse. And, fraught with potential difficulty, the relationship plagues whatever psychological or philosophical system is used for analysis. The relation can be either the vehicle that conveys patriarchal heritage or, as Irigaray argues, it can offer an alternative "female subjectivity."

> [T]he "mother-daughter" image...has emerged as a new paradigm. It is an imaginary couple that enacts the politics of female subjectivity, the relationship to the other woman and consequently the structures of female homosexuality as well as the possibility of a woman-identified redefinition of the subject... It attempts to invest the maternal site with affirmative,

positive force. (Braidotti 181)

Women's road narratives commonly explore the mobile, "affirmative" maternal site.

As I have continuously remarked upon, women's road narratives are often vastly different from those of men; the frequent presence of children in women's travel stories illustrates a primary distinction. In a great many instances, these children are daughters. Considering how different Kerouac's narrative might have been if children were constantly present provides fascinating speculation. Such contemplation is amusing but finally futile, for it is the very absence of children and domestic responsibility that make Kerouac's travel possible (or even attractive). Indeed, Kerouac's Sal travels in part to escape the mother figure of his aunt. The need to individuate and to separate from parental figures and especially male parental figures functions as one of the primary tropes of the male road narrative. In story after story, a young man sets out with an older and more experienced (father) figure.[4] (Frequently this pair becomes triangulated by the appearance of a female love interest.) In the course of the story, it becomes necessary for the hero to separate from the father. Typically, a fight—physical or psychic—is required. As Harold Bloom likes to insist in *The Anxiety of Influence*, an Oedipal streak exists in conventionally patriarchal literature. In traditional masculine road texts the male hero needs to defeat the father in order to supercede and finally become the patriarch.

Howard Hawks' 1948 classic film, *Red River* clearly depicts the road as the space of the young hero's identity quest, a quest that necessarily involves separation. *Red River* relates a paradigmatic, male coming-of-age road story. Montgomery Clift plays the young hero who signs up for a cattle drive led by the unsympathetic and older John Wayne. Initially friendly, the two men become alienated. They both are interested in the same woman, and they want to try differing routes to get to Abilene, Texas. The men fight, and Clift ends up with the girl and the right to select the direction of the drive. Defeated, Wayne goes his own way. The son and father must separate. In the same way, in Steinbeck's *Grapes of Wrath*, Tom Joad must finally leave his family and make his own way. Sal, despite his initial admiration and even love for Dean, ultimately scorns him. *On the Road* concludes with the aphorism "you can't teach the old maestro a new tune," as the now older and presumably wiser Sal and his friends drive off leaving Dean standing in the freezing cold.

> So Dean couldn't ride uptown with us and the only thing I could do was sit in the back of the Cadillac and wave at him. The bookie at the wheel also wanted nothing to do with Dean. Dean, ragged in a moth eaten overcoat he brought specially for the freezing temperatures of the East, walked off alone.... Old Dean's gone, I thought, and out loud I said "He'll be all right." and off we went...nobody, nobody knows what's going to happen to anybody besides the forlorn rags of growing old, I think of Dean Moriarty, I even think of Old Dean Moriarty the father we never found.... (Kerouac 306–307)

The father has been vanquished and surpassed.

The alternate aesthetic of maternal space offers a different traveling dyad. In women's nomadic literature, the road provides a space wherein daughters can reconnect and bond with the lost figure of the mother. For the authors and characters discussed here, the road becomes the place of rapprochement, the space where the lost love object of the mother can be recovered. Far from secondary, here the maternal body bears the potential for wholeness, forgiveness, growth and power. In these stories, the mother leaves the symbolic cabin of the masculine American road; she leaves the controlling shelter of domesticity and recovers her daughter and herself.

Outside of masculine control, the mother and daughter heal their divisions and find some space of potential growth. Many of these women's road texts suggest the rupture between mothers and daughters is the necessary result of patriarchy. These textual stories are consistent with much of feminist theory. Just as Nancy Chodorow contends in her *Reproduction of Mothering*, paternalistic institutions require that the girl-child turn away from the primary love object and replace her with a masculine attachment.

As Judith Butler frequently reminds us, patriarchy is invested in requiring a fixed heterosexuality. In these women's road texts, compulsory heterosexuality and the rejection by daughters of the primary love object is no longer a requirement. As Butler remarks, "gender consolidation" is a traditional Freudian aspect of individuation and adulthood. According to Freud in "Mourning and Melancholia," melancholy and mourning for the abandoned love object takes place as a result. (For Butler, this melancholy is a result of the repudiation of homosexuality.) But such melancholy and loss are not necessary on the woman's textual road. The mother figure can remain the primary love object. Moreover, while the masculine road narrative frequently requires decision between competing choices—which road to Abilene is best, should the travelers go to Mexico, how many people can fit in the car—women's road narratives tend to resist these choices. Because their travels often have no fixed destination, it isn't necessary to debate which road to follow. Choices are not binary or competitive; they are simply a part of the endlessly unfolding options and learning experiences. The masculine road tale is fueled by the hero's need to separate. The woman's road story often receives it textual energy through the need for unification. Thus, the hero of *Red River* becomes a man by defeating and separating from the father figure of John Wayne. In Mona Simpson's *Anywhere But Here* the fragile and temporary community of mother and daughter make Ann's journey possible. The novel begins with the mother leaving her daughter at the side of the road, but neither of them can make any progress in the story until the mother goes back and picks up her daughter. Separation is not a goal of the mother-daughter road story. Nor is it necessary for the daughter to defeat the mother; healing takes place in these texts through acceptance.

Frequently critiqued as a masculine construct, the maternal figure of the road text emerges as an alternative instead of a subordinate. Rather than existing within patriarchy, the textual mother inhabits an utterly different and matriarchal geography. Indeed, this textual matriarchal space is so powerful that, in many cases, the mother figure becomes associated with a deity. Anthropologists have long explored the mystical associations with the maternal body, and Kristeva reminds us, as a site of birth and death, the maternal body occupies a sacred space.

> [T]he maternal body as the site of the origin of life and consequently also of the insertion into mortality and death. We are all of woman born, and

the mother's body as the threshold of existence is both sacred and soiled, holy and hellish; it is attractive and repulsive, all powerful and therefore impossible to live with.... Kristeva emphasizes the dual function of the maternal site as both life-and death-giver.... the notion of the sacred is generated precisely by this blend.... (Braidotti 81–82)

The maternal body negotiates the space between these extremes.

It is a given that this negotiation is never complete or perfect. Few, if any of us, enjoy a relationship with the idealized maternal. Whether it is due to the interference of patriarchy, imperfectly balanced psyches or the disruptive pragmatics of everyday life, most of us feel we were not "mothered" perfectly. We have mothers, but we often fail to connect with the powerful, theoretical notion of the maternal. Indeed, the psychoanalytic community uses a nearly clichéd phrase to describe this condition. Repeating a term coined by the famous child psychologist, D.W. Winnicott, analysts speak of "good enough mothering." "Good enough" mothers are able to establish a bond with their children, however imperfectly. Such "good enough" relations between the infant and its mother result in the creation of the child's "continuity of being...a personal psychic reality and a personal body scheme" (Chodorow 68). But this mothering, while sufficient, is neither complete nor permanent. Like Lacan's mirror stage, the blurry and diffuse mother-child bond must give way. While a host of theoretical and psychoanalytic texts discuss this separation much more extensively than this work, it is perhaps women's road texts that most lyrically explore the problematic of "mothering."

In women's travel narratives, the road functions not as a highway to rugged individualism and separation, but as a path toward fulfillment, community and attachment between mothers and daughters. Chelsea Cain's *Dharma Girl*, Mona Simpson's *Anywhere But Here*, Barbara Kingsolver's *The Bean Trees* and *Pigs in Heaven*, Dorothy Allison's *Cavedweller* and Beverly Donofrio's *Looking for Mary (Or, the Blessed Mother and Me)* are all contemporary and powerful textual examples of mothers and daughters on the road. These texts search, each in a different way, for the maternal. The fictions engage with the idea of the maternal through itineraries that include encounters with Edenesque landscapes, beautiful monsters, comforting wombs and translucent deities. The mother they investigate is not simply the "good enough" (or not even good enough) mother of childhood experience. Each of these texts searches for an aspect of the idealized maternal; the protagonists find not simply their own lost mothers but the perfect maternal that is vanquished or hidden in the prosaic reality of the functional world. Thus, Cain finds not only her own mother, but also the maternal as goddess. Simpson comes to terms with the mother as the changeling monster of the unconscious. Kingsolver reveals the maternal as a primal womb of the world, while Allison explores this archetypal birthing maternal and makes it congruent with her own sexuality. For Donofrio, the maternal is not situated merely in her own mother or in her own motherhood but is found instead in the notion of a divine, salvation-offering mother figure. In each of these women's texts, mothers and daughters go on the road—albeit on a different road. In their quests they find one another, as well as a larger knowledge of the meaning of the maternal.

Re-Thinking Kerouac: The Road Leads Home

The very title of Chelsea Cain's *Dharma Girl: A Road Trip Across the American Generations* evokes Kerouac, simultaneously reminding the reader of Kerouac's consciousness-expanding travels, of the Beat generation, and of the fact women were largely excluded from Jack Kerouac's homosocial space. *Dharma Girl* is a memoir of a road trip, a road trip dedicated to Chelsea/Snowbird's reunion with her mother and a recovery of her lost and edenic past. Chelsea, known as Snowbird as a child, sees herself as a "psychonaut—a voyager into the soul." Like Kerouac, she crisscrosses the continent. But, her journey is more inward than that experienced by Kerouac. Kerouac pondered American culture, but Chelsea's trip takes her into her own psychic landscape. Says Chelsea about the impetus for her trip:

> And since she has read the *Tibetan Book of the Dead* she will soon realize that in order to find herself, she first has to create a self to identify. She has to tell the story. She has to find the child she was and the girl she became

to get the answers she wants. She has to see if she can find what she has
lost track of, before she can go on to anything else. (Cain 7)

To locate that lost girl of the past, Chelsea has to find her mother, a
woman once revered as the "Snowqueen." Cain's *Dharma Girl*
provides a lyrical account of how the road becomes the road back
toward reconnection with the maternal.

As she reveals in the early chapters of the text, Chelsea lives in
exile of her childhood garden. Inhabiting a monotone building in
Irvine, California, "a stucco city where it is illegal to paint your house
an unsanctioned color and you can be fined for leaving your garage
door open because it is unsightly," studying at the University of
California, Chelsea lives a life she finds "meaningless." Her existence
is defined by spending "two hours a day sucking down espresso
drinks at Starbucks" (30). When she mentions to a friend the name of
Mario Savio, the hero of U.C. Berkeley's Free Speech Movement,
Chelsea is told "Hello! The sixties are over... For all our sakes, please,
please, please let them go" (Cain 28). Feeling isolated and without a
sense of her past, she forgets to vote and calls her life "insignificant."
In the midst of this existential despair, she learns her mother suffers
from cancer, a rare form of melanoma that has metastasized.

Raised on an Iowa farm commune, Chelsea has changed her
name to Elizabeth and sought mainstream existence in the suburbs.
She lives far away from both her mother and her father, who have
been divorced for years. But "normal" life still eludes Chelsea; like so
many of the authors of women's road stories she is troubled by
restlessness. "I walk and walk," she says, and yet she can recognize
nothing. Her thoughts are disturbed by a kind of amnesia; she can
only remember small bits of her past. She retains just small blurred
images, and a recollection of a story that was integrated into her
childhood. In this story, her name is Snowbird and she inhabits a safe
universe ruled by the benevolent and loving Snowqueen. But this
story has little to do with her life in Irvine. Her California life is dull
and purposeless. Despite her friends' approbation, Chelsea decides to
go on a road trip with her mother, traveling back to Iowa. She wants
to re-experience the lost garden commune of her childhood. More
than that though, Chelsea wants to find once again her mother—"the

corn goddess," and the maternal Snowqueen of her youth.

Cain's narrative is not strictly linear. The text moves between the author's present—the time after the road trip, her travels with her mother, comments regarding pivotal moments in her more recent life, and vague, youthful memories. We learn Cain's early life was spent in a garden-like commune. In this Eden-like milieu, Chelsea, as Snowbird, once wandered between loving adults. The commune members were affectionate, kind, and indulgent. They resisted the Vietnam War and sometimes gardened in the nude. "The life they created for themselves existed entirely in the present" (61). Outside of the arbitrary constraints of time, the commune members dwelt within a kind of mythic space—a space defined by largely feminine generative principles. Gardening, collecting flowers, cooking, and bearing children were the celebrated activities. The emotional center of the commune, Chelsea/Snowbird's mother is described in terms that are nearly goddess-like. She appears as "beautiful," barefoot, surrounded by flowers, "her long brown hair hanging down her back" (70).

> The old, white farmhouse had been built in 1889, and stood at the end of an unfinished lane that led into tall grass. Behind the house, off the yellow kitchen, stood and ancient cottonwood tree that had been there for a hundred years, or maybe two hundred, depending who was telling the story...it would have been summer, so the air would have been hot and humid. The breeze, if there were any, would be warm, rustling the leaves of the trees and sending the rusty weathervane on top of the barn twirling. There would have been dogs asleep on the porch and two or three horses lolling in the pastures behind the barbed wire fence. At the base of the back porch would have been the vegetable garden—overflowing with tomatoes, beans, zucchini, cantaloupe, onions, basil and dill—and the corn in the field next door would have been green. (Cain 39–40)

Even death in this pastoral vision has no sting. Death is simply a natural part of life, Chelsea's mother, the Snowqueen explains to her daughter. She uses the garden's cyclical seasons as allegorical example. So successful is the Snowqueen in her explanation that Chelsea/ Snowbird, plays by burying her dolls in the garden. But the story enters a postlapsarian phase; the Garden is destroyed. The FBI discovers Chelsea/Snowbird's father, a draft resister. Agents watch the farm, and Larry's lawyer persuades his client to turn himself in. Fearing reprisals against his family, Larry complies. Patriarchy, in the form of the law, intrudes upon and wrecks paradise.

Eventually, alone, the Snowqueen leaves her fairy story identity and moves to town. After Chelsea's father, Larry, is released from prison, they divorce. Chelsea, Snowbird no longer, and her mother move finally to a different state where Chelsea (now Elizabeth) is forced to claim a new more mainstream identity.

> After my mom and I moved, I suddenly found myself an anomaly. I was a hippie kid in a conservative middle-class town—sort of like being Dan Quayle at a Hemp Fest.... These new lives we found ourselves living were startling. The kids at my school did not think about war and their parents were all married (I could tell by their matching sweater vests). My classmates all wore sneakers and jeans; I wore long multicolored skirts, sweat socks and clogs. They had no idea how to deal with me, just as I had no idea how even to start to be like them. It was as if I was speaking another language. (Cain 71)

This new identity never becomes fully comfortable and it leads Chelsea to her "meaningless" life in Irvine. The only way out of this empty life is to journey back through the past. Armed with a trip notebook that they share, Chelsea and her mother seek their mutual history.

At least to the visible eye, Chelsea is more "mainstream" than her mother. Although she is a vegetarian, Chelsea can eat at fast food establishments and diners. Her mother is a Buddhist; she meditates, listens to rock music and eats organic food. "My mother was dying," writes Chelsea, "but not yet" (24). As the journey begins, Chelsea and her mother exhibit different kinds of consciousness and divergent worldviews.

> This is what it's like traveling with my mother. She is a Buddhist and wants "to experience the place." I am an atheist and I want to find the nearest, cheapest lodge with coffee where I can sleep eight hours and then get back on the road. This slight difference in priorities has led to some discomfort in the past. My mother passes rest stops and wants to rest. I'd rather not make more than one stop per state. My mother gets hungry and wants to find a restaurant that she likes and eat; I get hungry and want to

go through a drive-through the next time we stop for gas. But this trip has
been different. I think we have both been so lost in our thoughts that
worrying about details—not to mention chitchat—has seemed incidental.
That sort of things is for tourists. We are travelers. (34)

The text's distinction between tourism and travel is significant.
Tourism suggests destination, purpose, and a final return to the
original place of departure. Travel is ambiguous and nomadic; it is
more about the process than the end.

As Chelsea travels and finally arrives back in Iowa, she begins to
reconstruct her childhood. Her mother explains the past and her own
motivations. Together they discover some of the people who once
shared the commune's space with them. Chelsea spends time with
her mother and her own pace begins to slow. She too becomes willing
to spend time, and to seek the experience rather than some fixed goal.
As Chelsea's early memories return, she begins to see her mother in a
more whole context. She remembers her as beautiful and goddess-
like. Chelsea remembers seeing her mother naked and unashamed in
their garden commune, as young and innocent Eve or as a harvest
goddess. Chelsea recalls when she drew pictures of her mother as a
child, that her mother was the corn goddess. She remembers too
when she was a child the Snowqueen, a goddess figure invoked by
her parents, used to leave her notes and give her reassurance. "You
were the Snowqueen," she says to her mother, acknowledging her
mother's earlier goddess status.

By the end of the text, Chelsea's mother is once again installed as
the Snowqueen, and Chelsea has reclaimed her name of Snowbird.
Pained as she is by the probable loss of her mother, Chelsea has once
again been taught to accept death. Chelsea has been rejoined to her
mother, and through this she can also accept herself. "She [Chelsea's
mother] is my wild abandon. My indestructible drop. My Original
Nature. I was as far away from her in Irvine, California as I have ever
been in my life" (Cain 167). Moved by her travels with her mother,
Chelsea settles in Iowa but frequently visits her mother.

As her mother becomes more ill, she takes away Chelsea's fear.
She informs her daughter that she lives without fear and regrets. "She
has been herself. She has been true to her own wonderful, Snowqueen

bodhisattva wisdom" (169). Frightened now of her own mortality, enduring her own biopsies, Chelsea is soothed by what her mother has taught her.

> I am not going to die of cancer, but sometimes I have to remind myself of this. So I think about what is important. About how I want to be. About those summer nights on the farm and my mother and how the Snowqueen always said she would watch over me. And I think about living. (169)

The Snowqueen has restored Chelsea both to her past and to a kind of youthful confidence that allows her to live. She has been saved and restored by her road trip with her mother, a trip that continues metaphorically as she visits her terminally ill Snowqueen. The road out becomes for Chelsea the road in. The road trip allows the completion of a psychic journey, a journey that leaves her, finally, permanently bonded to her once lost mother.

> My mother kept driving... There we were, my mother and me, out in the middle of nowhere, watching this natural phenomenon, and there were no other people out there. There were no other cars, no farms—just us. Because we had gone looking for it. Because we had driven into the dark, trusting in the experience. Because she kept driving.
>
> Self-knowledge is a funny thing—it is, I've decided, less discovery than acceptance. For me, it is the recognition of where I come from.... So I walk, and I remember... And it is with the knowledge that somehow I am still that blonde, little girl running naked through the vegetable garden. I am still Snowbird. (Cain 170–171)

The road has brought Snowbird back into the community of selfhood and the maternal.

Lyrical and seemingly simple, this text is nearly paradigmatic of mother-daughter's road narratives. In *Dharma Girl*, Chelsea Cain establishes the road as a space where that lost love object—the object without which life is melancholic and "meaningless"—is regained. The recovery of that lost love heals the wound that resulted from the original loss. The maternal recovery allows Chelsea to become reacquainted with what she termed her lost and "Original Nature." She has regained the Garden, from which she has been exiled not because of original sin but because of her loss of the maternal. And that garden is matriarchal; it does not subscribe to the fixed rules of patriarchy. It is not ruled by linear time or motion; it is circular and cyclical. The benevolent Snowqueen rules the garden, and in the garden all things are possible outside of patriarchy.

Cain's work finds resonance with Kristeva's consideration of women's identity and its textual representation in "Women's Time." Kristeva suggests notions of space, time and atemporality, and generative possibilities find expression within the maternal. "Matrix" and space are aspects of the feminine, contends Kristeva. Time and "Kronos" are masculine, while the eternal, the cyclical, the "extrasubjective," "cosmic time, occasion vertiginous visions and unnamable *jouissance*" are aspects of the female. In her essay, "Women's Time," Kristeva writes,

> "Father's time, mother's species," as Joyce put it; and indeed, when evoking the name and destiny of women, one thinks more of the *space* generating and forming the human species than of time, becoming or history.... As for time, female subjectivity would seem to provide a specific measure that essentially retains repetition and eternity among the multiple modalities of time. ...there are cycles, gestation, the eternal recurrence of a biological rhythm. ...one is reminded of the...myths of resurrection which...perpetuate the vestige of an anterior or concomitant maternal cult, right up to its most recent elaboration, Christianity, in which the body of the Virgin Mother does not die but moves from one spatiality to another.... (Kristeva, "Women's" 15–16)

Kristeva continues on to discuss once again the troubled status of maternity within contemporary theory, and continues to suggest despite its potential "alienating and even reactionary" qualities, the maternal can be a site of power. She points to the increasing numbers of single and lesbian mothers, contending they illustrate how "the refusal of the paternal function" (and thus patriarchy itself) can be concomitant with maternity itself. In Cain's memoir we see the attachment of the maternal to spaces outside of a narrow temporality—spaces like the cyclic and lost garden of Chelsea's youth and the ever-changing road itself. The Snowqueen, the maternal figure, explores even death, with its obvious associations with the eternal. As she negotiates these "extrasubjective" realms, her daughter links the Snowqueen's identity to both the matriarchal and the divine. Cain correctly understands her text to be a riff on Kerouac's road. She too takes to the road in search of identity and destiny; but, her heroine finds dharma housed within her own psyche and achieves redemption through affinity with the maternal.

"The Traveler Who Says, Anywhere But Here": Monstrous Mothers and Rapprochement with the Dysfunctional Maternal

An association between the maternal and the monstrous is a common theme in literature. Freud suggests this monstrosity is inherent in the mother's consuming love, sexuality and envy. He argues the female genitalia are manifest in the male's fantasies of monsters; moreover, Freud insists the basis of the mother-daughter relationship is hatred, a hatred that is based upon the monster-like behaviors of the mother figure.

> We will now turn our attention to the question of why this strong attachment of the girl to her mother comes to grief. We are aware that that is what usually happens.... The turning away from the mother occurs in an atmosphere of antagonism; the attachment to the mother ends in hate. Such a hatred may be very marked and may persist throughout an entire lifetime.... We will confine ourselves to studying this hatred at the actual time at which the turn takes place.... We are met with a long list of complaints and grievances leveled against the mother.... (Freud "New Introductory Lectures on Psycho-Analysis," *The Major Works of Sigmund Freud* 857)

Daughters hate their mothers for a number of reasons, Freud tells us. These reasons include: inadequate nourishment at the maternal breast and the perception that their early childhood weaknesses and illnesses are a result of maternal poisoning, rejection caused by the presence of another sibling, and a psychic castration that is blamed upon the mother (Freud 857–858). Freud's depiction of the maternal here is indeed monstrous; she is a woman who starves, poisons, rejects and finally mutilates her girl child.[5]

Rosi Braidotti maintains western lexicon associates what is

different with the monstrous, and the maternal body operates as the "sign of abnormality." Since Aristotle, masculinity has culturally functioned as the "human norm," continues Braidotti. The monster marks the space of differentiation. Even more extreme than the simply feminine body, the maternal body is sharply differentiated from the masculine "normal." She becomes a monster—that which is different. As symbolically different, as an alien in the linear space of the "normal" and thereby excluded from legitimate citizenship within the topos of patriarchy, the monster/mother is necessarily nomadic.

As Deleuze and Guattari remind us in their *Nomadology: The War Machine*, the nomad gives up citizenship in the *polis*, occupying instead the "fuzzy aggregate" of the *nomos*, "a space without borders or enclosure." The nomad eschews the "sedentary road...which is...a closed space," and, importantly, refuses the management of the territorial state (51–53). The "state," the patriarchal power structure, inevitably seeks to erase and discredit the nomad, and, in consequence, the nomad is placed outside symbolic expression. As an outsider, the nomad functions as a sort of cultural Frankenstein; she embodies difference and resistance. Thus, the nomad is a monster not only in bodily terms, but in social construction as well. The nomad functions as the barbarian and as the signifier of cultural difference.

While Chelsea Cain's text portrays the maternal as deity, other texts, even women's road texts, sometimes alternately represent the maternal nomad as deviant, dysfunctional and monstrous. But the *nomos* of the road is so open, so available to effacement, displacement, movement and change that the monstrous can be incorporated into the space of the road. While the maternal may emerge as less than saint-like, while she may indeed seem dysfunctional, this dysfunction and monstrousness is embraced by the vast and diverse topography of the highway. In this unregulated textual space, wherein monstrosity, "hate" and alienation are not culturally assigned, mothers and daughters can once again form a loving affiliation. Mona Simpson's novel, *Anywhere But Here*, provides perhaps the most resonant example of this textual and nomadic rapprochement.

Simpson begins her multivoiced novel with a nomadic declarative and a reference to Emerson and his insistence the "wants" of the traveler can necessarily never be sated by mere arrival at a fixed destination. And, Simpson's long and complicated journey never arrives at a concluding site. Instead, the text probes the relationships between the women characters, finding some resolution through their travels. Central to the text is the relationship between Ann and her psychologically troubled mother, Adele. The two drive to California, ostensibly so Ann "can be a television star," and so the two of them can find some more rich and elevated form of existence. But this particular road trip is only one of many drives undertaken in the text. Before moving west, Ann drives on the country roads outside Bay City, Wisconsin with both her mother and her grandmother. Later she will travel on countless "slow Greyhound buses during college, where there was always one very young woman in the back, her hair in a bandanna, hitting her kid, saying 'Shut-up' softly before each smack..."(Simpson 481). Estranged from her mother in adulthood, Ann returns to Adele after an absence of five years and drives through northern California and Napa Valley in search of some re-established connection. The very gifts Ann and Adele exchange are cars or the promise of cars, symbols of the space of their relationship. But the driving is not confined to Ann and Adele. Interwoven through Ann's story of her mobile adolescence with her mother are tales from her grandmother, Lillian, and her aunt, Carol. To one degree or another, all of these women travel, and the text thus emerges as a matriarchal lineage of interwoven paths.

"We fought" are the opening words of Simpson's text, and they describe the relations of Ann and Adele. Abandoned by Ann's father, Ann and Adele are bound together into a single, sometimes destructive unit. Muses Ann in the midst of her mother's violence,

> She hates you. She hates you more than anything she is and she's tied until she kills you, it's that deep in her. She will stay. And you know you will have to get up. You want to close your eyes and be dizzy, let this blur dark, tasting blood in your mouth like a steak, and let her come back to you and touch you softly, lead you to your bed, tuck you in, care for you. (Simpson 418)

"Give her to me. She's mine," insists Adele, when relatives try to protect Ann. The relationship between Ann and Adele is tightly woven, unbreakable even in its dysfunction. The two women fight in order to get away from one another, while knowing this escape is impossible.

There is no doubt that this is a particularly difficult relationship.[6] Even by her own mother's admission, "there has always been a wrongness" about Adele. A psychiatrist explains to Ann that Adele is incapable of assuming responsibility. No diagnosis is offered, but Adele suffers from extreme bi-polar mood swings, self-obsession, violent rages and an inability to control her behavior. She confuses her fantasies with reality, insisting, for example, that any day her psychiatrist is going to marry her and make them rich. Well educated, she has difficulty keeping a job. She is passionate about romance, yet her relationships are never sustained. She cannot cook and her more manic emotional stages are punctuated by wild shopping sprees. Adele loves Ann but is uncertain about how to mother. She treats Ann as a peer, taking her along on her own expeditions. She ignores boundaries, stroking Ann's back beneath her pajama top and asking the adolescent Ann to unfasten her mother's bra. In her bad moods, Adele beats Ann and ignores her. Like the monster vision of the mother, Adele will hurt her child, stalk men, lie to her husband, cheat her family, steal and manipulate anyone in her presence. "You don't have it easy with her," Ann's grandmother tells Ann. Ann, fully aware of her mother's insanity, counts the years that must elapse before she can become free.

However, difficult as Adele is, Ann recognizes their relationship is complex and is as loving as it is hateful. As a child, she admires her mother's beauty and longs to be like her. Ann pencils in freckles on her face so that she can more closely resemble her mother. "Nothing else mattered," Ann says about her mother. No one else was as much fun. As Ann gets older, she recognizes her mother's eccentricities and cruelties, but she remains attached to her mother. More than that, Ann sees herself in Adele.

> The thing about my mother and me is that when we get along, we're just the same. Exactly. ...we didn't talk about money. It was so big, we didn't talk about it. We lay on our stomachs on the king-sized bed, our calves tangling behind us, reading novels...we lay out from ten until two because my mother had read that those were the best tanning hours. That was what we liked doing, improving ourselves. (Simpson 9–10)

The mother who leaves Ann out on the side of the road, the mother who hits her, is also the woman with whom she is lovingly entangled. This affection, and the fact Ann claims they are alike, is as significant a part of the relation as the abuse. Imperfect and odd, Adele remains the most important person in her daughter's life. Considering her mother's impact, Ann says:

> Strangers almost always love my mother. And even if you hate her, can't stand her, even if she's ruining your life, there's something about her, some romance, some power. She's absolutely herself. No matter how hard you try, you'll never get to her. And when she dies, the world will be flat, too simple, reasonable, too fair. (17)

Adele is too complicated a character to be contained within middle-class culture.

Adele and Ann emerge as nomads in the text. Their drive across the country only begins the nomadic episode of their lives. Once in Los Angeles, they travel from hotel room to hotel room, from apartment to apartment. Focusing her romantic attention upon a Beverly Hills orthodontist, Adele makes daily drives past his Century City apartment and the home of his former wife. These nightly expeditions become a "habit" of which Ann is fond. The two women never make choices because, nomad like, they can never reconcile themselves to giving up one of their options. They drift. Because Adele avoids any sort of daily planning, there is never any food in the house, and each evening they drive in search of something to eat. Their belongings are moved about in an old suitcase, a suitcase that Adele unpacks and re-packs when she is upset. By the time Ann graduates from high school, the two women share a kitchen-less pool house in back of a mansion.

> We had habits, but we never admitted them. We ate out every night, but every night it was as if my mother felt freshly surprised that driving in the car and finding a restaurant was, at ten o'clock, our only alternative. We never bought food... All we had in the house was carrot juice and wheat germ oil. It was stubbornness. My mother didn't want this to be our life. She'd do it a day at a time, she'd put up with it, but she wasn't going to plan for it. We didn't pay bills, we didn't buy groceries, we bounced checks. Accepting our duties might have meant we were stuck forever. We

made it so we couldn't keep going the way we were; something had to happen. But the thing was, it never did. (Simpson 439–440)

The two women live a nomadic existence.

If Adele's nomadic eccentricity causes difficulty between Ann and her mother, then the road and its nomadic culture heal the ruptures in the relationship. For Adele and Ann the road first emerges as a kind of dream state, a path toward the fulfillment of fantasy. Trapped by their pedestrian, working-class life in Bay City, Wisconsin, the two begin to fantasize about driving to California and becoming celebrities. The road offers some promise of a space where anything is possible. When the Red Owl Wisconsin supermarket chain offers a prize to the winner of their lottery, Adele and Ann call in sick to work and school and drive through the countryside searching for the winning ticket. If they do not find the winning ticket, the two women do find at least a momentary peace as they drive.

But the road also brings Adele and Ann back together in some larger sense. After Ann leaves Los Angeles to go to college at Brown University, she refuses for five years to see her mother. While she visits her other relatives, she remains estranged from Adele. Then, somewhat abruptly, the two decide to go on a road trip together through northern California. They visit the wine country, collect antiques together, and dine out in Napa. At "Dr. Hickdimon's Mud Baths" Ann becomes aware again of how her mother's eccentricity is coupled with a unique sense of personal style, a singularity that is interesting if relatively worthless in the pragmatic contemporary world. "My mother's brilliance is in a lot of things you notice if you're around a person all the time, but which don't count for much in the world" (Simpson 480). Ann takes her mother's hand, remembering "how young" she was when they came to the West. A kind of acceptance emerges. In the novel's last encounter between the two women, Adele and Ann sit in a car at the airport, after visiting the old Lincoln they once drove west. The women turn toward one another and finally "see each other." Ann kisses her mother.

Ann receives a settlement check resulting from a union dispute with a television studio and Ann's earlier work there. She decides to send the check to her mother, so her mother can finally buy a house. Instead, Adele buys an expensive Mercedes station wagon, "all silver," so she can one day drive her grandchildren. Nomadic, she will never own a house (or even rent a nice apartment); she invests in her car. The novel concludes with Adele's rambling, self-congratulatory remarks on motherhood. Limited, even deluded, immersed in the clichéd, Adele's love for Ann is still evident.

> I never wanted to stay there [Wisconsin]... And now I've got my station wagon ready for my grandchildren... You carry a baby in the womb for nine months and then, when they're grown up, they call you collect, when they remember. She has her own life. And that's okay. I've learned to be patient. "Teach only love for that is what you are." The ups and downs; I live with it. And I've got a lot ahead of me and a lot to be proud of. I know: she is the reason I was born. (Simpson 534–35)

Ann and Adele are defined by each other.

Anywhere But Here is not a linear text. Instead, its story is recounted in several voices, with accounts that move back and forth, sometimes repetitively, in time. Some relatively brief moments are given pages of description, while some entire years are ignored. Stories are told, and then retold in a different way. The text itself is nomadic, zigzagging across the country and through time. Its plot wanders, finding and then abandoning its resolution. Contained within its primary nomadic tale, roam other nomadic stories. In addition to Ann and Adele's narratives, Lillian, Ann's grandmother speaks. She talks about her own seven aunts and how she spent every Saturday walking from house to house to make pastry. She talks too about Milton, her brother who was smitten with love for a circus girl and, as a result, ran away from home. She mentions her dead husband, Art, and how she fell in love with him when he told her a story about hobos. She suggests Adele's disturbed behavior was evident even in her childhood, but takes pains to also note Adele's good qualities. Lillian describes Adele's travels, and tells Ann she was fortunate not to be born in Egypt, because her mother had once moved there. She meditates on why her two daughters were so different—one seemingly content to stay at home and one a perpetual wanderer. Lillian's narrative ends with the death of her mother,

Granny. Carol, Adele's older sister and Ann's aunt also constructs several sections of the narrative. Carol's story too reveals a secret road life. Carol joined the service during World War II and quietly married an Italian communist who planned to assassinate Hitler. But the husband dies on their honeymoon, and Carol remains silent about him. She writes too about a trip she once made with Adele to Michigan's Mackinac Island.

> I only had a few times I was close with Adele...once, really, that I remember was when we were already grown. I sure remember fighting with her. That's what comes to mind. But once my parents sent us both off to Mackinac Island for a holiday...and we just had a wonderful time there. (289)

In travel, even the tensions between Carol and Adele are temporarily resolved.

The novel emerges finally a testimonial to the road and to the nomadic rather than the static. It is a compendium of road stories. And although, as the novel's title suggests, it is about never accepting a particular destination or fixed space, it is also about being in the dynamic moment of any space completely, if momentarily. In this shifting nomadic reality, the monstrous maternal is logical and appropriate. The unfixed space of the nomad matches the changing, other-ed self of the mother. Cruel, dangerous, and "abnormal" in the fixed world of mid-western middle-class existence, Adele is a survivor on the road. She lives in Deleuze and Guattari's *nomos*, rejecting the fixed and regulated *polis*. The way she looks, lives and acts is determined by the particulars of the individual space she momentarily inhabits. Adele's identity is derived from her situation, and is therefore mutant. It is easy for the reader to find Adele offensive, for she violates our cultural norms. She is a terrorist, moving outside of convention. We must see her as a kind of monster, for she marks the space of difference. She is mad, but as Deleuze and Guattari remind us, schizophrenia is the rejection of the status quo, of the production-oriented culture, a repudiation of the *polis*. Madness may be the resistance to regulation. Adele and her daughter inhabit the marginal space; they are the harbingers of cultural change. The nomad is about becoming, moving, never arriving. Monster and

Other, this is Adele's textual function. She operates outside the boundaries. For all her limitations, she emerges as the heroine of the tale, like the Snowqueen, the object of mystery, rapprochement and love.

The Road as Womb

The notion that the process of pregnancy is akin to a journey is a truism. Even the vocabulary of childbirth reinforces this idea. Infants travel down the birth canal and after months of bearing the burden of their bodies, mothers finally arrive at "their time." Mothers then labor to "deliver" their children. This natal passage finds literary representation in a vast number of texts. Birth imagery is a recurrent figure in women's writing, and road narratives provide no exception to this observation. In particular, mother-daughter novels often return to the birth scene as a kind of trope, finding that prenatal bond representative of the larger relationship. The textual figuration of the maternal woman laboring toward reproduction and the daughter sliding into consciousness find legitimacy in feminist theory. But in women's road literature, the passage is more than theorized; rather, the road depicts the birth process, albeit metaphorically. The road becomes the womb.

The road as womb—as the daughter's birth canal and the mother's movement toward understanding of maternity—finds depiction in the road novels of Barbara Kingsolver. In *The Bean Trees* and its sequel, *Pigs in Heaven*, Kingsolver tells the story of Taylor and her adopted daughter, Turtle. *The Bean Trees* relates how Taylor, young, free, resistant to the very idea of motherhood, takes to the road in search of adventure. But her quest for freedom is interrupted by the "delivery" of a Native American baby who is simply left with Taylor. Unprepared for this unannounced and seemingly fatherless child, Taylor initially resists maternity. But the narrow conditions of the road, the child's obvious need, and the mysterious development of Taylor's maternal love initiate Taylor into motherhood.

Even the physical difficulties of Taylor and Turtle mimic the discomforts of birth. Their bodies become cold, nearly in shock, like the body of a newly delivered woman. A victim of sexual abuse, Turtle has a violated vagina, a birth canal that is torn through delivery. Although Turtle is actually a toddler, she is developmentally still a baby. She wears diapers, and cannot speak or feed herself. She is diminutive and has the thin limbs of a newborn. Taylor and Turtle's mutual cuts and scrapes suggest a bruising passage down the birth canal. Taylor's difficulty in finding food for Turtle reminds readers of the trying day or two before a mother can begin lactating. Like another, more famous mother, Taylor embraces motherhood in a cheap inn (a roadside motel she can't afford), and the infant's survival is ensured by the assistance of kindly strangers. As Taylor and Turtle continue down the road, more obstacles confront them. Acknowledging the legal system will not permit her merely to accept Turtle as her daughter, Taylor constructs a mock adoption ceremony. Two tortured refugees of El Salvador name themselves as the parents and stipulate Taylor as the legal mother. By the close of the novel, Taylor understands motherhood requires stability and she begins to make a home. She retains her nomad consciousness through her work that takes place—naturally—in a car and tire shop just off the highway.

Pigs in Heaven takes place, ostensibly, several years later. Once again, Taylor drives the highways as she and Turtle enjoy a road trip in the southwest. In a strange confluence of events, Turtle sees an accident at Hoover Dam. Her reports of what she saw result in the rescue of a boy of diminished intelligence, and in brief televised fame. When Turtle appears on *Oprah*, a lawyer for the Cherokee Nation recognizes Turtle as Native American and understands the adoption is fraudulent. A long road sequence takes place as Annawake Fourkiller pursues Turtle and Taylor, in an effort to have the adoption adjudicated. Briefly accompanied by her own mother, Taylor takes to the road again. For Taylor, the road—the womb—becomes a condition of motherhood. Twisting and difficult, there is no legal claim upon her child outside this path. Name, custody and legitimacy are the province of patriarchy; it is only in the womb that a woman can claim her child. In Kingsolver's texts, motherhood is constructed by the womb. Taylor loses Turtle (temporarily) because she did not technically give birth. The only way she can continue to retain her child is to return to the womb of the road, retreating into the birth process. Only on the road can Taylor really be a mother; only the road reinforces her bond with her daughter.

As Nancy Chodorow reminds us, there is theoretical precedent for Turtle and Taylor's need to remain on the road and thus in the womb. Freud contends mothers and daughters can remain close and reconciled only in the girl-child's very early preoedipal, infantile stage. Once the child feels an Oedipal pull toward her father, her mother must become her rival. More moderate in this theoretical debate, Chodorow argues girls experience the Oedipal stage in a way that is quite different from the masculine models. Girls resist this triangular figuration much longer than boys, claims Chodorow. "A girl, by contrast, remains preoccupied for a long time with her mother alone. She experiences a continuation of the two-person relationship of infancy" (Chodorow 96). Until adolescence, according to Chodorow, girls internalize the mother figure. Only as they near adulthood, pressured by societal and sexual forces, do girls typically separate from their mothers. However, once this separation occurs, girls are forced to abdicate the mother as the central love-object.

Alone on the road with Taylor, Turtle's relationship with her unknown father, her tribe, and the larger nexus of Native American law are unimportant. Still in the metaphorical womb, her father and the larger paternal institution of culture do not matter to Turtle. Off the road, her connection to her mother becomes much more problematic, factored by litigation and racial origin. Off the road, Turtle is out of the womb and has entered the theoretically problematic arena of the Oedipal stage. The very idea of the Oedipal stage is rooted in a privileging of heterosexuality, as Judith Butler, Gilles Deleuze and Felix Guattari argue. Heterosexual culture requires the girl-child learn to make the male her central love object, and to accept the legitimacy of blood ties and the law. And, in the end, Kingsolver's novels return her two heroines to heterosexual culture. Taylor is reunited with her lover, Jax. Taylor's mother is allied with Apache Cash Stillwater, who conveniently turns out to also be Turtle's long lost, loving grandfather, Pop-pop. Turtle's grandfather claims legal custody, but agrees to share his granddaughter with her adopted mother. Jax will become Turtle's "official daddy." The mother-daughter dyad of the road is ruptured; traveling Turtle and Taylor bond solely with each other but off the road they are embraced by the broader and more paternal demands of heterosexual culture.

The road, like the womb is complex and fraught with danger. Dorothy Allison's *Cavedweller* is a nearly Byzantine novel about mother-daughter relations and the dangers of inhabiting and traveling through the spaces of the womb. In Allison's text, the path of the womb may lead out toward separation and a world where the child distinguishes between herself and her mother. On the other hand, the same path may remain internalized, ushering the girl-child into a matriarchal world where women remain the primary love objects.

The relationships in the *Cavedweller* are structured like the twisting, hidden passages of a cavern. "Tight passages are the subject matter," comments critic Minrose Gwin in her discussions of Allison's work (Gwin 138). Central to the text are Delia's relationships to her three daughters, Amanda, Dede and Cissy. Amanda and Dede are the offspring from Delia's first marriage to the abusive Clint. She leaves the girls when they are very young, hitching a ride on the tour bus of an aspiring rock and roll star. Cissy is the daughter of the musician, Randall. A drug addict and a cliché of the rock and roll life, Randall dies in a motorcycle accident and leaves an impoverished Delia barely clinging to sobriety. In the early pages of the novel, Delia decides to give up music and the decadence of Los Angeles. She climbs in her car with a furious Cissy and makes a manic road trip home to the south. Over a period of years, Delia re-forges her relationship with her two older daughters, one of whom is a fundamentalist Christian. Cissy remains obsessed with motion, wanting first to simply get back to LA, later to learn to drive, and finally to be a "caver"—an explorer of caverns—and to map out unknown paths. These relationships and trips are cast against the backdrops of Delia's newly matriarchal life. She eschews romantic entanglements and is most closely allied with her friends, MT and Rosemary. Delia's journey back home represents a reverse experience of the womb—nearly dead and in despair she goes home to be tended by maternal figures. The most interesting travels in the book, and presumably the source of the novel's title, belong to Cissy.

Initially deeply attached to her father, Cissy's travels move her to an alternative identity. Resentful of her mother and the forced move, Cissy is a loner. Although she has male friends, Cissy remains as an adolescent within a largely female circle. Before she begins venturing down into caves, Cissy tries to create cave-like spaces where she can feel safe. When her older sisters move away, she redecorates her room, removing windows and light, so it resembles a cavern. Only in these dark warm places can Cissy feel safe and find relief from her perpetual insomnia.

Although Cissy's anger at her mother seems to indicate she is more allied with her father, we learn her life with Randall was not safe. When Randall is around, Delia drinks, and Randall nearly kills Cissy, leaving her with scars, in an auto accident. Safety is not masculine, in this world. Increasingly, Cissy is drawn to the world of "cavers"—the community of people who explore the space of caverns. Most of the "cavers" are young men, competitive and prone to marking and destroying the landscape they examine. Instead, Cissy is attracted to two women "cavers," Mimi and Jean. The experiences with Mimi and Jean, as they travel underground pathways, return Cissy to the womb and ultimately to her mother and herself.

Clearly female in its associations, the landscape of caves becomes the manifestation of Cissy's unconscious.

> Flowstone settles down...it comes in shades from pure white to calcium yellow to mottled red. After the first trip down into Little Mouth, Cissy dreamed about flowstone, the slowly moving rock beneath the dirt. In her dreams flowstone was not hard but thick and soft as stale meringue. The white paste found in grade school libraries, dense and cloying and slowly stiffening against the skins, that was the flowstone in Cissy's dreams. She lay back into it and it took on the shape of her body, the warmth of her skin. It settled beneath her, gentry crept between her fingers and toes, rose to cradle her hips. ...growing slowly but growing.... She waited for it to wrap her around, slowly encase her body, and by that motion season her soul.... My country, Cissy thought, and in the dream the cave shaped around her as steadily as mud. ...the belly of Little Mouth... (Allison 324)

The cryptically named cave, Little Mouth is the maternal womb—with all of its implied sexuality, once again safely embracing

Cissy.

This womb can only be fully understood through struggle. Increasingly adventurous, Cissy suggests to her friends they sleep in Little Mouth. While the dark disturbs Mimi and Jean, Cissy finds that for the first time in her memory she sleeps deep and long. The dark feels entirely safe to her. Like an exploring infant, Cissy pushes the limits of the cave. She wants to chart out some unknown and never mapped path. She urges her friends to make progressively longer and more risky journeys. Eventually the women become lost. Trapped under the earth, suffering from hypothermia, it is only Cissy's relentless "panting and pushing, creeping progress" that saves the girls from their "yelps of fear" and delivers them from the cave. Trapped in a space where the white rocks "had dimpled centers with dripping points that looked like nipples...warm breasts sweating in the cool damp air," the three women must labor to be born. Looking at the breast-like rocks, the women become children in need of the maternal figure.

> She [Cissy] was tempted to slide back up the slope to a spot where the gap narrowed...and put her mouth to one of those bulges. She stared at the glistening center of the largest teat. She could imagine grainy syrup filling her mouth. That tit would sweat sweet. It would be like rock sugar. (Allison 414)

The need to be delivered from the passage and nursed is nearly irresistible. The exhausted, nearly dead Jean murmurs a suggestion that they are all "ice babies looking for ice tits" (414). They want to be embraced and held.

This impulse nearly proves deadly, for Jean wants to give up and huddle and sleep. But Cissy and Mimi know better. They strip Jean of her wet clothing, remove many of their own garments, and push themselves, swearing and tearing their flesh, out of the narrow confines of the earth. Bruised and ill, they emerge at sunrise, pushing aside a mass of kudzu vines that block their passage. The women have survived birth.

Cissy's sisters attack Mimi and Jean as "strange," "crazy" and as lesbians. At first Cissy resists this charge, but in the course of their adventures, she recognizes the truth of her friends' relationship.

Although she is outside their primary bond, she feels safe with it. She understands for her, the act of "caving"—of exploring the womb-like cavern—represents both recovery and sexuality. She has rejoined the maternal womb.

> Caving for her, Cissy understood, was like sex for most people. Though what other people thought about sex was nothing Cissy really understood. But in the dark she became for the first time fully conscious of her own body...she moved freely. In the dark her body moved precisely, steadily.... the unknown country.... (Allison 325)

Reborn through the cave of Little Mouth, Cissy looses her resentment and finds herself. No longer marginalized, she forms attachments to friends and achieves a sense of vocation. She lets go of the anger she has felt for her mother. It is no longer necessary for her to withdraw. Following her emergence and rebirth from the cave she moves into adulthood. She knows she will return to the West, that she will travel, but she no longer blames her mother for the necessity of this passage.

The road delineated by Allison's text is profoundly female, as is the textual space created by her characters. Her road is not linear nor is it open; she travels the twisting labyrinth-like paths of enclosed space. Within the metaphorical cave the characters shape what Haraway has called "the post-colonial terrain of women's liberating discourses" (Gwin 40). Allison's text is curiously akin to Kristeva's argument that maternity and its symbolic representations are closely allied with lesbian sexuality; Cissy's acceptance and attachment to the maternal have obvious sexual connotations. The bond with the maternal can refract in the construction of lesbian space. In refusing to reject the body of the mother, the maternal and the feminine become the love object. The unending womb of the road allows an alternative place to the heterosexual gendering of the postoedipal space. In that space, where the body of the girl is undifferentiated from the maternal body, where the mother is the idealized love object, it is not necessary to reject the maternal and adopt the masculine. The mother-daughter and feminine aesthetic define the sensibility of the road as womb. In this space both mother and daughter are constantly and again delivered, never coerced into patriarchy, never socialized, free to "slide" forever through the uncharted maternal caves.

From the Snowqueen to the Queen of Heaven: A Mother For Us All

As Kristeva correctly notes, discussions of the maternal necessarily move us finally toward conversations regarding the "power over origins," the "awe" aroused by the maternal body and the inclusion of a maternal representation within religious belief. This results, contends Kristeva, from the fact that "sexual difference—which is at once biological, physiological, and relative to reproduction—is translated by and translates a difference in the relationship of subjects to the symbolic contract" (Kristeva, "Women's" 32). This differing relationship to the symbolic naturally creates an alternative vision of origin or deity. Women of our time, suggests Kristeva, must ask "What can be our place in the symbolic contract?...How can we reveal our place?" The answer to these queries requires a new relationship to the world and to its legal and moral authorities. As "female subjectivity" asserts its self, the "aporia of the chora, matrix space, nourishing, unnamable anterior to the One, to God" is redefined as feminine.

Trinh T. Minh-ha argues the re-formulating of God, as well as the rethinking of a symbolic system, has philosophic consequence. Within patriarchal discourse, God is defined through an alliance between the lord and his priest. This relationship produces omniscient pronouncements; the literature resulting from this discourse is single voiced, centralized and authoritative. The woman writer engages a less centralized deity, producing a plurality of meanings. These pluralities are "the creation of womb," organic representations of the "linguistic flesh" (Minh-ha 37–38).

The maternal figure that results from this radically transformed symbolic system "has little to do with motherhood as experienced by men." The "year-round cook" and the "family maid" is replaced with:

> Mother of God, of all wo/mankind, she is role-free, non-name, a force that refuses to be fragmented by suffocates codes... In her maternal love she is neither possessed nor possessive, neither binding nor detached nor neutral.... The One is the All... (Minh-ha 38–39)

For Minh-ha, this new site of symbolic origin, this new deity, is the mother of us all. This site is quite consistent with Kristeva's awe-inspiring mother who dispenses life and death.

If one extends Minh-ha's argument, the search for rapprochement with the maternal exceeds the personal psychic needs of individuals. If, as we have seen in the texts discussed here, particular mothers and daughters seek one another in the nomadic space of the road, it is also possible they seek more than individual healing. Minh-ha suggests mothers and daughters look for a healing of the semiotic breach, a new way to exist within a symbolic system, and for a new notion of the maternal. The road then becomes a vast *nomos* indeed, for it is the site where patriarchy is remade and the lost mother found.

This search for the lost idealized mother is the basis of Beverly Donofrio's experiences and travel memoir, *Looking for Mary (Or, the Blessed Mother and Me)*. Donofrio's narrative relates her experience as she travels to Medjugorje, Bosnia, a village where the apparition of Mary is reputed to appear. But Donofrio's central travel tale is interrupted by fragments of other trips—journeys to Mexico, moves to Manhattan and to Orient, New York, as well as journalist's junkets. Her life emerges as a sort of travel narrative, and Donofrio clearly exhibits a nomadic sensibility. Despite her resistance to her own mother, maternity figures strongly in Donofrio's tale. Her life is shaped by her distance from her own mother, her teenage pregnancy and her relationship with her son, Jason, and her search to both find a mother and to learn how to mother on her own. Angry and wounded by patriarchy, Donofrio looks for another symbolic system, one that will provide her with legitimacy and forgiveness.

In an earlier memoir/novel, *Driving in Cars With Boys: Confessions of a Bad Girl Who Makes Good*, Donofrio tells the story of her adolescent drug use and pregnancy, arguing these actions should have been expected from a girl whose initials spelled B.A.D. The daughter of a policeman, Donofrio, is attracted by boys and cars. She becomes pregnant by her high school dropout boyfriend. When their teenage marriage (predictably) fails, Donofrio takes to "cruising" for male attention. Eventually she is arrested for drug use. Placed on probation, Donofrio finds herself impoverished, without a car, trapped by the demands of a baby. When a probation counselor finds the means to send her to college, provided Donofrio can procure transportation and a baby sitter, Donofrio is horrified because these are precisely the two elements she cannot supply.

> Not the goddamn car and not the goddamn kid. Let the problem be anything but the car and the kid. If I had a car and a baby-sitter to begin with, I wouldn't be sitting in this old coot's office…. How am I supposed to get there? (*Driving* 143)

Without a car she is confined in the cabin-like space of her small housing project apartment. Trapped with a baby and no money, Donofrio is rescued by the purchase of "Cupcake," a Volkswagen that will give her mobility. "I paused to look at Cupcake before making coffee. She shimmered like an emerald in the driveway. Behind her, a piece of paper skimmed along the gutter… I was joining the human race…" (147). The road sets Donofrio free. In fact, cars initiate liberation. As Sidonie Smith notes in *Moving Lives: 20th-Century Women's Travel Writing*, "automobiles are ubiquitous in the pages of Donofrio's memoir" because of their transcendent capabilities (S. Smith 185). Cupcake allows Donofrio to attend college. But although Donofrio "makes good" in conventional terms, she remains largely alienated and unhappy. Her first road trip, from Brooklyn to Wesleyan to Manhattan fails to supply her with meaning or fulfillment.

Looking for Mary, as a kind of sequel, opens with a monologue from a narrator whose life is empty and banal. As she enters Bosnia, Donofrio is surrounded by people "who all seem to wear glasses as big as windows and look like they feed from the snack isle at the supermarket" (19). Back home, her son has rejected her because of her failures as a mother. Her romantic relationships have all failed. Donofrio has come to Bosnia as a writer; earlier she traveled through the U.S. for National Public Radio investigating apparition sites and reported appearances of the Virgin Mary. A skeptic, who "hates God and Jesus," Donofrio is a lapsed Catholic. She despises God because of his paternalism and because she can't help but believe he punished her for having sex outside of marriage. She is a self-proclaimed feminist who despises working class morality. Still, unhappy as she is, Donofrio confesses she "is in the market for a spiritual conversion."

Although Donofrio disdains institutionalized Catholicism, in the years preceding her textual road trip she collects pictures and figures of the Virgin Mary. She is drawn by the "selfless" love that is associated with images of Mary. Donofrio may be, as she claims, an agnostic, but her house becomes a shrine to "the Blessed Mother." As she investigates dubious sightings of the Virgin, Donofrio says she "wants to believe." Her son and her lovers leave her because her faithlessness leaves her unable to really love. Reflecting upon Kip who has left her, Donofrio says,

> It wasn't only the physical [self] that repulsed him. It was the cold hard heart in the middle of me: too defended, too brittle, and too pockmarked by life. There'd been no soft pillow of comfort for him to sink into. No motherliness in me. (*Looking* 4)

Donofrio speculates that people leave her because she is incapable of love, and that she cannot give love because she never received "unconditional" love from her own mother. Despite her forays into promiscuity, therapy and meditation, Donofrio remains empty. Hoping faith can be learned and maternal love can be found, Donofrio signs up for the Bosnian pilgrimage. In the dark of the village night she acknowledges, "I know I did not come here only to write about the experience; I came because I want Mary to mother me and teach me mother things, like how to love" (2).

As the narrative's title suggests, Donofrio's travels eventually, at least in some limited fashion, return her to a beloved mother figure. She recalls in a doubled primal image that her own mother was "rescued" from drowning as a child by the Virgin. "My mother's Mary miracle was the first Mary story I ever heard" (114). As a child, Donofrio's orphaned mother sinks flailing into a lake. Suddenly she saw the Virgin Mary "aglow in the sky." The Virgin held out her arms and drew Donofrio's mother to the shore. But when Donofrio attempts to interview her mother on this subject, as a part of her work for National Public Radio, Donofrio's mother changes the story. "It wasn't Mary. It was my mother" (*Looking* 115). Sometime later the older Mrs. Donofrio returns to her original story and Beverly Donofrio reflects,

[I]t was interesting that Mary and my mother's mother had merged into the same person.... It was no surprise really that Mary and mother would be interchangeable; they answered the same needs: for comfort, warmth, unconditional acceptance, love. (115)

A discussion and acknowledgment of these needs slowly draw Donofrio to her own mother. Back from Bosnia, Donofrio and her son Jason attempt to mend their own breach. Donofrio expresses remorse for her limitations and tries to offer her son affection, an affection he begins to return appropriately enough on Mother's Day. According to the text, the Virgin teaches Donofrio to love. However, Donofrio does not adopt a conventional Catholicism. She continues to reject the primacy of God and Jesus, and of a trinity that does not include Mary. She believes in a Catholicism dominated by Mary as the Queen of Heaven. Her theology is interesting; she insists Jesus simply follows his mother's directions. "Mary, like any mother who knows what's best, tells her son what to do" (94). In the *Magnificat*, Mary's long speech in the *New Testament* of the *Bible*, Mary defines God as one who "lifts up the lowly," and Donofrio interprets this as Mary's directions to the masculine members of the trinity. For Donofrio, Mary is the leader of the real church. Mary, as the Queen of Heaven, becomes in Donofrio's theology, the principal deity.

Donofrio's memoir provides in many ways the apotheosis of the mother-daughter road tale. Traveling through Bosnia, its heroine seeks healing and connection with both her son and her mother. More than that, she wants to find representation of the maternal love object within her own symbolic system. "I was sick to death of the patriarchal American Church's blatant dismissal of the Mother of God," writes Donofrio (*Looking* 245). She wants to recover the "awe" that Kristeva associates with the maternal, and the alternate "real" womb that Trinh Minh-ha insists exists outside patriarchy. The long return trip to the Virgin Mary traces a return to a primary site of origin.

Donofrio is more than a mother involved in a dysfunctional family. She is a writer. Her memoir also attempts to find representation and textual authority within a system that marginalized her. By Donofrio's own account, her family was too poor to send her to college and her female status assigned her a less powerful position within the family. When she resists her father's control and becomes pregnant, she enters new forms of patriarchal power. To a great degree, her life follows from her young husband's whims. She recognizes his male authority when he resists giving her the cars keys and insists on driving while drunk, a decision that results in an accident that nearly kills both of them. Once separated from her husband, Donofrio becomes a subject of the welfare office and her (male) probation officer. She can claim no legitimacy within the system. Even Donofrio's writing is initially rejected. Her college English teacher who calls her in says,

> "You have trouble writing...." I could barely control my trembling lip in his office. I went into the bathroom and cried... I could not flunk out, I simply couldn't. I knew I was the poor relation being let in through the back door of this place.... The humiliation was even more intense because I'd fantasized that when I graduated from college, I'd move to New York and be a writer. (*Driving* 161)

Donofrio recognizes that she does not comply with the symbolic order.

But being on the road, and writing about being on the road in search of a mother provide Donofrio with a different venue. Within the genre of the road narrative, Donofrio's wandering nomadic style is effective. Writing about her need for a mother allows Donofrio to access what Trinh Minh-ha calls "organic and nurturing-writing." She gives voice to emotions and images exiled from conventional masculine road stories. She provides authorial authority for illegitimacy because on the road, in the *nomos*, nothing is illegitimate. On the road, looking for Mary, that amorphous mother figure, Donofrio enters what Kristeva calls the new generation of women writers.

> Essentially interested in the specificity of female psychology and its symbolic realizations, these women seek to give a language to the intrasubjective and corporeal experiences left mute by culture in the past...by demanding recognition of an irreducible identity...this feminism situates itself outside the linear time of identities...such feminism rejoins the cyclical.... (Kristeva "Women's" 17)

Within the context of these various road stories, the search for the maternal ultimately becomes a search for representation. Existing outside symbolic institutions, the road allows for this query.

On the road, outside "the desiring machine" of capital and the patriarchal quagmire of Freudian Oedipal theory, women find access to one another. They are released from the paradigms of individual production and competition into community. In the borderless, unlegislated space of the *nomos,* notions of authority and control become meaningless. Mother and daughter are released from the "dark continent" into *jouissance.* "We had fun," writes Mona Simpson.

CHAPTER FIVE

The Horsewomen of the Postapocalypse:
Where the Road Marks the
End of the Modern World

> ...at the periphery there roam the youthful gangs of
> the new nomads: the horsemen and the horsewomen
> of the Postapocalypse.
> Rosi Braidotti

Notes from the Postapocalypse

Contemporary women's fiction is often marked by a certain surprise regarding the condition of culture—a surprise experienced by the author. Prepared to live in a particular way no longer appropriate in the post-millennial world, such narratives suggest that their writers experienced cognitive dissonance. The niceties, the order, the expectations engendered in the wake of World War II and the rise of suburbia find only erasure in today's more apparently fragmented society. The lives we were taught to anticipate are not always—or perhaps even ever—possible.

To some extent, such vanished expectations and lost naiveté have always marked the passage into adulthood. But contemporary fiction—call it postmodern, post-structuralist, avant-garde or what you will—seems especially characterized by the sense that "something happened" and the world has become dramatically altered as a result. Within this post-apocalyptic context—the context of an irreversibly altered world—the road emerges as the site of recognition and reckoning. If the world women occupy has changed—a world now existent postmodern, post-capital, post feminism—then the road might provide direction without destination. Or, it may be the road simply provides some respite from a chaotic, ever shifting postmodern reality. Essayist and fiction writer

Joan Didion writes at some length, in a number of her works, about the subject of shattered expectations. She remembers an adolescence that now seems anachronistic, college years spent at Berkeley reading Lionel Trilling while contemplating "dates," "football lunches" and life in her sorority house. "Such an afternoon would now seem implausible in every detail," writes Didion in "The Morning After the Sixties", "so exotic as to be almost czarist" and "suggests the extent to which the narrative on which so many of us grew up no longer applies" (*White* 205). Things change; the historical moment shifts. When Didion mentions Henry Adams near the close of her essay, she does so purposefully, suggesting, like Adams, that we live in an era in which the central organizing principles and metaphors have been shattered.[1] As Didion remarks in *The White Album*,

> The only problem was that my entire education, everything I had ever been told or had told myself, insisted that the production was never meant to be improvised: I was supposed to have a script...and I no longer did. I was meant to know plot, but all I knew was what I saw: ...flash pictures in variable sequence...these images did not fit into any narrative I knew. (12–13)

In the chaotic world "after the barricades" a clear narrative script was no longer available and the re-written narrative of the post 1960s era resisted the formal requirements and rules of modernism.

Thirteen years after writing *The White Album*, Didion returned to this theme in the introductory essay in her collection, *After Henry*. Mourning the death of a friend and editor, she contends even with our personal experiences regarding the instability of the world, the knowledge that "benign experience was less than general," we resist recognizing the loss that constructs our lives. We close our eyes to change.

> I believed that days would be too full forever, too crowded with friends there was no time to see. I believed, by way of contemplating the future that we would all be around for one another's funerals. I was wrong. I had failed to imagine. I had not understood. (Didion, *After* 17–18)

This lack of understanding reflects our outdated educations and our misconstrued expectations. The world is different than we thought it would be.

Novelist and poet Kate Braverman makes a similar assertion. The apocalypse happened and we missed it, she repeats upon occasion in her poetry readings. We believe we inhabit one sort of world, only to learn we are utterly wrong in our preconceptions. She writes,

> By accident you turn a key and then you are there, removed from the world as it used to be. That other region is veiled in light purples and it inexorably recedes. You recognize you are an inhabitant of another terrain… You are riding in a car. You put your arm out and where the rain falls you begin to bleed. The rain is filled with thousands of tiny saws. Or perhaps they are fish with rows of teeth that glitter…. You decide to run away, to go back. But when you turn around you lose direction and the place where you were has been erased. (Braverman 34–35)

There is no safe site of origin, no space where things remain as they once were.

Indeed, the world that emerges in Didion and Braverman's texts is a world altered by the apocalypse. Something has happened—although the precise nature of the event is unclear. Origins and purpose remain obscured, perhaps erased while the natural world reflects confusion. Life confounds our expectations. Unprepared, we cannot read the signs that might allow us to understand. Language mutates; Didion finds the linear structure of the essay or history inadequate, while Braverman's pronouns falter for lack of a clear referent. Rosi Braidotti notes the "apocalyptic tone" of women's contemporary narratives, reading in their lack of fixed purpose and origin a sign of a shifting consciousness and the potential for a new culture.

Jacques Derrida considers at some length the significance of the apocalyptic sensibility in his essay "Of an Apocalyptic Tone Recently Adopted in Philosophy." He suggests the notion of apocalypse stems from the Greek word *apokalupsis*, and the word references revelation, "disclosure, uncovering, unveiling, the veil lifted from, the truth revealed about the thing." What is disclosed is the chaotic nature of existence, as well as the inevitability of rupture and change. The idea of apocalypse is rooted in the idea of waiting, but the precise nature of what will be sent and who will send it are necessarily vague.

Argues Derrida, the religious apocalypse itself, as accounted for by Saint John, is "a sending," a sign of what will come and, simultaneously, the coming itself. The signifier becomes the signified. For Derrida, this reasoning explains why the "apocalyptic tone" is increasingly popular in postmodern literature.

> As soon as we no longer know very well who speaks or who writes, the text becomes apocalyptic. And if the dispatches [envois] always refer to other dispatches without decidable destination, the destination remaining to come, then isn't this completely angelic structure, that of the Johannine Apocalypse... (87)

Derrida continues to argue apocalyptic writing, because it demands unveiling, is always subversive and always thus the enemy of fixed authority. For,

> [B]y its very tone, the mixing of voices, genres, and codes and the breakdown [le detraquement] of destinations, apocalyptic discourse can dismantle the dominant contract or concordant. It is a challenge to the established admissibility of messages and to the enforcement or the maintenance of order.... (Derrida 89)

Fragmented, displaced and violently severed, apocalyptic language seeks to reveal the shifting and changeable nature of truth. We see today, concludes Derrida, "the apocalypse without apocalypse," meaning we have the sense of the final catastrophe without some correlating final event. This is the same vision provided by Braidotti's comparison of contemporary women writers to the nomadic horsewomen of the apocalypse. Like Johannine of apocalyptic prophecy, women narrators comment upon some great catastrophe and change, and upon some shift that stands outside history.

Linda Hutcheon's discussion of metahistory and its relationship to postmodernism strikes a note not dissimilar to Derrida's "apocalyptic tone." She suggests contemporary narrative "dissipates its own referentiality," replacing the signified with an autonomous signified. The Sending—the symptom, the precursor—becomes the thing itself. Events and facts are replaced with a concern for subjectivity and intertextuality. Hutcheon contends in her essay "The Pastime of Past Time: Fiction, History, Historiographic Metafiction" that:

> [P]ostmodernism establishes, differentiates, and then disperses stable narrative voices (and bodies) that try to make some sense of the past. It both instills and then subverts... [it] is a desire to close the gap between past and present...and a desire to rewrite the past in a new context. (Perloff 67)

This desire to close the gap between past and present, between memory and hope, between prophecy and fulfillment, to make these impulses the same defines Hutcheon's sense of postmodern history. As she highlights the tropes of parody, fragmentation and ahistorical memory, Hutcheon describes a narrative that shares Derrida's "apocalyptic tone." Just as the apocryphal biblical books involve the reinterpretation and re-envisioning of biblical text, and the rethinking and revising of memory, the apocryphal nature of postmodern history—a history constantly reconsidered, revised and supplemented—requires new conceptions of the past and the re-remembering of experience (Hutcheon, *Textual* 19). The past becomes a vast expanse of free-floating signifiers—nomadic signifiers if you will—no longer attached to literal or fixed meaning. Their meanings are purely contextual, playful and transient. In that movement, freed from the autocracy of assigned meaning, the signifying narrative becomes revelatory and subversive. It speaks not of the old world, but of the absence of that older world. As Hutcheon contends in *A Poetics of Postmodernism*, the resultant narrative is one articulated by the "ex-centric." It is the narrative of "deterritorialization," the "enunciated discourse" of one who is always shifting focus and perspective as borders are necessarily negotiated. As the homogeneity of culture finds fissures and breaks, narrative becomes equally fluid, an expression of the mobile "flux of contextualized identities" (57–69). Examining the contemporary postmodern novel, Hutcheon suggests, "...we may be on the road to articulating a new theoretical model" (*Poetics* 86). In this sense, the women's road novel in its de-centered discourse emerges as a significant trope of postmodernism.

Notions of the de-centered and the apocryphal are nearly inherent to discussions of postmodern theory. Brian McHale returns to the topic in his own discussion of apocryphal history. Like

Hutcheon, McHale suggests postmodern narrative contains transformative powers in that it seeks to extend and "displace" conventional narrative and ideology. Like the apocryphal and frequently apocalyptic books that exist outside the liturgical canon, these subversive narratives refuse to recognize authority and boundaries. Writes McHale in *Postmodernist Fiction,*

> Apocryphal history, creative anachronism, historical fantasy—these are the typical strategies... Apocryphal history contradicts the official version...it operates in the "dark areas" of history...apocryphal history violates the "dark areas" constraint...[it] induces an ontological flicker between two worlds: one moment the official version seems to be eclipsed by the apocryphal version, the next moment, it is the apocryphal version that seems mirage-like.... (90)

That extra-textual "flicker between worlds" constitutes the real apocalypse, the transformative moment offered by revelatory contemporary narrative.

The disasters of the twentieth century have made the semiotic structures of modernism untenable, suggests Julia Kristeva in *Black Sun.* In this post-holocaust, post-atomic, post-nuclear world, the very notions of "project, continuity [and] resurrection" become impossible (Kristeva, *Black* 188). The linear language of narrative necessarily collapses. Our very conceptions of a linear scheme of time erode, leaving us with the circular, contradictory and simultaneous chronologies of "apocalyptic time" (188). As a result, literature must speak in a new dialect, voicing a "new rhetoric of the apocalypse" (233). In this new rhetoric, in its fractured tones and words, are both the larger representation of the apocalypse and its correspondent message regarding the future direction of culture.

Women's road narratives operate as the harbingers of change. The loss of certainty, alluded to by both Didion and Braverman, accompanied by the loss of history, origin, destination, meaning, fixed truth and stable narrative constitute the apocalyptic moment. The road novels of Didion, Braverman and Marilynne Robinson explore this ephemeral and spatial moment. All three authors relate "confessional" tales, each told after some catastrophe has leveled their personal worlds. Didion's Maria, in *Play It As It Lays,* writes from the mental hospital where she has been assigned after losing her family, her career and her identity, and after her involvement in a melodramatic death. Maria unsuccessfully plays all of her cards and thus forfeits the game. In Braverman's novel, the adolescent Jordan, dragged to California to witness the nonexistent "Wonders of the West" in the wake of cancer, radiation, death and nuclear disaster narrates the text. As radiation transforms cells, Jordan uses apocalyptic light to transcend the life she has been allotted. In Marilynne Robinson's *Housekeeping* the young protagonist, Ruth survives the failure of narrative. The granddaughter of a settler killed in a train accident, the daughter of a woman who committed suicide in the same lake that swallowed her father's train, the survivor of both flood and fire, Ruth relates a mythic tale. She describes for her readers another world, a world created after the civilized universe ends.

These postapocalyptic road tales operate prophetically. Road warriors, like the cinema's Mad Max, the female protagonists of these texts must negotiate a ruptured and untranslated landscape. They must read the signs and *be* the signs of a transfigured terrain. Call them postmodernists, poststructuralists or avant-garde girls; the characters in these texts epitomize the landscape of an altered world. The texts of Didion, Braverman and Robinson mark the end of an older culture.

Living on the Other Side of the Barrier: Driving with Joan Didion

Much of Joan Didion's work comprises a sort of elegy. She writes in memoriam, seeming to mourn a bygone world. "We live differently now," she writes in her essay "On Going Home." Returning to her parents' Sacramento home, Didion compares the stable materiality of her parents' house to her own more chaotic existence. She notes the collected Canton china, the faded photographs and the vast display of ephemera assembled by her maiden aunts. The house is surrounded by hundred-year-old cotton wood trees, and the family eats from antique dishes. As Didion celebrates her baby's birthday, she measures her own inadequacy against a nostalgia for her past. She wishes she could give her baby stability for her birthday.

> I would like to give her more. I would like to promise her that she will grow up with a sense of cousins and rivers and of her great grandmother's teacups...would like to give her *home* for her birthday, but we live differently now and I can promise her nothing like that. I give her a xylophone and a sundress from Madeira and promise to tell her a funny story. (Didion, *Slouching* 167–68)

The world has somehow shifted, and Didion cannot offer her child an idyllic youth.

The precise nature of the change and loss is never fully defined by Didion. "In the Morning After the Sixties" she recalls there was a time when she would "go to the barricades" to defend her ideals. Indeed, Didion insists, she would still be more than happy to return to the barricades if she could discover a sufficient cause. But that greater cause eludes her. She meditates upon the fact that the time for idealism is gone.

> Most of us live less theatrically, but remain the survivors of a peculiar and inward time. If I could believe that going to a barricade would affect man's fate in the slightest I would go to that barricade and quite often I wish that I could, but it would be less than honest to say that I expect to happen upon such a happy ending. (Didion, *White* 208)

Didion resides on some other side of the cosmic barricade; the old world is lost to her.

The concept that one is a survivor of nearly overwhelming catastrophe is a common trope in the elegiac narrative. Genre critic Alastair Fowler argues in his work on elegy that the mournful and warning voice of the survivor is a conventional motif. The elegiac narrative becomes didactic, counseling attention and change on the part of the listeners. Similarly, Peter Sacks contends in *The English Elegy: Studies in the Genre* that the elegiac text is marked by the narrator's "need to draw attention, consolingly, to his [the elegist's] own surviving powers" (Sacks 2). Didion's work would appear to fall within Sacks and Fowler's generic definition, save for one problem. Didion never notes a specific catastrophe. Marked moreover by textual irony, Didion's long lost past proves to be as dismal as the present.

Critiquing her own nostalgia in "On Going Home," Didion quickly dispenses with the antique china and reflects on the fact that family life is really an "ambush," and that we are "veterans of a guerilla war we never understood" (Didion, *Slouching* 16). Beneath the surface, flaws disturb the bucolic family life—even this suburban, 1950's family life. There is no past to romanticize, to mourn, or to idealize. "I had by all objective accounts a normal and happy family situation, and yet I was almost thirty years old before I could talk to my family on the telephone without crying" (165). Snakes crawl in the grass. Her family members drink too much and refuse to refer to her husband directly by name. They spend hours discussing the neighbors or the price of real estate. Dust drifts everywhere. Sighing over her baby's birthday, Didion still suggests she mourns the loss of something that never existed, something that even if it had existed she would never have wanted anyway. Thus self-consciously ironic, Didion's elegy mourns an apocalypse that she cannot recall. In this sense she resembles Derrida's "sending." Didion's words, mourning, and her texts themselves become the apocalypse and the revelatory call for change.

Whether Didion's apocalypse is real or perceived, textual or biblical, her characters must still inhabit and traverse this problematic zone. A novel about the difficulty of living after some final catastrophe, *Play It As It Lays*, concerns the life of the fictitious Maria Wyatt and the problems resulting from an irrelevant education and falsely engendered expectations. Maria shares this trait with Didion, for like the author she was raised to live in a nonexistent world. Like Didion, Maria has "trouble with how it was" and how it is. The novel tells the story of how the beautiful Maria was raised on hope and great expectations in a small town just outside Las Vegas, how she becomes a starlet, marries a famed film producer, bears a child with a genetic defect and misplaces her identity in the dead-ends of her life. Espying no solution for her increasingly meaningless life, Maria takes to the road. Nomad-like, she perceives the space of the road as a blank and in its undesignated turns she can find some small salvation. For her, the road does not lead anywhere; the virtue of the highway is that it is outside the fixed and corrupted world. The road leads nowhere; it is only in this unnamed space that she can hope to recover her self and to perhaps find some alternate way to live.

Maria is a wayfarer and a gambler. She has no real vocation and recognizes the transience of her passage. As the novel's title suggests, Maria rejects long-term expectation and simply plays her cards. Her situation dictates her choices. Erased by death and destruction, Maria's early optimism evaporates. Raised on the lyrically named Silver Wells Ranch, Maria recognizes her life falls short of her youthful expectations. Razed to the ground, the Silver Wells no longer exists and public policy converts the nearby town to a missile site. Maria's mother is dead, killed in an automobile accident and then consumed by coyotes. Her father, a wide-living gambler dies, massively in debt. Her producer husband proves faithless and her baby possesses the attributes of a kind of post-atomic mutant. Maria is ill equipped for contemporary life.

> I was raised to believe that what came in on the next roll would always be better than what went out on the last. I no longer believe that...NOTHING APPLIES...they misread the facts, invent connections, extrapolate reasons where none exist...it [the past] leads nowhere. (Didion, *Play* 2–4)

Like Didion herself, Maria has been provided with an out-of-date script.

As Maria opens her story from the mental hospital where she is incarcerated for reasons made clear later in the novel, she makes evident hers is a post-disaster story in which the present and the past fail to rationally connect. Her life is fractured. She inhabits an aberrant universe.

> The facts are these: My name is Maria Wyeth. That is pronounced mar-eye-ah, to get it straight at the outset. Some people here call me Mrs. Land, but I never did. Age, thirty-one. Married. Divorced. One daughter, age four. (...Kate is where they put electrodes on her head and needles in her spine and try and figure out what went wrong... Kate has soft down on her spine and an aberrant chemical in her brain...) From my mother I inherited my looks...from my father I inherited an optimism which never left me until recently... I might as well lay it on the line, I have trouble with as it was. (Didion, *Play* 3–5)

With her disdain for "how it was," Maria lives outside of history, in the timeless condition of the nomad.

Like all nomads, Maria sacrifices her very legitimacy. As she attempts to express her fractured state of being, her narrative becomes fractured and broken. Drugged and hysterical, Maria no longer speaks in a linear manner. Her words possess no power. In despair, Maria asks her estranged husband, Carter, if he believes in God. Disgusted at her old-fashioned sentimentality, he turns away. She is able to make no moral claim. There is no god in this new world, her doctors suggest. In the place of religious certainty, the physicians offer Maria Valium and antidepressants. Her desire for answers is dismissed as psychotic. Maria discovers she was a "fool" for believing in meaning or in coherent rules for the game. "I was holding all the aces," says Maria, "but what was the meaning of the game?" (8). Finding no place for herself in the world, Maria stops eating and her slender body dwindles to eighty-two pounds. It seems the larger empowered world seeks to eradicate Maria. But Maria discovers an alternative lexicon; she "drives the freeways" and in that driving—past the rusting remains of the postapocalyptic world—finds freedom.

A series of driving episodes structures *Play It As It Lays*. Significantly, each of these episodes occurs after a period of trauma. Each trauma alienates Maria from herself and, typically, involves some aspect of sexuality that Maria regards as debased. The car becomes Maria's vehicle for expression. Through the car window she can see the sights of the empty and devastated world. She can navigate the banality of the new world order. She is a horsewoman of the apocalypse, narrating the coming demise and, simultaneously, living proof of that already shifted and transformed globe.

The first road episode occupies the entire third chapter of the text. Alone, separated from her husband and her daughter, at odds with her lover, Maria deteriorates. Unable to sleep and unable to rise, she spends her days and nights lying on the chaise lounge near the neglected pool. She does not dress or wash her face. The narratives of marital expectation, romance and motherhood have all failed her. Then, as an inspiration, Maria splashes water on her face, ties back her hair with a ribbon and goes driving. Thus, driving becomes its own sanity-restoring litany.

> In the first hot month of the fall after she left Carter (the summer Carter
> left her, the summer Carter stopped living in the house in Beverly Hills),
> Maria drove the freeway... She drove the San Diego to the Harbor, the
> Harbor the Hollywood, the Hollywood to the Golden State, the Santa
> Monica, the Santa Ana, the Pasadena, the Ventura. She drove it everyday
> as a river man runs a river, everyday more attuned to its currents, its
> deceptions... Again and again she returned to an intricate stretch just
> south of the interchange from the Hollywood onto the Harbor...and the
> afternoon she finally did it without once breaking or losing the beat on the
> radio she was exhilarated and that night she slept dreamlessly... (Didion,
> *Play* 13–14)

For Maria, the road emerges as the space of regeneration. On the road
she is baptized, crosses the mythical water, consumes hardboiled eggs
and Cokes in a parodic fertility rite. When the road necessarily runs
out, "in a scrap yard in San Pedro or on the main street in Palmdale or
out somewhere no place at all where the flawless burning concrete
just stopped," Maria "skillfully" maneuvers the car back onto some
alternate route (15–17). Nomad-like, Maria marks the failure of
predetermined roads, makes her own course and finds salvation not
in her Beverly Hills home, but on the road. The automobile becomes
the verbiage in her transgressive vocabulary.

Another of the novel's road scenes occurs after Maria attends a
party held in Beverly Glen. She is distraught and disconnected.
Forced to undergo an illegal abortion, Maria now dreams of fetuses
and believes the plumbing in her Beverly Hills house malfunctions
because of its infusion of body parts. She moves out of the house, acts
in a television program called *Interstate 80*, appropriately, and tries to
reorganize her life. She attends a party. An icon of the nineteen-
sixties, Maria is barefoot, wears a silver vinyl dress, drinks, smokes
marijuana and uses drugs. She leaves with an actor who "she did not
like very much" and succumbs to his persistent sexual advances and
offer of amyl nitrites. Repelled by everything, Maria waits until the
aptly named Johnny Walker is asleep.[2] Maria then takes the actor's
Ferrari and drives through the San Fernando Valley to the freeway, to
Las Vegas, Silver Wells and Tonopah. Maria is arrested, but her

estranged producer/husband pressures Walker into dropping his charges. "I don't understand girls like you," says Maria's agent, Freddy as he and Carter shake their heads over Maria's misdeeds. But that lack of comprehension is exactly the point; driving permits Maria to transgress borders—geographical, moral, societal—and to establish an alternative existence that is outside common habits and understanding.

Constrained by her husband and limited to a movie set and small desert motel, Maria makes a final effort to escape the degradation that has become her life. She makes a list of resolves, things desperate as she is she will never do. She will not walk through Las Vegas casinos alone after midnight; she will only engage in "S-M if she wants to," she will not wear borrowed furs or carry a Yorkshire. But as the novel nears its close, the only resolution she has kept involves carrying a Yorkshire through Beverly Hills. Her resolves and identity dissolve. She leaves the motel and arrives in Las Vegas.

> [S]he wore dark glasses. She did not decide to stay in Vegas: she only failed to leave. She spoke to no one. She did not gamble. She neither swam nor lay in the sun. She was there on some business but she could not seem to put her finger on what the business was. All day, most of every night, she walked and she drove. ...she was constantly thinking about where her body stopped and where the air began.... She began to feel the pressure of Hoover Dam.... (Didion, *Play* 169–171)

Nomadic, Maria's identity shifts. She travels in the disguise of sunglasses. She has no agenda and no destination. Only the possibility of movement provides safety.

But Maria returns against her will once again to her husband, the motel and the film industry. Disaster results, and the novel concludes with Maria's soliloquy from a psychiatric hospital. Empty, her identity fully eroded, she exists outside language, narrative, relationships. "I know what nothing means and keep on playing," Maria tells the reader (Didion, *Play* 213). Her nomadic history is indicative of the cultural apocalypse. It is interesting to note Didion's much newer, non-fiction book, *Where I Was From*, casts Didion herself as a sort of survivor of warped mythologies. In this text Didion confesses her earlier writing sprang from a "tenacious" and "pernicious mood of nostalgia," a nostalgia that made her misunderstand the past (160). "There is no real way to deal with everything we lose," she writes later (Didion, *Where* 224). Didion may attempt to distance herself from her earlier work, but her tone, like Maria's, remains apocalyptic.

"Nothing" is the signifier for that which lies outside of linguistic representation, Kristeva tells us. That unrepresentable space is the very space of the apocalypse.

> [M]onstrous and painful sights do damage to our systems of perception and representation. As if overtaxed or destroyed by too powerful a breaker, our symbolic means finds themselves hollowed out, nearly wiped out, paralyzed. On the edge of silence the word "nothing" emerges, a discreet defense in the face of so much disorder, both internal and external, incommensurable. Never has a cataclysm been more apocalyptically outrageous; never has its representation been assumed by so few symbolic means. (Kristeva 223)

The "nothing" that Maria understands lies outside of traditional experience and narrative. "Nothing" marks the fractured representation of cultural shift and apocalypse. The vast emptiness of "nothing" signifies the subject of Didion's novel.

A Book of Revelation: Kate Braverman's
Wonders of the West

Named for the biblical river, the adolescent protagonist of Braverman's broken road trip, *Wonders of the West,* Jordan travels to the Eden of the West with her mother. A woman "who plays with edges" and borders as she seeks to escape poverty, banality and a bad marriage, Roxanne demonstrates few maternal traits. With a dedication to the road and Kerouac, the novel explores the women's travels and their hopes that Roxanne's gambler brother will provide for them. But Uncle Louie is dying of cancer, a cancer caused and fueled by the residual flotsam of the nuclear age, suspects Jordan. Housed in a public facility reserved for those "receiving treatment," Uncle Louie and his family live amidst filthy asphalt and the mutant, polluted sunsets that surround the center. Jordan notices a large number of the afflicted are the offspring of the witnesses of atomic blasts. These marginalized inhabitants emerge as the literal children of the apocalypse. The story that results is one of "inhumanity and time travel" (Braverman 279). A survivor of the cataclysm, Jordan tells her readers early on,

> At the moment of impact at Hiroshima, during the actual flash, people had the pattern of their kimonos tattooed to their flesh. Everything stalled.... Time and measurement were factors. It was an intricacy that proved worthless. It didn't help anyone survive...it's possible to be ambushed by revelation. ...You would recognize the constellations and where they were going... You would remember everything. You would know what they were saying. Nothing would require translation. (22)

The "nothing" that exists outside translation that is apprehended only in the final destructive moments of revelation finds expression in Jordan's experience. Like Didion's Maria, Jordan too knows "what nothings means and keeps on playing." The space that exists beyond language and representation, outside of legitimacy and the borders of regulated discourse, finds definition in "nothing."

Roxanne and Jordan have left Ernie "the drag, the square" and are on their way west. Roxanne who was once named Ruthie has re-christened herself and she is moving to California to find glamour, wealth and maybe even romance.

> [W]e are driving in the red convertible. It is me and the person who used to be my mother, me and the stranger named Roxanne... Now she knows about maps. I wonder how she learned this. She must have read about these things in magazines and saw them in movies. ...Everything is behind us. My father. My school. ...We are driving into America. (Braverman 111–112)

But the "America" encountered by Roxanne and Jordan fails to match their expectations. Roxanne's friends have moved away, fallen into drug addiction or simply died. There is no free lodging and assistance available to the women. Jordan assumes the geography and terrain must correlate with the maps they carry and her own preconceived ideas, but the country she encounters is utterly foreign and unknowable.

> I imagine the states will resemble my puzzles of America. The states will
> be red or blue, pink or yellow or green. Their various products will be
> displayed. ...A lady with a starched apron the color of clouds will hold up
> a tray of round cheeses and smile. A man with faded blue overalls will
> stand alongside a field of corn. There will be a scarecrow at the edge of the
> field. (112)

Instead, Jordan sees a world that is really a sort of cosmic junkyard
pass by. Empty sheds, broken equipment and even desiccated
carcasses flung upon the parched land comprise the Midwest.
Dilapidated fences and collapsed barns punctuate the flat earth. The
suburbs of eroded hills, ugly, twisted subdivisions and empty
boulevards speak of some disaster. As Jordan consults the map in
disbelief, she realizes the road is a "prophetic wound" running
through a nation that must be conceived of as a disaster zone.

For Jordan, America emerges as the place of catastrophe and
collapse. The road provides her with hope and a potential freedom
from the mortal illness of American bourgeois life. Raised on popular
and romantic images of a robust American frontier dotted with fertile
farms and bustling metropolises, Jordan instead encounters another
less vital and picturesque nation.

> America is trucks with killer faces, with yellow and red streaks on their
> cabs, like Indian war paint. Or the tattoos certain tribes engrave on the
> faces of their children. Then the groves of trees seem abandoned. And the
> derelict farms that look like people ran from them. There are craters in the
> field near the highway.... There are ruins of stockyards.... (117)

From Jordan's point of view, some terrible apocalypse has occurred,
something that drove people from their once bucolic farms and
homes. The survivors are muted, shell-shocked and docile. Roxanne
leads Jordan to believe the West will be different.

Enthralled with the idea of the West—describing in affluent
terms the life they will have in Hollywood with her rich brother
Louie—the generally cynical Roxanne decides they should take a
detour and visit the widely advertised "Wonders of the West." Nearly
out of money, Roxanne and Jordan sleep in the car, delay eating, and

sometimes mix catsup with water and pretend that it is soup. Roxanne pawns her belongings, including a diamond watch that was once a gift from Ernie, "the drag." Their lives are tolerable because they are certain they are on their way to some place far superior. Sunburned and dirty-haired, the women follow the road signs and drive through several states to see the "wonders." After all, on the road they are free to change their destinations, as no one expects them anyway. After a great deal of driving, the women arrive in an unidentified rural town. The town is filled with rusted and abandoned railroad cars, lethargic women with lined faces and discarded farming equipment. But the real "wonders" require a fee; Roxanne pays and Jordan and Roxanne enter a courthouse that has been turned into a museum.

> We are edging closer to the Wonders of the West. ...Upstairs is a room littered with random junk. The lady with the eyes of an isolated midnight express explains the objects to us. She shows us a pony express mailbag and antique dentist tools. ...Roxanne wants to ask for her money back..."If this is what you learn from the ancestors, no wonder everybody runs from the land." ...We are walking down the steps and we don't look at each other. We continue down the street where everything is closed... The street is empty. We walk for blocks and don't see anyone. We have seen something horrible in the courthouse. (Braverman 228–229)

The "Wonders of the West" are an illusion, a lie. The museum confirms the women's worst fears; some unreported and terrible disaster has happened. Weak, hungry sick and destitute, they hasten back to the road.

The "real" West fails Jordan as well. Los Angeles proves to be a city of molecularly charged air and mutants. Even before they arrive, Jordan sees ahead of them the vast orange cloud. The sky is scarlet and "abnormal," "spread above us like a mutilated body." The city appears as some both abandoned and futuristic space, utterly uninhabitable. Worst yet, Uncle Louie and his wife, Doris, impoverished by Louie's cancer, wear cast-offs and live in public housing. They eat the leftovers brought home by Doris, broken bits of rolls and frayed pieces of pressed turkey. All they retain of their former glory is an aggressive cynicism and an insistence they not be viewed as "hicks." Roxanne continues on the road; she gets a job at a film studio and travels incessantly, always "on location." She flies with boyfriends to Hawaii, Mexico and Jamaica, in pursuit of "the most prestigious of tans, the winter tan." She is "making up for lost time."

Jordan remains for a time in the projects. She associates with the other "project kids" and comes to believe the cancer that afflicts each family in the project is the result of a "flash," of radiation, of the thermal energy situated in L.A. Jordan assumes Roxanne's favorite phrase, "on location," refers both to travel and to a particular bodily site where cellular mutation has resulted in cancer.

But Jordan too goes "on location" and takes to the road again. She believes insistently there must be another way to be, some better way to live in the radically transformed new world. Aptly, the novel is set in the late nineteen sixties, and Jordan leaves school to hitch a ride on a painted "hippie" bus, carrying her guitar and her poetry books. She is an inter-galactic traveler, on her way to a new space. As she boards the bus she sees her school's guidance counselor "dissipated in gray smoke." "He is lost in a veil of nerve gas" (Braverman 280). Jordan vacates the apocalyptic landscape. "I am walking down the stairs, through the corridor with its ruined metallic air, with its sunken broken air. Then I am passing through the fence. I get into the van. Someone turns on the radio. Someone begins to drive" (280). The road that once appeared to Jordan as a scar upon the map, as a beacon of approaching disaster, is the road that will carry her away. The road is both the signifier of this vast cultural collapse and a pathway beyond. Jordan and flame-haired Roxanne are naming the disaster, calling out omens as they ride across the landscape. Braverman's women are Derrida's "envois," "charged with a historic mission of whom nobody has requested anything," "sending" word of a new aesthetic (Derrida 86).

This new aesthetic is subversive and outside the discourse of the state and culture. Just as Jordan must speak from the marginal space of the projects, apocalyptic discourse emanates from a subversive posture.

By its very tone, the mixing of voices, genres, and codes, and the

breakdown [le detraquement] of destinations, apocalyptic discourse can
also dismantle the dominant contract or concordant. It is a challenge to the
established admissibility of messages and the maintenance of order....
(Derrida 89)

As Jordan and Roxanne blend their voices into a single tale, as they
merge time frames and the genres of poetry and prose, as they defy
authority, they challenge the structures of their culture. They must
take to the road as nomads, speaking of their rebellion and
transcendence.

The apocalypse is a matter of tone and perception, argues
Derrida in "Of an Apocalyptic Tone Recently Adopted in
Philosophy," a genre and experience characterized by a notion of
ending, of eschatology, and rupture. This revelation is not based on a
particular historic vision, but rather, upon a sense that that rupture
has already happened. The Derridean apocalypse is the
understanding that origins and destinations are meaningless, that we
have surpassed some final judgment and live on in some new
undefined way.

Now here, precisely, is announced—as promise or threat—an apocalypse
without apocalypse, an apocalypse without vision, without truth, without
revelation,...of addresses without message and without destination,
without sender or decidable addressee, without last judgment.... Our
apocalypse now: that there is no longer any place for the apocalypse as
the collection of evil and good...to an event of certainty.... (94)

The mutant red sky over Los Angeles and the radiated bodies of the
cancer victims are Braverman's sendings. Disaster has happened; we
simply don't know which phenomenon to identify as the precursor of
the end. Freed from discourse—from identified senders and
addressees—Braverman's characters emerge as postmodern nomads.

Surviving the End of the World: Robinson's *Housekeeping* and the Creation of a Nomadic Discourse

Didion's Maria fumbles to recover her lost identity in a brave new world wherein mothers desert their children, water faucets leak blood and love is always about betrayal. Her life unfolds against a barren desert terrain, reminiscent of the wasteland. The apocalypse is marked by the failure of social systems and Maria attempts to escape on the road. Similarly, Braverman's Jordan relinquishes all faith in the cultural institutions meant to sustain her. Science, family relationships and the social order of schools, agencies and the medical profession prove incapable of assistance. Both the codified language of the state and her family's cynical "hipster" lexicon are out of date. The age of domesticity is over and scientific reason is dead (bombed at Hiroshima). For Jordan, the "Wonders of the West" crumple beneath a polluted sky. To survive, Jordan adopts a new discourse—a discourse that is marked by a "new" style and aesthetic—and takes to the road. In Marilynne Robinson's lyrical novel, *Housekeeping*, the "ordinary" modern world is marked by such catastrophes—family tragedy, flood and fire—that conventional life seems banal and false. Like Noah after the biblical flood, the novel's heroine, Ruth requires some new covenant and some alternate discourse. The road provides Ruth with this transcendent vocabulary.

Unfolding in the ominously named town of Fingerbone,[3] Montana, Ruth's "civilized" and domestic life is curiously circumscribed by death. And indeed, perhaps this should not be surprising. As Jane Tompkins remarks in *West of Everything*, in the West "death comes more and more to the fore" (27). Insists Tompkins, the story of the West is necessarily, always, about violence and death; it is a morality play cast against the rugged landscape of Manifest Destiny and colonial expansion. In Tompkins' reading, the western is always masculine; men narrate the conflict between civilization and the frontier while women are confined within domestic havens. Ruth's childhood in Fingerbone is consistent with Tompkins' commentary. While violence composes the periphery of her life, Ruth lives in seeming tranquility within a female enclave.

Ruth's grandfather first brings the family west to Fingerbone. A railroad worker who is most happy when traveling, he settles his not entirely happy wife in the town. In Fingerbone, his wife waits with the couple's three daughters for his visits. But the locomotive jumps the track as it crosses the black water of the lake just outside

Fingerbone and the entire train disappears into the depths. Ruth's grandmother then raises her daughters in an edenic household of pressed linen and braided hair. The family is silent and slow moving and there is some sense they will always live in the same manner. But the girls abruptly leave their mother; one becomes a missionary, one a sort of hobo, and the prettiest—Ruth's mother—marries. What happens on these various expeditions is never narrated, but a few years after giving birth to Ruth and her sister Lucille their mother leaves the girls with a babysitter and drives her own car into the now familiar waters of Lake Fingerbone. The girls are left at first with their grandmother who raises them as she did her own daughters.

> Ruth and Lucille pass their early days in Fingerbone in relative peace. An avid housekeeper, their grandmother cooks and cleans for them. She teaches them property—a house—is the only security in an insecure world. A house is kept, she implies, through a combination of domestic and financial skills.
> My grandmother loved to talk about these things.... "Keep the house. So long as you look after your health and own the roof above your head, you're safe." (Robinson 27)

The grandmother teaches the girls about canning, cooking, and the seasons of cleaning. She washes and starches the doilies that protect the furniture. She takes pride in the perfection of her house and grounds. No discussion concerning the violence of their lives, and the town and its proximity to familial death takes place. Confined and "kept" by the house, the girls separate from the violence of the lake. Yet, they grow increasingly silent, withdrawn and even melancholy.

The house cannot permanently preserve the elderly grandmother and she eventually dies. At her request, two maiden cousins stay briefly with Ruth and Lucille but they find children untenable. The "hobo" sister, Ruth and Lucille's Aunt Sylvie is sent for. Sylvie (her name suggesting an association with that woods and sylvan nature) is a committed transient. Despite her real efforts, she cannot accommodate herself to the house. She naps on public benches with a newspaper over her face, sleeps at home in her clothes, eats from tins, wears men's shoes, wanders off and is friends only with the women she meets riding boxcars.

As the girls endure their erratic domestic lives, nature intervenes. Winter brings unprecedented rain and snow, and the spring is accompanied by a great flood. Water rises everywhere. It is impossible to go to school. The entire bottom floor of the house fills with water while the grounds also flood. The house sits like a great ark upon the sea of Fingerbone.

> Days of rain at just that time were a disaster. They hastened the melting of the snow but not the thawing of the ground. So at the end of three days the houses and hutches and barns and sheds of Fingerbone were like so many spilled and foundered arcs...we lived on the second floor for a number of days. (Robinson 61)

"It's the end of the world," Sylvie tells Ruth and Lucille. And as Ruth ponders the flood and her dead mother and grandfather lost in the lake, she suggests, "perhaps we all awaited a resurrection" (96).

Slowly the water recedes. The sun comes out with a blinding light. The girls are left with the sodden furniture and the disapproval of visiting ladies. They sense the disapprobation of their neighbors and wander together, missing school. Lucille, the oldest, reads the signs and knows their world cannot continue as it has. The flood has marked some change. She wants to learn the vocabulary of domesticity and eventually goes off to live with her home economics teacher. Ruth is left alone with Sylvie.

Increasingly like her aunt's, Ruth's behavior begins to raise the ire of the community. The sheriff announces Ruthie will probably be removed, placed in a foster home so she can grow up conforming to the rules of domestic culture. But before Ruthie can be claimed by the authorities, a second disaster occurs. The house and orchards burn. Ruthie and Sylvie set the fires in order to initiate a plan of escape. They stage their own deaths, escape the confines of patriarchy and take to the road. Indeed, they nearly die when they walk across the railroad ties that span Fingerbone Lake, buffeted by wind and narrowly missing an oncoming train. As the women traverse the water that houses the graves of their relatives, their old identities die. Reborn as nomads, they no longer can be called "housekeepers;" instead, Ruth and Sylvie opt out of the confines of domesticity.

An adult by the end of the novel, Ruth ponders her nomadic

status. She wonders what made the common vocabulary—a clean house, curled hair, balanced meals, a well-tended yard—impossible for her. Why could Lucille speak that language without difficulty while it remained alien to Ruth? "When did I become so unlike other people?" asks Ruth.

> Either it was when I followed Sylvie across the bridge and the lake claimed us, or it was when my mother left me waiting for her, and established me in the habit of waiting and expectation which makes any present moment most significant for what it does not contain. Or was it at my conception? (214)

Ruth becomes a nomad as the only tenable response to disaster. She suffers the loss of grandparents, the desertion of her father, the suicide of her mother, flood and fire. She sees the lost civilization of Fingerbone as "a Carthage sown with salt" (152). Ruthie understands too that the loss of her earlier life may presage some new healed vision of the world.

> What flowering would there be in such a garden? Light would force each salt calyx to open in prisms, and to fruit heavily with bright globes of water...where the world was salt there would be even greater need of slaking. ...And here again is the foreshadowing—the world will be made whole. (152–153)

After the apocalypse, suggests Ruth, some new and better era will dawn. Lot's wife who was turned to salt as she left Sodom "full of loss and mourning," will in the new era no longer be "salt and barren" but instead "here rare flowers will gleam in her hair" (153).[4] A new covenant will yield a new edenic world. Ruthie walks away, looking for a new way to be in the world.

In this new world she does not have direction or destination. She and Sylvie simply move. Ruthie reflects, "now truly we were cast out to wander and there was an end to housekeeping" (209). They reject the confines of domesticity. When a job or town begins to seem confining, they leave. They do not talk to their (temporary) neighbors and co-workers, and they do not "keep house." They carry old newspaper copies of their fictive obituaries. Mostly, the women evolve into "silent," "drifters," inhabiting a different terrain from everyone else.

> We are drifters. And once you have set your foot in that path it hard to
> imagine another one. ...When my own silence seems suddenly
> remarkable, then they [acquaintances, café customers] begin to suspect me,
> and it is as if I had put a chill on the coffee by serving it. What have I to do
> with these ceremonies of sustenance, of nurturing? (Robinson 213–214)

Phoenix-like, Ruthie and Sylvie rise from the dead. In the wake of
flood and fire they walk away from the domestic graveyard of
Fingerbone.

"Go out into the highways and ledges," Jesus instructed his
apostles—male and female.[5] His apostles were to wander as they
spread the word of the second coming. Similarly, Ruth and Sylvie
"face the terrors of the crossing" as they move across the lake and
enter a new territory. They speak of the failure of domesticity and of
the violence that is its corollary. Ruth and Sylvie have heard some
other language, listened "like blind women groping their way...[to]
some sound too loud to be heard, some word so true we did not
understand it, but merely felt it pour through our nerves like
darkness or water" (215). The language they hear is Kristeva's new
rhetoric of the apocalypse—silence mixed with a new lexicon that
signals an entirely alternate sensibility. Like Derrida's "envoys," they
too signify the failure of the world as it is conventionally constructed.
In their rejection of the common vernacular, they offer another
language, another sensibility and an alternate aesthetic in the world
to come.

CHAPTER SIX

A New World Made:
(Re)Envisioning Utopia from the Road

Where We're Going Is Where We Are

The impulse toward utopia might be considered a distinguishing aspect of western, Anglo-European literature. In particular, however, the notion that with just a bit more effort, utopia could be established within our continental borders marks American literature—indeed American literature. Some have contended, as does Sacvan Bercovitch, that this urge toward utopia springs from the Puritans' conception of the "Alabaster City on the hill" and that the fantasy is perpetually reconstructed in a material and even vulgar manner. Cotton Mather himself refers to John Winthrop as "Nehemias Americanus," paying tribute to the first Puritan governor as the leader—the biblical Nehemiah—who would lead his people to find and build the Promised Land (Bercovitch 5). The allure of potential utopia empowered the Puritan enterprise and its "errand into the wilderness," and was later translated into a political vocabulary of national expansion.

Richard Slotkin along with a host of other cultural critics, comments upon how the ideas of Manifest Destiny and material democracy propelled the American establishment across the continent and ultimately into Vietnam and the "final frontier" of space. National and economic interests required the continual movement toward some larger and more utopian idea of statehood. The United States was necessarily, always, in the Hegelian process of becoming some larger and more perfect nation. Utopia waited just around the next bend in the road. As Ronald Reagan said to much applause at the 1984 Republican Convention, "You ain't seen nothing yet."

But utopian claims are not the sole province of the American political right. The Transcendentalists also adopted the idea that paradise could be claimed (although their conception of this paradise was obviously radically different than that claimed by Reagan). Walt Whitman wrote of "democratic vistas" that would put to shame "Old West dynasties." As Bercovitch notes,

> World history. ...[It] meant simultaneously a total assertion of the self, a jeremiad against the misdirected progress of the "dead" present and an act of prophecy, which guaranteed the future by celebrating...[and expanding] the regenerate "Americanus." (184)

The mythology of American culture was built upon the concept that we are always enroute and always on the road to Utopia. And, in fact, the road to the American West hosts numerous (frequently failed) utopian communities, with perhaps the Transcendentalists' Brooke Farm being the most famous. In his text, *Walking*, Henry David Thoreau suggests the seeker escape the clutches of familial life and take to the road to find a spot where one might recover the soul. By the middle of the nineteen sixties, idealists recited Thoreau's words as they took to the road, Woodstock, the commune and "Yasner's Farm" in an effort to "get back to the garden."

> What for Mather had been the purifying wilderness, and for Edwards the theocratic garden of God, became for Emerson's generation the redemptive West, as frontier or agrarian settlement or virgin land. Every stage of this long development bespeaks the astonishing tenacity of myth.... A self-proclaimed people of God subsumed the facts of social pluralism...in a comprehensive national ideal.... (Bercovitch 186)

Even today, we invest a large portion of our national identity in the belief that we collectively engage in the construction of a utopian project. The elusive nature of this project seems unimportant; like Gatsby we resist the idea that the green light is behind us and expect to establish the democratic vista in the future.

The utopian vision manifests the "Dis-ease of the West," insists Ihab Hassan in *Selves at Risk: Patterns of Quest in Contemporary American Letters*. Americans believe in "the power of travel" writes Hassan. We believe the present day intolerability of our own lives is subject to immediate change, particularly if we keep moving. Thus, travel constitutes an attempt to "wrest" utopia from "Destiny." We seek, claims Hassan, like the mythic Grail King, to heal some psychic wound through the process of geographical discovery.

> The Dis-ease of the West is nonetheless real, prompting men and women to risk their lives far from societies they disavow. Often they elude their own sahib-kind, whom they find more dangerous and repugnant than any "natives"...they flee the contemporary world, flee Western history, hoping to discover another time in another place. Their journeys are as much in quest as escapes, no less judgments on occidental reality than assays in utopia. (Hassan 68)

From the Oregon Trail to the "Green Hills of Africa" the American traveler and writer, according to Hassan, looks to find a garden without a "serpent" and to escape the wound of bourgeois culture. Yet, according to Hassan, the wound finally produced by cultural violence, materialism and the desire for domination causes the real societal pain, and since this violence and materiality are a necessary part of the colonial project, utopia must always recede.[1]

In her text, *The Anatomy of National Fantasy*, Lauren Berlant suggests utopian fantasy allows the erasure of present day political and economic disruptions, "obscuring the political activity and power relations in American civil life" (32). Where we are doesn't matter because our national identity is embedded in a promise about where we will eventually arrive. We accept "imperfect formations" because their importance fades against the possibility of larger utopian horizons. Indeed, posits Berlant,

> [T]he agents of the law and civil society can enforce inequity because of our transient state. The National Symbolic sutures the body and subjectivity to the public sphere of discourse, time and space that constitutes the "objective" official political reality of the nation...an official technology of memory whose purpose is to burn into the minds of subjects their intrinsically social existence and responsibility.... (Berlant 34)

The law then, as well as civil discourse, concerns the process of becoming, of traveling the road toward that utopian community, rather than a protective mechanism.

But for the true nomad—that person who resides between

borders, who recognizes no national identity and no defined destination—the notion of becoming is nearly impossible. The nomad must reject the possibility of a civilly constituted utopian society, for a significant aspect of nomadic identity is the rejection of the power of civil society and the polis. The nomad has no confidence civil society can produce a more just and less marginalizing world, so the nomad opts out of the various governmental forms created by the *polis*. If the nomad credits at all the notion of utopia, it is a post-structuralist, post-humanist utopic vision. The nomad cannot conceive of a future destination or take comfort in the possibility of the *polis*. Instead, the nomad conceives of a utopia rooted in the present—a utopian form in the now. This subjectivity does not exist within the linear time frame of phallogocentrism, but in the circular continuousness of the present moment. For the nomad there is no mythic past, there is no promising future; there is only the negotiation of subjectivity. The agency of the self and the community replace the law of the *polis*.

Women's contemporary road fiction frequently explores what might be regarded as the utopia of the road. For the road—that place between destinations—allows for the creation of a feminine subjectivity. Paula Sharp's *Crows Over a Wheatfield* contends there can be a community that exists outside the National Symbolic. In her novel, the laws of the *polis* are undermined and their promise of future good ignored. The law is reconstituted. The novel's heroine, who is an actual lawyer and judge, adjudicates within an alternative system and time frame. That alternative nomadic space is utopian. Similarly, Paule Marshall's novel, *Praisesong for the Widow*, does not wait for the law to address civil injustice. Rather, the novel with its notion of time that is simultaneous instead of linear, offers an alternative and mobile republic of the spirit. Zora Neale Hurston leads her heroine, Janie, out through the garden gate and into a mythic life that is finally concerned with the embrace of the self. In the same manner, Sandra Cisneros' "Woman Hollering Creek" liberates its subject and subjectivity itself by reversing patriarchal expectation. In the work of women nomadic writers, visions of utopia are claimed in the present tense. Utopia is not pursued in outlying territories; it is claimed in the immediacy of the present. This present may be conceptual rather than actual. These are not narratives of the expectant; these contemporary fictions explore what emerges in the instant in which citizenship in the established *polis* is relinquished.

"Be here now," American seekers have preached since Ram Dass coined the phrase in the nineteen sixties. And while none of the texts included here directly address notions of eastern philosophy and spirituality, the nomad seems curiously aligned with the practitioners of eastern metaphysics. Post-colonial critic, Gayatri Spivak comments upon this indirectly when she suggests French postmodernists —notably Derrida, Lyotard and Deleuze—"reach out to all that is not the West, because they have, in one way or another, questioned the millennially cherished excellence of Western metaphysics" (Spivak 7).[2] For, while the true nomad subscribes to no fixed world-view, religion or political persuasion, she also rejects linear temporality and centralized narrative. Her aesthetic is not contained within the "Grand Narratives" of western culture; she lives instead in shifting and parallel universes. In the final analysis, the nomad cannot be, strictly speaking, utopian. For the essence of utopia suggests an attained perfection and a resulting stasis. The nomad lives a dynamic existence; yet, where she is, at any given moment, can perhaps be "good enough."

The Problem of Atticus Finch: *Crows Over a Wheatfield* and the Rejection of Law

Paula Sharp's troubled protagonist, Melanie Ratleer, recalls that her first major confrontation with her famous and abusive attorney father occurred shortly after the film *To Kill a Mockingbird* was released. To her discomfort, the novel became required reading for adolescents.

> Gregory Peck, as Atticus, the benevolent lawyer-father of the child telling the story, made my teacher's heart flutter, and even my father went to a movie theater with a pack of defense attorneys to see the film. It was a movie that everyone talked about and that lawyers loved. ...the *Chicago Tribune* described my father..."as a figure with a presence as formidable and arresting as a Harper Lee character." (Sharp 22)

But Melanie finds the novel and film disquieting. She is troubled by the relationship Atticus maintains with his daughter Scout, and by the glamour that surrounds Atticus at the expense of his client. The fact that Atticus' client, Tom, is killed does not seem to detract from Atticus' heroism. Melanie concludes that Atticus and the novel celebrate the triumph and power of the law rather than protecting actual victims. Forced to write an essay on Lee's novel, Melanie conspires with her brother, Matt. Killing a mockingbird, Lee's novel reminds the reader, is evil, for a mockingbird does nothing but sing. This is sentimental nonsense, says Sharp's Matt.

> The killing of mockingbirds is a necessary evil because they are actually miniature hawks that lie in wait in trees, ready to attack us. Alfred Hitchcock would have made a better horror movie if he'd used mockingbirds instead of seagulls. (26)

Only in fairy tales are mockingbirds loveable, suggests Melanie. Similarly, only in the nation's fantasy life are (white) lawyers like Atticus heroic. Harper Lee's novel, like its metaphor of the mockingbird, uses sentimentality to disguise the fearsome power of the law. Atticus Finch emerges as an emblem of the law's patriarchal origins and its regulatory offices.

This notion of the law is significant in both Sharp's work and in larger philosophical discourse concerning legal structures. As Michel Foucault points out throughout his writing, the law always connects repression and the regulation of the body. The cost of violating the law is the incarceration (or execution) of the body. Criminality is most often associated with the unauthorized use of the physical body. "For a long time," Foucault tells us "sovereign power" and the law dealt with the power of the Roman patriarch to dispense life or death to his wife, children and slaves (Foucault 135). The law literally meant the "power over them of life or death." More recently, the "juridical form" of power is exercised as "essentially the right of seizure: of things, time, bodies, and ultimately life itself" (136). Increasingly, this legal power addresses the notion of family, for it is within this domestic structure that the law attempts to regulate sexuality (108). This process of regulation is neither concerned with protection or ethics; the law is purely concerned with utilizing the body in all ways to benefit the "deployment of alliance"—a "system of kinship" between the focus of power and it subjects, between political structure and possessions (106). The agent of power, the law regulates bodies, most particularly as they are claimed for production with the construction of the family.

Such laws, as Deleuze and Guattari have already reminded us, revolve around capitalist production. Within this social, "desiring machine" each member of the culture is organized to produce and consume in highly specific and regulated ways. Like the factory worker at his designated station, we are each given particular productive functions.

> For each member in a global system of desire and destiny that organizes the productions of production, the productions of recordings and the productions of consumption. Flows of women and children, flows of herds and of seed, sperm flows, flows of shit, menstrual flows, nothing must escape coding. The primitive territorial machine, with its immobile motor, the earth, is already a social machine.... (Deleuze and Guattari 142)

Within this factory vision of the world, we organize into families with the purpose of regulating discourse, sexuality and, hence, production. To maintain power and increase production the state must provide "specific codes"—laws—that regulate all interaction. All relationships are named—"designated"—by the law, and these "designations" replace natural affinities and relationships. The law regulates the body; one might even contend that the body of law—its entirety—displaces the vitality of the human body. Sharp's narrator tacitly acknowledges this when she agrees that entering the legal profession and eventually becoming a judge "meant that I had opened the coffin lid of the law and walked in" (Sharp 63).

It is important to note that unlike earlier writings that delineated the so-called "social contract," Deleuze and Guattari do not suggest that the relinquishment of individual power to a sovereign state takes place in order "to preserve the common good." For them, it is mere illusion to believe that law preserves the individual. The power of the sovereign state is used to protect and benefit the state; the law benefits the larger body of the law. Law emerges as the *Urstaat* (Deleuze and Guattari 221). Citizens are subject to the state. Argues Lauren Berlant,

[C]itizens...are all merely subject to the law: within its symbolic order but outside direct control over its legislation. These citizens' bodies are not protected by the law that administers to them; these citizens' minds are not fully engaged in support of the state's manifest legislation. (101)

At the apex of the state's mechanisms of control, lies control of the body. Control of the body, insists Foucault (along with legions of contemporary cultural critics), lies in control of sexuality. "Sex without law," Foucault tells us, would be like conceiving of power without a centralized authority (91). And indeed, Deleuze and Guattari argue it is precisely the regulation of sexuality that creates and defines the larger super-structure of capitalist culture. Paula Sharp's novel emerges as a critique and subversion of the power and process of the law.

Abused by her tyrannical lawyer father, Melanie, the protagonist and narrator of *Crows Over a Wheatfield*, eventually becomes a lawyer and a judge. Her brother, groomed to be a "brilliant" legal mind, rebels by withdrawing into schizophrenia and then escapes further regulation by climbing through a window in the state mental institution.[3] Melanie adopts the role that was meant for Matt. However, as the novel, which is divided into four sections, moves into its second half, Melanie's ironic distance from the law evolves into serious misgiving. For, as the text of the novel makes clear, the law is not concerned with protection of the helpless; the law is concerned with the preservation of (patriarchal) power. Melanie's father is a defense attorney and (like Atticus Finch) by all outward appearances is dedicated to the protection of liberal ideals. Yet, he protects killers, rapists, and in his most famous case, a woman who drowns the small children in her care. This pattern repeats itself in Melanie's later experiences. Melanie visits the small Midwestern community where her escaped step-mother Ottilie and Matt have taken refuge with a radical Marxist minister who is dedicated to the assistance of Latin American refugees.[4] When Melanie first arrives, the community is excited about the imminent arrival of Daniel Munk, a theologian preaching liberation theology in Brazil. But, Munk is not what he appears. Charismatic and popular, claiming an impressive degree from Yale, Munk is actually controlling, violent and sexually abusive. He attacks his wife Mildred and demonstrates particular cruelty toward their young son, Ben. Mildred tries to leave her husband and to remove her son from his care. But the law is impervious to her pleas and offers of evidence. If Mildred divorces or leaves her husband, he retains custody rights to Ben. If she remains married, Daniel Munk can continue the abuse. The realities of the state create a legal conundrum.

Melanie Ratleer initially attempts to help Mildred and her son through the application of the law. She works with a well-known attorney, Vogelsang, and attempts to mount a legal argument that would provide Mildred with custody of her child.[5] But Melanie's attempt is doomed to failure. Daniel's piety proves too convincing, while the revelation Mildred's long-dead mother suffered from mental illness rocks the courtroom. The taint of Marxism corrupts the image of Mildred's father. Reared by middle-class "moral" Americans, Daniel insists his outlook is "conventional" and "conservative," and unlike his liberal wife he simply wants a life of order and discipline. He argues that she spoils Ben. If Mildred will return and be a "true wife" to him—providing him with access to her body, he will drop his own custody suit. Daniel asks for counseling and judicial intervention in the preservation of his family. Mildred insists upon separation and the custody of her son; such demands mark her as willful, defiant of the court, and selfish. Vogelsang urges Mildred to cooperate with the court, to allow Daniel visitation with his son, and to devise "strategy." But Melanie knows they will lose.

> Judge Bracken did not want extra work. ...the judge would find the further suggestion of Daniel's lack of sexual boundaries with his son distasteful, and shun our papers and dismiss evidence of Daniel's violence.... Even now it is unnerving for me to remember how effectively a man like Daniel, who subverted every code, fit the law into his hand like a well-worn tool. It was as if the law had been designed specifically for him all along. (Sharp 285)

The law *has* been designed for people like Daniel, Melanie discovers, and it is this discovery that changes the course of Melanie and her friends' lives and makes this novel a road text.

Confronted with the real nature of the law, an institution that cannot even enter Ben's name correctly in the court proceedings but that must protect the status quo, Mildred seeks another solution. "Every last one of them [judges, lawyers, and court appointed psychiatrists] is crazy! Any one of them could have protected us! They all had the power to help us, but none of them did" (293). Assuming a false identity (provided by her father who routinely did this for political refugees), Mildred takes her son and becomes a nomad, living restlessly without identity on the fringes of American culture. She and her son alter their appearances, their ages and their names. They remain mobile and aloof, and Ben grows up outside of the law. The road saves Mildred and Ben; they relinquish all legitimating documents.

Outside the *polis,* Mildred creates what Melanie will regard as a "parallel universe." Following the model of the nineteenth century's abolitionists, Mildred creates a modern "railroad" for victims of fear and domestic violence forced to live outside the law. In this new universe, relationships are forged out of commitment and desire; here, the marginalized bond together in order to create a free world. Matt, Melanie's schizophrenic brother, becomes an expert computer hacker. Other members trace the complicated network of "safe houses." Unmarried couples live together. Lives are characterized by constant motion—mad dashes to airports and rides lying down in the back seats of cars. Despite the circumstances of its conception, life on Sharp's railroad is characterized by joy, egalitarianism, community and rebellious pleasure. Writes Sharp,

> Some people are lost in life's turbulence, while some buoy up in tact, above water and swim to shore. I thought she [Mildred] must have made it to the shore long ago.... With time I would come to understand that Mildred's Railroad was essentially anarchistic, a recalcitrant entity that existed in part for the sheer pleasure of savoring its own lively rebelliousness. It was a natural extension of Mildred's personality. In every instance where Mildred would be accused of leading the railroad, she would deny it, not out of false modesty, but because she did not see herself in that role or desire it. She envisioned the railroad as a spontaneous community of women and children and some men, just as her father envisioned a self-made world of madmen living in harmony with the sane world. (378)

"We don't need leaders," Mildred proclaims, and, amazingly, she is correct. The new world, created outside the law, does not require centralization.

This world is nearly utopian, and yet, because it defies all regulation, order and description, because what it is constantly changes, this new world that exists on the (rail) road can claim no name or designation.

As the novel nears its close, Melanie receives an appointment to the federal judicial bench. Despite the prestige attached to this accomplishment, Melanie feels her life, like the law, is sterile and banal. She attempts to find ways to manipulate the law for good and writes legal articles on the need to protect the victims of domestic violence. But her efforts seem pointless.

> I felt a growing ambivalence toward my career, for while outwardly I displayed an attitude of commitment excitement and gratitude for my ascendancy to the federal bench, inwardly I had to experience an increasing aversion to my work. Even the word career made me think not of the trajectory of profession, but instead of reckless speed, of a life careening crazily toward a fatal consequence.... I found myself sinking beyond the small print of pages into a dark maze of legal reasoning where I searched not for knowledge of the law, but instead for its weaknesses and vulnerabilities, the soft tunnels that it pressured, could crumble and bring the mighty edifices of the courts tumbling to the earth.... (Sharp 324)

In vain, Melanie seeks to find a way to use the law against itself and for victims. But the law, she believes, is devised to protect itself.

In the end, Melanie learns the obvious; the way to undermine the law is to ignore the law. She resigns from the bench, and takes to the railroad. Outlaws, the railroad community moves about the world. They use the computer as means of obtaining information and feeding misinformation to the authorities. Asked by her new lover, Henry, Matt's friend and fellow hacker, if she wants to lend legal advice, Melanie decides she must help in some other manner. "I could not leap into a new life with the old one encasing me like a husk" (444). Instead, Melanie becomes a traveler, an escort for children, a provider of false documents, and an historian of the movement. She lives with delight and imagination, free of the limits of the law.

> I had plotted thousands of miles of travel. Ben had recommended the
> Iguacu water falls in the south [of Brazil], more immense than Niagara's,
> and the interior's swamplands where lily pads with ten-foot diameters
> scattered like planets across boundless dark water and a red-clay road that
> ran to a small stucco house in which eight Brazilian women lived in hiding
> together, exchanging stories and ideas as outrageous as our own. After
> that, I contemplated nothing—just a vastness, spreading out before me
> with limitless possibilities. I would dedicate myself to the underground, I
> would turn myself into a minky animal and hole up with Henry, I would
> never marry, I would lead school tours through Dr. Eatman's [a madman]
> Paradise by day, and write *The Ratleer Chronicles* by night. I would play
> poker until early morning with Mildred and other escaped women in
> unlikely cities. (Sharp 449–450)

Melanie and her fellow nomads roam the world, incognito, exploring
fantastic lily pads, playing cards, free from the regulation that
constructs ordinary life. In the end, Paula Sharp's novel, *Crows Over a
Wheatfield*, evolves not as a polemic regarding the victimization of
women, but, rather, as a meditation on the nature of the law. Like
Braidotti's nomads, Sharp's characters live in the "in between"
spaces, outside the gates of the *polis*.

These are the zones that have no fixed law, and hence where
bodies and their inherent sexuality are not regulated. Because it is the
function of law to control bodies, the continuance of domesticity is a
legal concern. While domestic violence might receive some trivial
verbal attention, it is not the purpose of law to support the
withdrawal of women and children from the domestic union. Rather,
the law must seek to preserve that union and to regulate women's
sexuality so it is confined within the marriage contract. Sharp's
characters are symptoms of this legal and regulatory condition.
Because the novel does not focus much upon the individual moments
of abuse, the text necessarily turns its readers' attention toward a
larger and more philosophical purpose. *Crows Over a Wheatfield*
emerges as a novel about the law and the undoing of civil society and
the breaking of the social contract. It is a text about the undermining
of regulation. Nomads who have either too many passports, or no
documentation, Sharp's heroines possess numerous fraudulent
documents and no fixed identity. Sharp's women are the girls of the
railroad, in between zones, making that un-named space free.

Crossing To the Other Side of the Border: Sandra Cisneros' "Woman Hollering Creek"

Like Sharp's novel, Cisneros' story, "Woman Hollering Creek," interrogates our notions of social justice and our sense of North American legal superiority. And like Sharp, Cisneros subverts our expectations; while Sharp suggests law and the creation of the *polis* are not about the protection of the individual, Cisneros contends that the crossing of the border into the United States as a legal citizen does not necessarily engender freedom. For Sandra Cisneros, it is once again the road where the self finds some sovereignty—and it is a road shared with a community of other women.

Cisneros' seemingly simple fable concerns the history of Cleofilas Hernandez, the only daughter in a family of men, who crosses the border from Mexico to marry Juan Pedro Sanchez and live in the United States. The understanding—on both the readers' part as well as Cleofilas'—is that she is leaving a limited patriarchal culture to live more freely and fully in Texas. Brought up watching the Cinderella-like, romantic *telenovelas*, Cleofilas marries with an expectation of extravagant love and lifestyle.

> But what Cleofilas has been waiting for, has been whispering and sighing and giggling for, has been anticipating since she was old enough to lean against the window displays of gauze and butterflies and lace, is passion... (Cisneros 44)

Money and enduring love will be hers within the U.S. borders, believes Cleofilas. She has been educated, albeit in Spanish, in the dominant myths of western culture: a man is her destination and he alone can give her life meaning.

But, reality smashes Cleofilas' romantic expectations. Her new husband, Juan Pedro, is not a prince. Instead, he is an over-weight, acne-scarred man given to flatulence, alcohol, infidelity and violence. While the reader is not surprised at the ruin of Cleofilas' romantic hopes, we are perhaps somewhat startled at the failure of her financial dreams. Cleofilas' home in Monclova, Mexico spoke of much more affluence than that possessed by her new American life. In the United States she does not own a television set, much less her own house. She can't afford medical care and her baby must wear shoes that are too small. With no access to the books and music she enjoyed as an unmarried woman in Mexico, Cleofilas' journey from one destination to another leaves her only further impoverished. Even worse, Juan Pedro routinely beats Cleofilas, and his friendship with an alleged wife-killer suggests a further incipient threat.

Cleofilas knows should Juan Pedro kill her, there will probably be little consequence. The town and its legal agencies protect its male workers. Juan Pedro's friend, Maximiliano, "the foul smelling fool from across the road," killed his own wife but is exonerated because of what is deemed to be self-defense. His late wife was "armed with a mop" (51). As Cleofilas ponders the problem of women's helplessness, she comes to believe the law will always support men. Domestic violence is either ignored or attributed to the failings of the wife.

> Was Cleofilas just exaggerating as her husband always said? It seemed the newspapers were full of such stories. This woman found on the side of the interstate. This one pushed from a moving car. This one's cadaver, this one unconscious, this one beaten blue. Her ex-husband, her husband, her lover, her father, her brother, her uncle, her friend, her co-worker. Always. The same grisly news in the pages of the dailies. (52)

There is, it seems, no recourse for Cleofilas.

Cleofilas is afraid for her life, but is without resources. Her only friends are two sad and widowed neighbors, aptly named Soledad and Dolores.[6] Contained within a patriarchal culture, still defined by their absent husbands, these women can offer Cleofilas little assistance. Overwhelmed by her loneliness, grief and foolishness, Cleofilas sits by the creek in the arroyo and watches her little boy. She considers the name of the creek, *La Gritona*, and imagines a woman crying out in pain. She believes the creek and arroyo are inhabited by the spirit of La *Llorona*—the weeping woman, a mythical and disaffected bride who drowned her own children. Despair and loneliness color everything. As she sits by the creek, Cleofilas believes *La Llorona* calls to her, and the reader is forced to anticipate a story with a similarly tragic conclusion. We expect the suicide of Cleofilas and her baby.

> The stream...a thing with a voice all its own, all day and all night, calling
> in its high silver voice. Is it *La Llorona*, the weeping woman? *La Llorona*,
> who drowned her own children. Perhaps *La Llorona* is the one they named
> the creek after, she thinks. ...*La Llorona* is calling to her. She is sure of
> it...*La Llorona*. Wonders if something as quiet as this drives a woman to
> the darkness under the trees. (Cisneros 51)

As readers, we wait for the loss, we mourn Cleofilas' journey north and can barely stand to turn the pages of the text.

But the text confounds our expectations. Just as Cisneros crosses linguistic and stylistic boundaries, mixing prose and poetry, Spanish and English, she also disturbs genre-produced expectation. The text has established a tragic trajectory. Yet, at the moment the reader expects the worst, the story shifts in tone. Pregnant with a second child, Cleofilas requires medical attention. She persuades her husband to take her to a clinic, promising not "to shame" him or to allow the doctor to discuss her bruises. She will not alert the authorities to her predicament. When examined, however, by a woman at the clinic, Cleofilas' bruises document violence. Graciela, the clinic attendant, immediately plans Cleofilas' escape.

Graciela and her friend, Felice, have also been raised by soap operas and talk shows. But these television programs, unlike the romantic *telenovelas* of Cleofilas' youth, provide empowerment, It is "A regular soap opera sometimes," remarks Graciela about her own life, as she plans with Felice about how to get Cleofilas safely on the road. They acknowledge Cleofilas' helpless state—no money, no language skills, no hope, but believe that together they can overcome these difficulties. Cleofilas has landed safely within the mobile community of women.[7] As the women speak, they allude to the community of women saints, evoking the Virgin Mary in their conversation.

For Cleofilas, Felice represents a new kind of womanhood. When Felice meets Cleofilas at the designated Cash N Carry convenience store, she drives a truck. Not her husband's, Cleofilas remarks in wonder, but her own.

> Everything about this women, this Felice, amazed Cleofilas. The fact that
> she drove a pickup. A pickup, mind you, but when Cleofilas asked if it

was her husband's, she said she didn't have a husband. The pickup was
hers. She herself had chosen it. She herself was paying for it.... I used to
have a Pontiac Sunbird. But those cars are for viejas. Pussy cars. Now this
here is a real car.... What kind of talk was that coming from a woman? (55)

Felice drives Cleofilas and her baby to the city of San Antonio, where
they can catch a bus home or continue on in their travels and start a
new life. As Felice drives across the arroyo, *La Gritona*, she emits a
loud, Tarzan-like and joyful yell. Cleofilas is startled, both by the
sound and by the information Felice provides. They are crossing
Woman Hollering Creek, a border Cleofilas has previously
misunderstood. The creek marks not a limit but a negotiable border.
The creek and arroyo are nearly the only spaces that commemorate
women, Felice informs Cleofilas. The bridge that spans the creek
marks the space of transgression, a passage that leads to liberation
and joy. On the road finally, Cleofilas begins for the first time to laugh
and holler herself. On the road, in the community of
women—defined by Felice, Graciela, all of the resources that they and
their friends command, and the powerful history of women
saints—Cleofilas finds freedom.

The nomadic notion of a fluid community proves more
compelling than a fixed hierarchy. Like Sharp's commune, the
undefined connection between women provides an alternative
highway toward freedom. Interestingly, the women on this particular
highway find their connection through television. Critic Tanya
Modleski comments on the community-building and empowering
aspects of television in her text, *Loving With a Vengeance: Mass
Produced Fantasies for Women*. Modleski contends television soap
operas and romance novels do not simply serve as means to reify
patriarchal society; rather, according to Modleski, these "mass
produced fantasies for women" offer women new models and can
thus serve as tools for empowerment. Within these texts, women
frequently appear as primary protagonists. As does nineteenth
century domestic fiction, soap operas and romance novels focus
largely upon the home and on relationships. And, in the same way
that nineteenth century novels celebrated so-called women's issues,
these contemporary texts place value not upon masculine

accomplishment but on tasks and values traditionally associated with women. As Ann Douglas notes in her *Feminization of American Culture,* domestic fiction was considered by many as emblematic of the increasing role of women in American cultural life. Resultantly, at least in fantasy, American males resisted the valorization of domestic life by seeking to replace domestic fiction with more "masculine" texts depicting rugged frontier life.[8] Similarly, argues Modleski, our own patriarchal culture patronizes and rejects soap operas and romance novels. Televised football games, cop shows and detective novels have no necessarily larger social purpose and are no more worthy of praise than soap operas. Yet, because such texts have large male audiences they retain a more privileged status within the culture and are far less derided than "soaps" and Harlequin romance novels.

In particular, the soap opera focuses on what we perceive to be women's interests, and like earlier domestic fiction the soap opera does not hesitate to introduce social concern into the fiction. Just as nineteenth century women's novels often examined the politically charged categories of slavery, prohibition, poverty and suffrage, soap operas do not hesitate to explore topics including domestic violence, molestation, phobias, absent fathers and unequal familial distribution of wealth. Unspoken and hidden issues thus find voice in a larger community.

> Their [soap operas] enormous and continuing popularity, I assume, suggests that they speak to very real problems in women's lives. The narrative strategies, which have evolved for smoothing over these tensions, can tell us much about how women have managed not only to live in oppressive circumstances, but also to invest their situations with some degree of dignity. (Modleski 14–15)

Soap operas, then, can be viewed as performative meditation on women's lives.

But, Modleski continues, soap operas do more than simply give voice to repressed topics. They also provide women with a wide variety of strong female characters, characters who often have control over the lives of others as well as their own. A plethora of strong maternal figures appear weekly on television. More over, even the "evil" villain provides a powerful female role model. Typically, these "bad" female characters reject traditional definition. Society deems them "bad" precisely because they view their own needs as more significant than those of their husbands and children. In this sense, the soap opera subverts sexual stereotypes.

> The spectator...continually tunes into soap operas to watch the villain as she tries to gain control over her female passivity, thereby acting out the spectator's fantasies of power. ...the spectator constantly returns to the same story in order to identify with the main character and achieve, temporarily, the illusion of mastery denied him or her in real life. (Modleski 97)

While such identification is short-lived and even uncomfortable to the viewer, it does provide another collective model for ways of being in the world. If on the most obvious levels these soap opera texts reaffirm traditional values, they simultaneously interrogate and even reject these values. Because the soap opera follows generic patterns, the program empowers the viewer, enabling her to predict future actions and consequences. In terms of the narrative and its expectations, the viewer becomes omniscient and again enjoys an increased feeling of power.

Perhaps even more significantly, soap opera viewing is a collective act. Viewers talk about episodes, write fan letters, read about the actors, and engage in a discourse about their favorite programs. Such discourse leads to community. If mass culture appears to be escapist, it is because the culture posits the possibility of escape into a better world (Modleski 112). Such is the role of the soap opera; even as it reifies culture it suggests ways in which that culture can be remade. Sandra Cisneros' text is concerned with exactly this point; "Woman Hollering Creek" is a short story about the ways in which women can connect with one another in order to subvert traditional expectation and outcomes. With the help of Felice and Graciela, Cleofilas can re-envision her life. Felice teaches Cleofilas to reinterpret the cultural semiotic; a truck is not necessarily masculine nor does a woman holler only in pain. The discourse of the soap opera allows this feminist connection, as Felice and Graciela plainly understand.

The space of the road provides the arena of action, the site where this new community can grow. The house contains and constrains Cleofilas. She understands things—often incorrectly—only within the discourse of tradition. In the house she belongs to her husband or father. On the road she finds the freedom to understand the larger joyful meaning of the creek. In the truck, bound for no long-term destination and noisily negotiating the road, Cleofilas comprehends her emancipation. For Cleofilas, finally connected to the discourse of women—saints, the Virgin and the women at the clinic—the road is utopia. It is the space of laughter and *jouissance*. "Then Felice began laughing again, but it wasn't Felice laughing. It was gurgling out of her own throat, a long ribbon of laughter, like water" (Cisneros 56). As Cleofilas laughs, her voice merges with the creek, her laugh becomes a band of water and she becomes Woman Hollering Creek. She not only transgresses a border or limit, she becomes the border and the creek that is constantly in motion. Cleofilas *is* Woman Hollering Creek, a woman in transit and a part of the historic continuum of women's community.

Paule Marshall's Praisesong for the Widow: Flying Home to a Better World

There is a persistent story in the archives of slave folk tradition, a tale often referred to as the story of the flying Africans.[9] According to this legend, slaves working in the vicinity of the Georgia or South Carolina Coasts put down their hoes one day and simply took flight. "Den dey rise off duh groun an fly away. Nobody ebuh see um no mo. Some say dey fly back to Africa," contends a Georgia resident whose grandfather knew the slaves in question (*Drums and Shadows* 78). "Dey rise in duh sky an...fly right back to Africa," adds another older man who witnessed the flight. Unhappy and unable to adjust to the conditions of slavery, these members of the West African Ibo tribe took to the highway of the sky. Some storytellers maintain the slaves flew back home to Africa while others are less clear about their destination. The flying Africans left their narrow circumstances and went to search for a better world.

Western epistemology and American pragmatism have difficulty in accepting the idea of actual flight. Even the interlocutors conducting the W.P.A. interviews regarding slave tales were forced to ask if the story meant the slaves actually flew. Couldn't flight be a metaphor, the interviewers seem to suggest. But former slave Wallace Quarterman is not interested in metaphor.

> Wut, you ain heah bout um? Ebrybody know about um. Dey sho lef duh hoe stannin in duh fiel an dey riz right up... I knowd plenty wut did see um, plenty wut wuz right deah in duh fiel wid um...dey done fly way. (*Drums and Shadows* 150–151)

But if Quarterman and other interviewees insisted upon the actuality of the flight, other historians provide a slightly less fantastic version of the story. They believe a number of newly captured slaves, all members of the Ibo tribe, refused to acknowledge the power of their new owners. These slaves, led by their former chief, walked into the water singing West African songs and were finally drowned in the water off Ibo's Landing. But the notion of flight and a refusal to commit to a life of slavery and degradation continues to capture the imagination.[10]

Based on the story of the Flying Africans, Paule Marshall's novel, *Praisesong for the Widow,* explores the ways that actual travel allows the individual to experience correspondent psychic change. Such change is so powerful it forces the traveler into continued motion and pursuit of a more equitable world. Marshall's heroine is Avey—Avatara—Johnson, a middle-aged, middle-class African American widow who has taken refuge from life in the suburbs of White Plains. There, Avey votes Republican, tries to hide her black skin and works at the Department of Motor Vehicles. In the wake of her husband's death, Avey has started taking tours and cruises, and, as the novel commences, Avey and her numerous pieces of luggage are bound for the Caribbean on the ironically named *Bianca's* [white] *Pride.*

As readers, we know some sea change is about to happen. Surrounded by the mirrors of the Grand Salon's Versailles Room, Avey feels uncomfortable, anxious and restless. She ascribes this discomfort to a bad night spent dreaming of great-aunt Cuney and of her long-ago childhood on the coast of South Carolina. In her dream,

Avey recalls the story of the Flying Africans and of a visit to the site of "Ibo's Landing," a dock near her great-aunt's house. She recalls her great-aunt's version of the story.

> They just kept walking...just kept on walking like the water was solid ground.... And when they got to where the ship was they didn't so much as give it a look. Just walked on past it.... They feets was gonna take 'em wherever they was going that day. (Marshall 38–39)

Even as a child, Avey found the story unconvincing, to her aunt's great disappointment. But in her dream, Avey's aunt appears insistently, bothering Avey, as she stands dressed for lunch in her new spring suit and hose. The aunt drags Avey in the direction of the landing until Avey finally wrests free and fights her elderly aunt. Her aunt's hand is a summons, Avey recognizes, but it is a summons she rejects. Now awake on the ship, Avey feels haunted.

Unsettled, Avey decides to leave the ship at the first available port. Afraid of a possible heart attack or even simple irritation, her mood increasingly darkens when she dreams of her aunt's African dancing. She wakes to remember the embarrassing dancing of her roommate, Thomasina Moore.

> It had been Cartagena, Columbia, where, to Avey Johnson's disgust the woman had abandoned them to dance in a carnival parade they were watching with other passengers from the *Bianca' s Pride*. Had gone off amid a throng of strangers swishing her bony hips to the drums...with their fellow passengers watching. White faces laughing! White hands applauding! Avey Johnson had never been so mortified. (25)

Thomasina's willingness to appear black is horrifying to Avey. For, Avey makes every effort to cover her blackness and, indeed, to cover her very identity. She is always carefully dressed, "everything in muted colors. Everything in good taste" (48). Her legs are covered by stockings, her body by dresses and suits in restrained hues; she wears long sleeves and hats, frequently with an attached veil. Outside, she always wears gloves, even in the casual heat of the Caribbean. Inevitably encased in a girdle and rigid undergarments, Avey forgets her history. As she gazes in the mirrors of the Versailles Room, she recognizes her companions but remains bewildered by her own reflection. "For a confused moment, Avey could not place the woman in beige crepe de Chine and pearls.... This wasn't the first time it had happened" (48). Avey's very identity has been erased.

Avey attempts to reject self-knowledge and the summons of her ancestor, but her struggle is to little avail. Once off the ship she is lured into a further excursion and her travels will make her more conscious of her past—her childhood and her life with her now dead husband. Sailing outward through the islands, Avey reverses the historic middle passage and reconnects to her African history. She learns to feel and to dance again.

Off the ship, but still on the road, Avey must spend the night in a hotel while she waits for a flight home. This hotel stay provides her with little ease. She dreams of her dead husband, Jay, and of her early affection for him and their easy sensuality. She recalls the blues clubs and the dancing in Harlem. She remembers, too, their descent into poverty after the birth of their three children, and the fights that then resulted. Things changed; Jay became distant and obsessed with work. They both embraced respectability. Jay took classes at night and with tremendous difficulty finally became a C.P.A. They left New York and "the house in White Plains lay ahead."

Jay becomes someone else. He shaves his mustache, exposing "the vague, pale outline of another face superimposed on his, as in double exposure...this pallid face whose expression was even more severe" (131). Remaking himself as a white man, Jay attacks the civil rights movement and voices the wish that all the dance halls in Harlem could be burned down. When Jay dies, Avey does not weep. She cannot mourn a man truly dead already for so many years. She remains numb. But sleeping on the recliner in the hotel, Avey holds a wake. In her dreams she mourns Jay and feels his presence. She wakes to find herself still dressed, soiled like a baby and unable to deny the past anymore.

A few hours later, out on a walk, Avey is persuaded to join the locals in the Carriacou Excursion. A trip taken annually in canoes to the outlying islands, the Excursion requires that people leave their jobs and forget their regular lives. They dance and connect to their particular lost tribe, reaffirming their African heritage. Avey, who suffers terribly during the voyage from seasickness and remembrance, has to be carried ashore and nursed. As her naked flesh is tended, Avey begins to remember who she is. She begins to dance again.

But Marshall's novel is not limited to the story of her heroine's brief vacation. As the novel closes, Avey continues to further explore her lost identity. She decides to sell her house in White Plains and to move back to the landing. Further, she will go on other Excursions. She decides too to use her aunt's old house as a kind of camp or commune for unwanted or impoverished African Americans, "for the sweetest little lepers." Previously alienated from her youngest daughter, Marion, a child she had tried to abort and had little in common with, Avey decides to make this grown child her confidant. Marion, who dresses in African clothing and wears her hair in an Afro, will understand.

> She would enlist Marion in her cause. Marion whom she had tried to root from her body by every means possible, repeatedly throwing herself one day down the five flights of stairs.... Of her three children, Marion alone would understand about the excursion and help her spread the word. (Marshall 255)

With Marion and like-minded individuals, Avey intends to "spread the word" and to teach younger African Americans to confront their real identity, an identity derived from the fact that they are nomads in this country and must travel outward on "excursions" to learn the truth about themselves.

Just as the Middle Passage sought to erase language, history and identity from captured slaves, the rites of the Excursion seek to reverse this process. Historian Sterling Stuckey notes in his text, *Slave Culture*, the essential quality of this recovered sense of history. Contrary to popular history, Stuckey argues, rather than erasing African identity, the slave ships frequently served as "an incubator" for slave identity. This identity, manifested in song and dance, was repressed, first by slave owners and later by the culture itself. This same "resistance [to African culture] was widespread among blacks" as well, contends Stuckey. Like Avey and her husband, many African Americans aspired to America's white middle class and subsequently repressed this West African self. This "foreign" self was seen as pagan, extravagant, primitive, emotional and un-Christian.

Avey initially shared these prejudices with the result that, like her husband Jay, she was in some ways dead to experience and feeling. It is the road that allows her to transcend this narrow and limiting perspective, the road that will finally liberate her. Travel makes Avey remember both her repressed personal history and suppressed culture. This recognition of history can afford a new life, a new way to be in the world. Nomad-like, Avey learns holding things—houses, silver, clothing, all the accoutrements of bourgeois life—produces a static and unreal existence. Only movement and the release of material belongings permit freedom. This is Avey's legacy and she plans to pass it on. She will teach other African Americans this history, making them aware of flight and the necessity of reversing the Middle Passages' tragic consequences with their own "Excursions" outward.

The Truth is the Dream: Zora Neale Hurston and the Vision of a Better World

In *Their Eyes Were Watching God*, Zora Neale Hurston's heroine, Janie, begins her realized life within the safe enclosure of her grandmother's yard. There, in the Eden of pre-pubescence, she sits beneath the fertile pear tree dreaming. She watches the "tiny blooms" of the garden that correspond to her awakening self. She leans over the garden gate, the boundary that confines her, and contemplates marriage and love. But her romantic longings do not find much space for expression. Much as her grandmother loves Janie, she remains convinced that only through being confined can Janie be safe. But Janie's own road toward self-identity leads her otherwise; over and over in the novel she takes to the road in the hope of finding some new and more beautiful world.

Janie's hope was not foreign to the mind of Zora Neale Hurston herself. By her own admission, she had "a lot of hope," and an ambition "to jump at the sun" as she made her own journey toward New York. Hurston's novel and story of Janie is widely read as a rejection of racialized oppression and the erasure of women's sexuality. Barbara Christian makes this point in her discussion of *Black Women Novelists* while Hazel Carby traces a similar history in *Reconstructing Womanhood*. Thadious Davis notes:

> Consciousness of a woman's right to self-hood and self-definition, so that it is an expression of freedom from the constrictions of black folk life, even while it celebrates that life...she [Hurston] could represent through Janie's development and maturation the unpacking of multiple layers of domination and oppression.... (Davis 428)

"Her conscious life commenced at Nanny's gate," decides Janie. For it is at the gate that she wonders about the "struggle with life" from which she feels excluded, and asks "where were the singing bees for her?" (11). In her effort to escape, she leans over the gatepost to kiss Johnny Taylor. Horrified, her grandmother punishes her and forces her to take the older, more prosperous and boring Logan Killicks as her protective husband. But within two months, Janie is disillusioned, still wanting romance and the gilded world promised by the peach tree. Her husband is old, abrupt and bossy, and shows no sign of romantic heroism. She loses interest in the possibility of marriage, once again frustrated by the boundaries that surround her. "The familiar things had failed her so she hung over the gate and looked up the road towards way off" (24). Looking over the gate, once again, she contends "God tore down the old world every evening and built a new one by sun-up" (24). She longs for that new world.

Before the year is over, the road reasserts itself in Janie's life, through the personage of Joe Starks. Briefly, Janie enjoys the excitement offered by the road and by romance, as she travels by buggy and train. Too quickly, Starks settles them in a town, where, as the years progress, he becomes the mayor and eventually prospers. Janie is confined. She covers her head, seldom speaks, and is, for the most part, subservient to her husband. Seeing no other option, she plays a supporting role to her popular spouse. She leads a life of repression and her psyche nearly perishes. Joe Starks falls in her esteem from a romantic idol, to a foolish antagonist. "Her image of Jody [Starks] tumbled down and shattered" (68). Janie's sense of self becomes nearly non-existent. The road with Joe Starks has lead nowhere.

> The years took all the fight out of Janie's face. For a while she thought it
> was gone from her soul. No matter what Jody did, she said nothing.... She
> was a rut in the road. Plenty of life beneath the surface but it was kept
> beaten down by the wheels. ...mostly she lived between her hat and her
> heels.... Now and again she thought of a country road at sun-up and
> considered flight. To where? To what? (72)

The road hovers in Janie's unconscious only as incoherent possibility.

But with the death of Joe Starks, Janie is again free—if she
ignores popular opinion—to travel the road once again. "Ah jus'
loves dis freedom," remarks Janie to her friend, Pheoby (89). In the
wake of Joe Starks' amazing and lavish funeral, God remakes Janie's
world. While tending Starks' store, Janie meets the young and
handsome Tea Cake and ultimately takes to the road with him,
despite her neighbors' disapprobation. Their mutual road through the
Florida Everglades is romantic and sustaining, despite Tea Cake's
occasional violence toward Janie. But a tremendous and mythic
hurricane interrupts bliss. In a nearly biblical manner, water floods
their world. Their landscape appears overwhelmed. Pieces of houses
sail by on the wind, trees and wagons float. Vast serpents hang from
the floating cypress trees. Tea Cake saves Janie, but in doing so is
bitten by a rabid dog. Janie, in love and in self-defense, shoots Tea
Cake.

Despite this seeming tragedy, Janie's life is not tragic. She makes
this clear in the frame story. A persistent belief in possibility saves
Janie from despair. Even in the beginning of the novel, the road that
opens out from the closed garden gate suggests an alternative reality.
Within this mobile space of the possible, Janie dreams. These dreams,
suggests Hurston, are more real than the fixed and finite boundaries
accepted by a linear world. Janie possesses no fixed destination or
purpose. She embodies "a mood come alive. Words walking without
masters; walking altogether like harmony in a song" (2). She is alive
to unfettered possibility and in that unfettered moment experiences
the utopia of the world "God has remade." Pinning her existence on a
spot outside the gate, down the road somewhere to a spot outside
linear possibility, Janie lives outside boundaries. This border-less
existence is feminine, argues Janie, for men are linked to the fixed, the
defined, the linear and the limited.

Ships at a distance have every man's wish on board. For some they come in with the tide. For others they sail forever on the horizon, never out of sight, never landing until the Watcher turns his eyes away in resignation, his dreams mocked to death by Time. That is the life of men. Now, women forget all those things they don't want to remember, and remember everything they don't want to forget. The dream is the truth. (1)

For men, suggests Hurston, the line of the horizon is always present and unbendable. For women, this possibility lies on the other side of the horizon; it is flexible and unnamed. Owned in the moment of its contemplation, possibility lacks any connection to time. For Hurston, it is the dream, the inchoate thought that results in change, that is the real. Janie realizes this as she walks down the dusty road in her overalls, mourning Tea Cake's passing. Tea Cake is with her yet, she concedes for Tea Cake—the notion of love and selfhood—is not dependent upon time or actuality. Janie looks down the road, past the fixed horizon. "Here was peace. She pulled in her horizon like a great fish-net. Pulled it from around the waist of the world and draped it over her shoulder. So much of life in its meshes! She called in her soul to come and see" (184). Janie's travels down the road outside the gate have allowed her to transcend the limits of actual experience. Like God, she sits at dusk to remake the world. The garden gate is the point of entry.

Like all the other nomads in this text, Hurston's Janie uses the road to escape the confines of patriarchy, sexism, racism, violence, domestic abuse, and the simple lack of imagination. In *Crows Over a Wheatfield*, Paula Sharp creates an "underground" traveling world, a road of the "parallel universe" where painful, patriarchal law is obviated and women are free. For Cisneros, the road is the joyful gurgling of Woman Hollering Creek; it is a joyful and incoherent cry that exists outside language and outside fixed borders. Paule Marshall creates a watery road that leads back into a recovered and beloved history, and this history has pragmatic utopian value. Her heroine, Avey Johnson, returns to the Landing to find rapprochement with her daughter, her dead relatives and her lost, dancing self. In turn, she uses this recovered self to create a less repressive, more aware world for African Americans. Like the Flying Africans of folk tales, Avey takes flight. It is that same internalized road toward selfhood that Hurston's Janie travels, learning as she moves through the gate that the road out is the road in. In that mobile fluid understanding she finds possibility.

For the nomad, fixed notions of the utopian must remain implausible and empty, since every place lacks further destination and is thus *the* place. Utopia lies between departure and arrival, in the nameless spaces traversed between where one goes and where one's been. To be a nomad is to find a nearly miraculous space outside.

The End of the Road

Fascinated, I sit and watch the *House and Garden* channel on my television set. All day, every day, one can watch nervous home buyers finally acquire the space of domestic bliss, watch giddy couples compare granite to tile as they replace their kitchen counters, watch designers teach a devoted audience the importance of something called "curb appeal." Foolishly, living in my narrow academic world, I failed to realize I could view this homage to domesticity 24-7. Now, a recent convert, I tune in daily. My favorite show, *House Hunter*, airs nightly and recounts the tribulations of upwardly-bound young couples seeking their own houses in a world grown far too expensive. In each episode there is a moment when the couple (it is nearly always a couple, although the occasional single man or solitary mother might make an appearance) starts to give up, starts to believe the miracle of home ownership will never happen in their lives. But always too the plot turns; the couple gets a telephone call that tells them their "offer was accepted." Their lives change and the final closing scene inevitably depicts the couple happily ensconced, assuring the interviewer their purchase of the house was "meant to be." The program and the network establish a clear principle: everyone wants, pines even, to settle down.

And I think this might be true, because the *House and Garden Network* is not the only channel newly devoted to domestic bliss. Once the channel of armchair travelers and those who dreamed of the exotic, the *Discovery Channel* now frequently focuses upon the mystique of the house. In shows like *Surprised by Design* (that seems to be on for several hours each day) kind-hearted family members race to redecorate homes within a single day so their deserving spouses, mothers, sisters, husbands, sons or fathers can register amazement at the transformation of the homes. An urgent, repetitive quality marks these programs; wives—and it is usually wives—race home to redecorate so when their husbands return from the office they find their houses remade into a familial Eden. Should the viewer not fully understand the message, *Discovery Channel* also hosts multiple hours of *Rally Round the House, Monster House* and the *Christopher Lowell Show*. Lowell's doctrine is particularly intriguing for he combines gentle antiseptic comedy with a nearly Pentecostal approach. Each episode concludes with a homily as the host urges his viewers to have courage as they attempt to recreate his modeled arts and crafts efforts in their own homes. The principles of design, he assures them, have meaning within their own personal lives. The audience bursts into spontaneous and daily applause. If one accepts the message of these programs, it seems that women have once again taken up residence in the frontier cabin, albeit a cabin with upscale improvements, lots of feng shui and faux painting techniques.

I make inquiries and ask my friends about this shift. All professional women, all women who fought for inclusion, they laugh, shrug, tell me they too watch the design shows and obsess about the right shade of upholstery for the couch. Big weddings are coming back, they tell me. Interior design is a new status profession. I wonder if this fetishizing of the domestic is altogether healthy. Perhaps sooner or later we all succumb; perhaps, finally, the road is too difficult a place for permanent residence.

Other mediums explore the renewed interest in the home. Any news-stand displays numerous magazines dedicated to the domestic arts. Of these journals, *Martha Stewart Living* is by far the most ubiquitous. Nagged by financial worries, felony charges, potential prison and the collapse of her financial empire Stewart still provides the most vivid example of this new empowered domesticity. Transcending her working class origins, Stewart quickly moved from fashion model to stockbroker to entertainment savant. Intuitively, she grasped the exchange value inherent in the systems. In the final years before her fall, Stewart captured the exotic—Indonesian food, Brazilian music, Javanese art, reducing them to mere commodities that could be purchased for the home. Stewart provides for a sort of literal cultural consumption, a kind of postmodern cannibalism. We consume the food of another place and thus acquire the location. We eat Martha Stewart's rare mole chicken, prepare the themed centerpiece, and feel we possess some superior knowledge of Latin America. We learn to make our own Egyptian rag paper and on some level we come to own the Egyptians. The entire exterior world becomes accoutrements for the domestic; the domestic becomes the province of finance. This progression is important; we tend to regard the domestic as a feminine and even matriarchal space. Thus, the revived interest in what Stewart calls "home-making" appears to reflect increased power for women and the previously disenfranchised. Celebrating the home seems to be a celebration of a counter-point to business, but this is only appearance. As television and mass media suggest, the home is a marketed product of the corporate. Rather than a counter-point to business, the house is the selling point of capital.

With the rise of the all-inclusive corporate structure and the new mystique of the domestic, the road reverts to a subordinate position. Within this scheme, the road simply provides new themes for interior decoration. Continuing with this logic, decoration improves curb appeal and curb appeal increases value. Defined within this marketing scheme, the globe shrinks. Michael Hardt and Antonio Negri address this issue in their controversial text, *Empire.* They suggest that the postmodern exchange system must reduce the world to commodity items.

Postmodernism is indeed the logic by which global capital operates. Marketing has perhaps the clearest relation to postmodernism theories,

> And one could even say that the capitalist marketing strategies have long been postmodernist...certain postmodernism theorists, for example, see perpetual shopping and the consumption of commodities and commodified images as the paradigmatic and defining activities of postmodern experience, our collective journeys through hyperreality. On the other hand, postmodernist thinking—with its emphasis on concepts such as...celebration of fetishism and simulacra, its continual fascination with the new and with fashion—is an excellent description of the ideal capitalist schemes of commodity consumption... (Hardt and Negri 151–52)

The road mutates into an object, both consumable and marketable. As mere object and fashion statement, the real road ceases to exist, replaced by its simulacra.

As the global economy expands, the spaces at the margins shrink. The subversive gesture becomes the mere property of mainstream capital. The traditional markers of the counter-culture—blue jeans, tattoos and piercings—become elements of fad and fashion, marketable and devoid of political content. In this era of late capital, no outside—no exterior of the marketplace—exists. The *Internet*, instant messages and worldwide-marketing link the world in a defined, ordered and controlled grid. In the age of the cell phone no one is out of reach. Cultural critic Naomi Klein in her manifesto, *No Logo*, addresses the power of the marketing web. Perhaps a kind of road woman herself, Klein concludes her text by noting the growth of the anti-globalism movement. She follows demonstrations from the city of Rosario in the Philippines to Washington, Toronto, London, Berkeley, Port Harcourt in Nigeria, Cologne, Bangladesh, and Geneva, joining in the "global carnival against capital" (Klein 444). Euphorically, coalition groups attempt to "Reclaim the Streets" (444). Intriguingly named, this reclamation project literally tries to establish zones—streets or roads or enterprises—that lie outside the corporate structure. While Klein's final account reflects a nearly extreme optimism regarding resistance, the earlier pages of her text are more convincing. Most of the chapters in her rather long work deal with the successes of global capital as it seeks to remake the world. Noting the emergence of a newly diminutive world, domesticated by corporate growth and power, Klein contends we live in a globe of "no space" where one can see the "surrender of culture and education to marketing" (Klein xxi). "The global web of logos...the global village...laptop computers" and E-business reduce the world to IBM's "Small Planet," a space of "world-wide style culture" (Klein xvii). And if the whole world is a village, there is little place for the road. Real nomads live outside the polis. Reduced to simple accoutrement, the road becomes now an aspect of style, a marketable trope, a commodity, like a pair of designer jeans.

Commodity or not, the road has been particularly apparent in popular culture since the 1992 release of Ridley Scott's *Thelma and Louise*. In its wake, a roster of women's road films have found release, notably *Leaving Normal; Gas, Food, Lodging; Tumbleweeds; Smoke Signals and Anywhere But Here.* Interestingly, most of these films are directed and written by men, and it is perhaps because of this that so many of the films end predictably. Thelma and Louise die. Other road heroines, like the character played by Drew Barrymore in *Gas, Food, Lodging,* eventually find love, get married and settle down. In the cinematic version of *Anywhere But Here,* unlike the novel, the mother Adele is only mildly eccentric; the film is finally about good, traditional, self-sacrificing motherhood. More recently, director Ron Howard dabbled in the genre of the road. His western captivity narrative, *The Missing* addresses the re-establishment of patriarchy. Ostensibly on the road to find her abducted daughter, Howard's heroine really needs to bond with the father who deserted her. "Let's go home," are the final words of the film's main character, as she leads her daughters homeward to bury her self-sacrificing father. The men in the movie may be dead, but the women understand themselves and find identity through patriarchy.

But, of course, these girls from popular culture, be they rebels or the most conventional of young ladies, have destinations and fixed destinies, destinies intuited by every viewer. In the end, these girls must return home. *The Searchers,* a film that may perhaps be the most famous women's cinematic road story, the necessity of the heroine's return finds full explication. The film, a classic captivity narrative, concerns a woman who was taken from her home at a young age by Indians, and has begun to identify with her captors. She resists re-integration into the frontier community. Debby (played by the young Natalie Wood) initially defies attempts to bring her home. But the audience knows the film can only end one way; nice girls eventually come home (and bad ones die). Fathers, brothers and husbands await the return of the prodigal (and as the Beach Boys used to sing, the relinquishment of the car keys). The road represents a diversion in popular culture, not a form of female identity. This more popular road, this mere stylistic figuration, can be marked and sold. My fear is that this commodified road must erode the nomadic pathway. But nomadic women may refuse this co-optation; they stand outside popular narrative. By definition they occupy that space this is unclaimed. Through subversion and absence they remain at the margins.

Nomadic literature is ultimately emancipatory. It provides an annunciation of newly defined relations between subject and object, the ruler and the ruled, the two sides of a constructed border. In her discussion of border texts, critic Emily Hicks contends "border writers" are those authors whose texts are able to "cross over into another set of referential codes...in Derridean terms, the Ear of the Other must be heard; some readers of border texts may become border crossers" (Hicks xxvi). While Hicks' text concentrates largely upon the crossings of Latin American and Chicana authors, she suggests any author who, like Franz Kafka, "experiences the deterritorialization of language and...signification" negotiates the permeability of borders.

> The border crosser is both "self" and "other." The border crosser "subject" emerges from double strings of signifiers of two sets of referential codes, both from both sides of the border. The border crosser is linked, in terms of identity, activity, legal status, and human rights to the border machine. (Hicks xxvii)

Like Paula Sharp's heroines, who move from the constructed legalisms of American life into their own more free "parallel universe," nomadic women operate within competing territories and ignore any notion of exclusivity. In their rejection of fixed purpose—and thus fixed power relations—nomadic women, are, at least in the moments of their crossings, free.

In her strange and lyrical text, *In Memoriam to Identity*, the late Kathy Acker manipulates the texts, language and biographies of Arthur Rimbaud and William Faulkner to tell a twisted tale of rape, murder and travel. Through the characters of her own Capitol and Airplane, as well as a reconfiguration of Faulkner's Caddie, Acker meditates upon the road, arguing the road finds definition finally internally, rather than externally. These roads lead to a repossession of the self, an acknowledgement of pain, tragedy and objectification. For Acker, women can literally re-claim the territory. This becomes the nomad's task. At the end of *Memoriam* the character Capitol is put on trial for the crime of beheading her Nazi dolls (and thus defying both the political power structure and the requirements of femininity). A final plea is made on behalf of Capitol. A disembodied, deterritorialized voice speaks:

> "Fuck you," said aloud. The waste isn't just me. It's not waste. It's as if
> there's territory. The roads carved in the territory, the only known, are
> memories. Carved again and again into ruts like wounds that don't heal
> when you touch them but grow. Since all the rest is unknown, throw what
> is known away. "Sexuality," she said, "sexuality." (Acker 264)

Ambiguous as Acker's words may be, she makes several points quite
clear: Memory and experience carve correspondent trails. Unknown
territory still exists. Gender and sexuality fix and contain narrative
and identity. The domain of the grand narratives of the past finds
persistent re-enactment, as painful power dynamics repeat
themselves. But, insists Acker, if one travels into uncharted territory
and finds new roads free from the ruts of historic repetition, new
identities and new constructions of the world become possible. When
one eschews the limits of a single passport, existence is revised. Reclaim it and own it, Acker's texts finally advise.

Such reclamation may not be easy but it is necessary. As Minrose
Gwin contends in her *Woman in the Red Dress: Gender, Space and
Reading*, space can be "nonfelicitous." As Gwin discusses at some
length, home can be a dangerous place for women, and she reviews
the tropes of domestic abuse and incest as they appear in women's
literature. For Gwin, the road—the self-contained home of the
nomad—becomes a replacement of the domestic and offers a real if
transient "home." Writes Gwin,

> [F]or some daughters, home may be grounded not in place but in the
> replacement of the displaced self elsewhere, in an aptitude for travel.
> What such writing as this...can do is to point to that other space, that
> "elsewhere" in which the daughter can begin to write her own cultural
> story, create her own felicity. Call it home; call it travel. The way in and
> the way out. (Gwin 115)

The road offers here an alternative rehabilitative space.

Marilyn Wesley continues this theme in her conclusion of *The
Trope of Women's Travel in American Literature*. She suggests travel
constructs for women a new way of being in the world. This new way
allows for the empowerment of literary heroines, and, by extension

for the readers of their exploits. Insists Wesley,

> Her [the woman traveler] movement beyond the known limits, a
> metaphor enacted as the narrative journey, is a vehicle for conceptualizing
> alterations and realizing change. ...Thus, the narrative trope of women's
> travel does nothing less than create an effectual feminine self and define a
> place for women in a reconceived world. (Wesley 137)

From the accounts of Mary Rowlandson through postmodern fiction, this new empowered self has been central to the discourse of travel narrative. Through travel, the fixed and determinant proves to be only situational and contingent. Mary Rowlandson can be dowered, sold and ransomed; but she can also participate in an economy, moving from commodity status to that of the proprietor. Similarly, Paule Marshall's fictive Avey *in Praisesong for the Widow* can return to the sites of slavery and captivity—the sea crossing and the coastal landing docks. She can understand these sites as the spaces of her enslavement and, simultaneously, she can reclaim these spaces as places of personal and historical transcendence. Like the slaves in the folk tale of the flying Africans, Avey too can just fly away.

All this brings us back to several final points. Within popular culture, the road serves for women as a kind of space of temporary adventure, a space from which women must finally return restored to patriarchy. In a slightly more subversive sense (and often in slightly less popular texts), the road also becomes the solace for the marginalized and unhappy woman. As Gwin remarks, "We are left with a lonely woman who plans to break down another wall. Her loneliness compels her to travel" (Gwin 174). Finally though, in its most subversive sense, the road marks the space of exaltation, power, and what might be conceived of as joy.

This joy coincides with what others have defined as postmodern space. Critic Carlton Smith in his *Coyote Kills John Wayne* maintains, "...the fetishes and power of patriarchy continually endeavor to reassert themselves. But in the small breaks...narrative expression changes course" (C. Smith 147). Even in the most fixed firmaments, shifts happen and cracks appear in monolithic culture. And in those shifts and fissures, change and resistance unfold. As quickly as culture claims the space at the margins, the margins unfold to reveal new ground. In the most ardently constructed domestic space, the garden path opens. It may be that there is always a road out.

And what of the *House and Garden Network* and the renewed power of the domestic? Have we really arrived at the end of the road? Is the subversive exuberance of the road absorbed in the every widening web of capital? Certainly one can make such an argument. But I prefer to maintain that just as global capital of necessity unceasingly co-opts, the subversive impulse must forever continuously resist, like Penelope unraveling each day's weaving. It may be that every seeming site of patriarchy teems with small efforts toward revision. Such is the nature of the postmodern condition. In *Postmodernist Fiction*, Brian McHale explores the ontology of contemporary texts, citing Annie Dillard and her famous phrase that contemporary literature is "unlicensed metaphysics in a teacup." McHale continues this line, arguing postmodernist fiction "gives us a pretext for doing unlicensed ontology in a teacup" (McHale 25). To be postmodern is to be unlicensed, an outlaw within the local and seemingly domesticated space. By extension this may mean, perhaps, that to be perfectly postmodern is to tread the path hidden in the marketed garden of a homemaking television show. Indeed, discussing television and soap operas in her *Loving with a Vengeance: Mass-produced Fantasies for Women*, Tania Modleski argues popular "mass art" always operates on two levels. Mass media both reifies contemporary power structures and it also informs viewers of the ruptures within their own lives. Television shows viewers the "conflicts at the borders" (Modleski 111). Popular culture demonstrates the discrepancy between the real and the imagined. Soap operas, says Modleski, and I would argue even the *House and Garden Network* "act as 'indispensable informers' which reveal the contradictions in women's lives under patriarchy" (111). It may be that what looks like the end of the road is only a detour, a shift, a quick blurring of borders. We know from the works of Braverman, Simpson and Didion that the places that look as if the freeway has run out are really only brief stops, a place to take refreshment before fording the little avenues and tributaries that feed into another highway.

Somewhere, heedless of encroaching globalism a teenager waxes a car to a new verdant green; somewhere too a young girl—a student perhaps—scribbles in her journal, then tosses the volume into her backpack and climbs into her car. She drives the freeway without destination. All of the women in this book—authors and characters—suggest the existence of an outside space. Such texts tell us to find the keys, start the car, pick up our feet and begin walking, to transgress borders and forget itineraries. They tell us the only possible reaction to oppression is subversion. Thus, these alternative texts explored here are ultimately performative and their performance is an act of liberation. I think the road continues.

NOTES

CHAPTER ONE: Points of Departure

1. The less Eden-like aspects of Dean/Neal Cassady's life are explored in Carolyn Cassady's *Off the Road*. As she describes it, Neal Cassady died in 1968, alone on the railroad tracks near San Miguel de Allende, Mexico. Cassady remains central to road literature so much so that *The Grateful Dead* wrote commemorative lyrics about him, immortalizing his time with them in the Magic Bus, "Cowboy Neal at the wheel of the bus to never-ever land" ("That's It for the Other One," music and lyrics by Bob Weir and Bill Kreutzman).

CHAPTER TWO: Resistance and Revisions in the Wilderness: Women's Road Narratives and the Mythologies of Frontier Space

1. Kolodny borrows here from Joel Kover's *White Racism: A Psychohistory*. New York: Pantheon Books, 1970.

2. See Dee Brown's *The Gentle Tamers: Women of the Old Wild West*. Lincoln: University of Nebraska press, 1958.

3. Women write entirely new and spectral frontier texts. See this text, page 27.

4. This aspect of Rowlandson's narrative has been amply documented elsewhere. Her work is anthologized in nearly every collection of early American writing. See Katherine Zabelle Derounian's "The Publication, Promotion and Distribution of Mary White Rowlandson's Captivity Narrative in the Seventeenth Century," *Early American Literature*, 23.3 (1988).

5. Derounian details much of this in her article. See also Mitchell Robert *Breitwieser's American Puritanism and the Defense of Mourning: Religion, Grief, Ethnology in Mary White Rowlandson's Captivity Narrative*. Madison: University of Wisconsin Press, 1990, p17–20, and see too Richard Slotkin's *Regeneration Through Violence*.

6. Mitchell Robert Breitwieser fully develops this argument in his *American Puritanism and the Defense of Mourning*. See, in particular, pp 4–9. In his book, *American Puritanism and the Defense of Mourning: Religion, Grief, and Ethnology in*

Mary White Rowlandson's Captivity Narrative, Breitwieser provides a detailed analysis of both the political conditions surrounding Rowlandson's writing and her repression of sorrow. He finds Rowlandson's position analogous to that of Lot's wife.

7. This point is made in a variety of places. See Derounian's "The Publication, Promotion, and Distribution of Mary White Rowlandson's Captivity Narrative," David L. Greene's "New Light on Mary Rowlandson," *Early American Literature*, 20.1, Spring, 1985, and Breitwieser's *American Puritanism and the Defense of Mourning*.

8. For a much more in depth discussion of this point see the chapter entitled "Lot's Wife: Looking Back," in Breitwieser's *American Puritanism and the Defense of Mourning*, pp 71–129.

9. There is some disagreement among historians regarding this resistance. Elizabeth Jameson discusses in *The Women's West* (Norman: University of Oklahoma Press, 1987) the possibility that some women were more delighted by the possibility of travel. Lilian Schlissel argues in her *Women's Diaries of the Westward Journey*. New York, Schoken Books 1982, that newlyweds and single women were much more enthusiastic than women with children.

10. In the "Private Life of Public Women," *The Women's West*, Mary Murphy discusses Montana prostitutes and alcohol, 194–202.

11. Mary Ellen Williams Walsh has written a very detailed essay that cites numerous incidences where Stegner's text simply repeats, with nearly word for word accuracy, Foote's correspondence and autobiography. Walsh contends that this use of Foote's work represents "an ethical issue." See Walsh's "*Angle of Repose* and the Writing of Mary Hallock Foote: A Source Study," *Critical Essays on Wallace Stegner*. Boston: G.K. Hall and Co., 1982.

12. See the letter from Mrs. Marian Conway to Mary Ellen Williams, 1/11/80, in Walsh's "The Writings of Mary Hallock Foote: A Source Study."

13. For more information regarding Mary Hallock Foote's relationship with Harry Tompkins, see Lee Ann Johnson's book, *Mary Hallock Foote*. Boston: Twayne Publishers, 1980. Read pages 144–148 in particular.

14. Foote evidently was reluctant to discuss this event much, finding it too painful. Because of this reluctance, a number of her biographers were not familiar with the factual fate of Agnes, a situation that led greater credence to Stegner's account. In

reality, Agnes was taken ill while on a train trip, in May of 1904. She died surrounded by her family members. Her adolescent death, while painful and tragic, lacked the sexual dimension of Stegner's account. Strangely it is the fictitious Agnes who appears real.

15. These lines are quoted by Deleuze and Guattari from Marcel Griaule's "Remarques sur l'oncle uterin au Soudan," *Cahiers internationaux de sociologie,* January, 1954.

16. This editorial pressure is commented on by Lee Ann Johnson in her *Mary Hallock Foote.* Boston: Twayne, 1980. See page 50 in particular.

CHAPTER THREE: Reclaiming the Territory: Mary Austin and Other (Un)Natural Girls

1. See William Wordsworth's "The Solitary Reaper."

2. See Roderick Nash's *Wilderness and the American Mind.* New Haven: Yale University press, 1967. See in particular pages 4–45 for a longer discussion of American Manifest Destiny.

3. Powell's system included plans for damming and redistributing the water from the Colorado River, one of the world's most ambitious water and dam projects. The eventual construction of these dams, most famously Hoover Dam, celebrates Powell's vision. Lake Powell is, of course, named to commemorate his effort.

4. Vera Norwood discusses Austin's emergent feminism. See "The Photographer and the Naturalist: Laura Gilpin and Mary Austin in the Southwest," *Journal of American Culture* (Summer, 1982): 1–28.

5. Austin repeatedly separated from her husband, largely because of his drinking and his lack of emotional support for her work. In 1899, Mary Austin contacted the influential Charles Lummis, and inquired as to whether he might be interested in her work. Encouraged by Lummis, Austin moved to Los Angeles where she met and was deeply influenced by Charlotte Perkins Gilman, Helen Modjeska, and David Starr Jordan, then president of Stanford University. Excited by these contacts, Austin tried to persuade Stafford Austin to move to Los Angeles with her. He refused however, and noted in his response that Ruth's illness was Mary Austin's fault (Fink, 103). Mary Austin returned to the Owens River Valley and built a house in Independence, near the site of today's museum. In 1903 however, she moved to Carmel, California. In 1905, Mary and Stafford Austin separated,

although the couple did not formally divorce until 1914. Eventually settling in Santa Fe, New Mexico, Mary Austin became the companion of Willa Cather and Mabel Luhan Dodge. For more discussion of these biographical points see *Earth Horizon*, and Augusta Fink's account in *I-Mary* (Tucson: University of Arizona Press, 1983), especially pages 100–125.

6. It is interesting to note that Austin's literary career was launched by her 1899 publication in Bret Harte's *The Overland Monthly*, a journal dedicated to western and frontier life and named for one of the most famous westward wagon trails. Again, readers may find Fink's discussion of Austin's literary career helpful, particularly pages 95–100.

7. Austin herself claims that the inspiration for this story came from an actual "Mrs. Walker." In the unpublished *Tejon Notebook* Austin remarks, "Over on the Temblor we met the Walking Woman...nobody knows her name... They say she has just as good sense as any body, except that she is a little bit crazy" (21).

8. This is a complicated argument. For a more detailed analysis, readers should read the entire essay, "Melancholy, Ambivalence and Rage" in Butler's *The Psychic Life of Power*. Readers should consult as well Homi K. Bhabha, "Postcolonial Authority and Postmodern Guilt," *Cultural Studies: A Reader*, Lawrence Grossberd, Ed. New York: Routledge, 1992.

CHAPTER FOUR: In Search of the Maternal: Mothers and Daughters on the Road

1. Kristeva discusses this point at some length in her essay "Women's Time." *Signs: Journal of Women in Culture and Society.* Vol. 7, 1981.

2. Chodorow's controversial and seminal text was reissued in 1999. She addresses in her new preface the difficulties inherent in conversation regarding feminism and motherhood.

3. Butler discusses this at great length. See particularly Butler, *Gender Trouble*, 136.

4. The obvious resonance that this discussion has with the notion of homosocial space is too complex to be explicated at any length here. Clearly, as has been enumerated elsewhere, sexuality is at issue in regard to this masculine pair. The masculine dyad is sexualized and the minor female romantic interest simply underscores the primacy of couples' relationship. This third party, the woman, allows the masculine sexuality of the couple to be triangulated and thus made

socially safe. For more discussion consult Eve Sedgwick's *Between Men: English Literature and Male Homosocial Desire* and *Epistemology of the Closet.*

5. We must not take Freud's monstrous depiction too seriously. In the same lecture, Freud insists, "It must be admitted that women have but little sense of justice, and this is no doubt connected with the preponderance of envy in their mental life... We say also of women that their social interests are weaker than those of men, and that their capacity for sublimation of their instincts is less...A man about thirty seems youthful, and in a sense, an incompletely developed individual of whom we expect that he will be able to make good use of the possibilities of development, which analysis lays open to him. But a woman of about the same age frequently staggers us by her psychological rigidity and intangibility... There are no paths open to her for further development..." (Freud 863).

6. The 1999 film version of *Anywhere But Here* presents Adele simply as a kind of unconventional free spirit. For interesting reasons of its own, the film does not show the abusive and psychologically disturbed behaviors that are an important aspect of Adele's character.

CHAPTER FIVE: The Horsewomen of the Postapocalypse: Where the Road Marks the End of the Modern World

1. The chapter regarding "The Virgin and the Dynamo," in Henry Adams' autobiographical *The Education of Henry Adams* fully addresses this theme. In Adams' case, the historical rupture he senses lies in the late nineteenth century and the rise of Modernism. While attending an exhibit at the World's fair, Adams realizes that the metaphor and organizing notions of religion are replaced with the image of the engine. Antiquity is giving way to modernity. Like Didion, Adams finds his education insufficient to the task of coping with historical shift.

2. The actor, Johnny Walker, shares his name with a well-known brand of Scotch, both seemingly offering a particular brand of escape.

3. Fingerbone suggests the cliché of the beckoning finger of a skeleton, silently signaling our necessary end. The town signals the arrival of the Grim Reaper.

4. This reference to Lot's wife calls to mind Mary Rowlandson's comparison of herself to Lot's wife, as she mourns her captivity. Like Robinson's heroine, Rowlandson failed to identify with the so-called "good" domestic women of her day and recognized her alliance with the woman who was damned for a lack of obedience.

5. This reference is taken from Jane Tompkins, *Sensational Designs* (42–43), as she examines a speech by Carry Nation and a rejection of domesticity.

CHAPTER SIX: A New World Made: (Re)Envisioning Utopia from the Road

1. Annette Kolodny makes a similar argument in *The Lay of the Land*. Like Hassan and Joni Mitchell she contends that the practice of finding paradise necessarily wrecks it. We tear down paradise and "put in a parking lot." It is significant that both Hassan and Kolodny address their remarks largely in reference to masculine discourse. The contemporary texts that Hassan discusses are almost entirely masculine—male authored—narratives.

2. Spivak discusses this idea at some length with her interlocutor in *The Post-Colonial Critic*. She contends here that there is a "command" to turn away from binary thought, and for the West to examine the "non-West" and for the East to consider western terminology. She also considers this topic in her article "French Feminism in an International Frame." It is natural for theorists to look elsewhere, she suggests, as their confidence in a single Hegelian narrative fades.

3. It is also interesting to note that Deleuze and Guattari address, in *Anti-Oedipus*, the notion that schizophrenia and localized fragmentation are what capitalism attempts to regulate within its unifying and totalizing principles. By being schizophrenic, Sharp's character Matt leaves the desiring machine fostered by his father, and eschews involvement in the larger system of production. Like his sister Melanie, Matt finally decides to live within a self-acknowledged Marxist community.

4. While not central to the discussion in this chapter, Sharp's use of bird imagery in *Crows Over a Wheatfield* is striking. Attorneys, like Atticus Finch, are characterized as celebrating the mockingbird, a notorious bully in the bird world. Like Atticus also, attorneys are types of finch—songbirds that define themselves through their vocal powers. Crows, although ominous in appearance and reputation, are protective of their terrain and their young. Ottilie is the name of the tragic swan princess in the Russian fairy tale *Swan Lake*. While Sharp's ornithology is made simplistic in this note, it is quite the opposite. She suggests that our very way of seeing and naming the natural world is often flawed and that some birds must defy man-made law to protect their selves.

5. Vogelsang, the name of Mildred's attorney, is a cognate for bird song, an interesting commentary on the seemingly soothing speech of lawyers. This

commentary becomes slightly disturbing when we recall that for Sharp's narrator the song of a bird is not necessarily gentle, peaceful and restorative in nature. We are reminded of the "real" nature of the mockingbird (according to Matt and Melanie Ratleer). For Sharp, the birdsong is predatory, masking possessiveness and violence with melody.

6. Again, many of the names in Cisneros' text are cognates. Cleofilas' name suggests her filial qualities while her neighbors are named for loneliness and sadness. Cleofilas' misunderstanding of the name of the creek in the arroyo is based upon translation. She believes that the creek is correctly labeled Woman Weeping Creek, as opposed to Woman Hollering Creek.

7. Like Dolores and Soledad, Felice and Graciela's names are obviously cognates. The community of women is defined by women of happiness and grace.

8. Owen Wister's novel, *The Virginian*, commended by Theodore Roosevelt for its depiction of "rugged masculinity," is a striking example of the effort to resist domesticity. The novel's heroine, Molly, threatens to give up her fiancée—the novel's Virginian hero—if he does not renounce revenge, violence and other "masculine" vices. The hero refuses to be domesticated; he invites Molly to leave him if need be, for "a man's gotta do what a man's gotta do." In tune with the novel's aesthetic, the heroine loves the Virginian even more for resisting her "school marm" morality and remaining a real "man."

9. As is the case for nearly all, oral narratives, there are vast number of variations of this tale. Indeed, *Drums and Shadows*, the exhaustive WPA collection of African American folk narrative, contains more than two-dozen versions of the story. Yet, despite variation, the stories share the idea of literal flight and the longing to travel away.

10. This image, for example, and the notion of escape are central to Toni Morrison's novel, *Song of Solomon*, as well as to a host of contemporary film and song. Indeed, "getting away from it all" has become a Madison Avenue short-hand in order to sell affluent vacations as real escape.

BIBLIOGRAPHY

Abbey, Edward. *Abbey's Road*. New York: Penguin/Plume, 1991.

Acker, Kathy. *In Memoriam to Identity*. New York: Grover, Weidenfeld Press, 1987.

Adams, Henry. *The Education of Henry Adams*. New York: Oxford University Press, 1999.

Allison, Dorothy. *Cavedweller*. New York: Penguin, 1998.

Armitage, Susan and Elizabeth Jameson. *The Women's West*. Norman: University of Oklahoma, 1987.

Austin, Mary. *Earth Horizon: An Autobiography*. Boston: Houghton, Mifflin and Co. 1932.

———. *The Land of Little Rain*. New York: Viking/Penguin, 1988.

———. *Lost Borders*. New York: Harper and Brothers, 1915.

———. *The Outland*. New York: Boni and Liveright, 1919.

Bartkowski, Frances Bart. *Travelers, Immigrants, Inmates: Essays in Estrangement*. Minneapolis: University of Minnesota Press, 2001.

Baudrillard, Jean. *America*. Translated by Chris Turner. London and New York: Verso, 1989.

Bercovitch, Sacvan. *The Puritan Origins of the American Self*. New Haven: Yale University Press, 1975.

Berlant, Lauren. *The Anatomy of National Fantasy: Hawthorne, Utopia and Everyday Life*. Chicago: University of Chicago Press, 1991.

Bhabha, Homi K. "Postcolonial Authority and Postmodern Guilt," *Cultural Studies: A Reader*. Lawrence Grossberg, Ed. New York: Routledge, 1992.

Bible, The New Testament. King James Version. London 1611.

Bible, The Old Testament. King James Version. London 1611.

Bloom, Harold. *The Anxiety of Influence: A Theory of Poetics*. New York: Oxford University Press, 1973

Bohls, Elizabeth A. *Women's Travel Writers and the Language of Aesthetics, 1716–1818*. Cambridge: Cambridge University Press, 1995.

Boyle, Kevin Jon, Ed. *Rear View Mirror: Automobile Images and American Identities*. Riverside, CA: University of California/California Museum of Photography, 2000.

Braidotti, Rosi. *Nomadic Subjects: Embodiment and Sexual Difference in Contemporary Feminist Theory*. New York: Columbia University Press, 1994.

Braverman, Kate. *Wonders of the West*. New York: Random House, 1993.

Breitwieser, Mitchell Robert. *American Puritanism and the Defense of Mourning: Religion, Grief, and Ethnology in Mary White Rowlandson's Captivity Narrative*. Madison: University of Wisconsin Press, 1990.

Brown, Dee. *The Gentle Tamers: Women of the Old Wild West*. Lincoln: University of Nebraska Press, 1958.

Butler, Judith. *Bodies That Matter: On the Discursive Limits of "Sex."* New York and London: Routledge, 1993.

———. *Gender Trouble: Feminism and the Subversion of Identity*. New York and London: Routledge, 1990.

———. *The Psychic Life of Power*. Stanford: Stanford University Press, 1997.

Cain, Chelsea. *Dharma Girl: A Road Trip Across the American Generations*. Seattle: Seal Press, 1996.

Carby, Hazel. *Reconstructing Womanhood: The Emergence of the African American Woman Novelist*. New York: Oxford University Press, 1987.

Castiglia, Christopher. *Bound and Determined: Captivity, Culture-Crossing and White Womanhood: From Mary Rowlandson to Patty Hearst*. Chicago: University of Chicago Press, 1996.

Chodorow, Nancy. *The Reproduction of Mothering: Psychoanalysis And the Sociology of Gender*. New Preface and Edition. Berkeley: University of California, 1999.

Christian, Barbara. *Black Women Novelists: The Development of A Tradition*. New York: Greenwood Press, 1980.

Cisneros, Sandra. *Woman Hollering Creek and Other Stories*. New York: Vintage Books, 1991.

Cooper, James Fennimore. *The Last of the Mohicans*. New York: Penguin Books, 1986.

Davis, Thadious. "Race and Region." *The Columbia History of the American Novel*. Emory Elliott, Ed. New York: Columbia University Press, 1991.

Deleuze, Gilles and Felix Guattari. *Anti-Oedipus: Capitalism and Schizophrenia*. Minneapolis: University of Minnesota Press, 1983.

———. *Nomadology: The War Machine*. Translation by Brian Massumi. New York: Columbia University Press/Semiotext(e), 1986.

Derounian, Katheryn Zabelle. "The Publication, Promotion and Distribution of Mary White Rowlandson's Captivity Narrative in the Seventeenth Century." *Early American Literature*, 2.3, 1988.

Derrida, Jacques. "Of an Apocalyptic Tone Recently Adopted in Philosophy." *Semia: An Experimental Journal for Biblical Studies*, 23. Robert Detweiler, Ed. Chico: Society for the Study of Biblical Literature, 1982.

Didion, Joan. *After Henry*. New York: Simon & Schuster, 1992.

———. *Play It As It Lays*. New York: Farrar, Straus & Giroux, Inc., 1970.

———. *Slouching Toward Bethlehem*. New York: Farrar, Straus & Giroux, 1961.

———. *The White Album*. New York: Simon & Schuster, 1979.

———. *Where I Was From*. New York: Alfred A. Knopf, 2003.

Doane, Janice and Devon Hodges. *Nostalgia and Sexual Difference: The Resistance to Contemporary Feminism*. New York: Methuen Press, 1987.

Donofrio, Beverly. *Driving in Cars With Boys: Confessions of a Bad Girl Who Makes Good*. New York: Penguin, 1990.

————. *Looking for Mary (Or, the Blessed Virgin and Me)*. New York: Viking Press, 2000.

Douglas, Ann. *The Feminization of American Culture*. New York: Alfred A. Knopf, 1977.

Emerson, Ralph Waldo. *Selections from Ralph Waldo Emerson*. Stephen Whicher, Ed. Boston: Houghton, Mifflin and Co., 1960.

Etulain, Richard. "Mary Hallock Foote," *American Literary Realism*. 5, Spring, 1972.

Farnsworth, Martha. *The Diary of Martha Farnsworth, 1882–1922*. Marlene Springer and Haskell Springer, Eds. Bloomington: University of Indiana Press, 1986.

Federal Writers' Project. *Drums and Shadows: Survival Stories Among the Georgia Coastal Negroes*. Athens: University of Georgia, 1940.

Filson, John. *The Adventures of Colonel Daniel Boone*. Washington D.C.: National Archives, 1794.

Fink, Augusta. *I-Mary*. Tucson: University of Arizona, 1983.

Flint, Timothy. *Biographical Memoir of Daniel Boone: First Settler of Kentucky*. New Haven: College and University Press, 1967.

Foote, Mary Hallock. *The Chosen Valley*. Boston: Houghton, Mifflin and Co., 1892.

————. *Coeur D'Alene*. Boston: Houghton, Mifflin and Co., 1892.

————. *The Cup of Trembling and Other Stories*. Boston: Houghton, Mifflin and Co., 1895.

————. *Edith Bonham*. Boston: Houghton, Mifflin and Co., 1917.

————. *In Exile and Other Stories*. Boston: Houghton, Mifflin and Co., 1894.

————. *The Led-Horse Claim*. Ridgewood: The Gregg Press, 1968.

————. *Letters of Mary Hallock Foote*. San Marino: Huntington Library Archive.

————. *A Touch of Sun and Other Stories*. Boston: Houghton, Mifflin and Co., 1903.

————. *A Victorian Gentlewoman in the Far West: The Reminiscences of Mary Hallock Foote*. San Marino: The Huntington Library, 1972.

Foucault, Michel. *The History of Sexuality*, Vol. 1. New York: Vintage, 1990.

Fowler, Alastair. *Kinds of Literature: The Theory of Genre and Modes*. Cambridge: Harvard University Press, 1982.

Frederick, Bonnie and Susan McLeod, Eds. *Women and the Journey: The Female Travel Experience*. Pullman, WA: Washington State University Press, 1993.

Freud, Sigmund. *The Major Works*. Robert M. Hutchins, Ed. Chicago: Britannica Press, 1952.

————. "Mourning and Melancholia," *The Standard Edition of the Complete Psychological Works*. J. Strachey, Trans. London: Hogarth Press, 1953–74.

Gates, Henry Louis, Jr. *The Classic Slave Narratives*. New York: Signet, 2002.

Gilbert, Sandra and Susan Gubar. *The Madwoman in the Attic*. New York: Columbia University Press, 1979.

Greene, David. "New Light on Mary Rowlandson." *Early American Literature*. 20.1, Spring, 1985.

Gwin, Minrose C. *The Woman in the Red Dress: Gender, Space and Reading*. Urbana and

Chicago: University of Illinois Press, 2002.

Hall, Sands. "Fair Game? — or Fair Use?" *Internet.* 9.2.03. www.sandshall.com/fair-more.htm

———. *Fair Use.* Nevada City, CA, 2001.

Hardt, Michael and Antonio Negri. *Empire.* Cambridge: Harvard University Press, 2000.

Harper, Lila Marz. *Solitary Travelers: Nineteenth Century Women's Travel Narratives and the Scientific Vocation.* Cranbury, N.J.: Associated University Presses, 2001.

Haraway, Donna. "Gender for a Marxist Dictionary: The Sexual Politics Of a Word." *Simians, Cyborgs, and Women.* London: Free Association Books, 1991.

Hassan, Ihab. *Selves at Risk: Patterns of Quest in Contemporary American Letters.* Madison: University of Wisconsin Press, 1990.

Hicks, Emily. *Border Writing: The Multidimensional Text.* Minneapolis: University of Minnesota Press, 1991.

Hurston, Zora Neale. *Their Eyes Were Watching God.* New York: Perennial Library Series, 1990.

Huston, Pam. *Cowboys Are My Weakness.* New York: Washington Square Press, 1992.

Hutcheon, Linda. *A Poetics of Postmodernism: History, Theory, Fiction.* New York: Routledge Press, 1988.

———. "Beginning to Theorize Postmodernism." *Textual Practice,* 1987.

Irigaray, Luce. *Speculum of the Other Woman.* Ithaca: Cornell University Press, 1985.

———. *This Sex Which Is Not One.* Ithaca: Cornell University Press, 1985.

Johnson, Lee Ann. *Mary Hallock Foote.* Boston: Twayne Publishers, 1980.

Kerouac, Jack. *On the Road.* New York: Penguin, 1976.

King, Clarence. *Mountaineering in the Sierra Nevada.* Lincoln: University of Nebraska Press, 1970.

Kingsolver, Barbara. *The Bean Trees.* New York: Harper Perennial, 1988.

———. *Pigs in Heaven.* New York: Harper Perennial, 1989.

Klein, Naomi. *No Logo: Taking Aim at the Brand Bullies.* New York: Picador Books, 1999.

Knight, Sarah Kemble. *The Journal of Madam Knight.* 1825. New Jersey: Literature House, 1970.

Kolodny, Annette. *The Lay of the Land.* Chapel Hill: University of North Carolina Press, 1975.

Kristeva, Julia. *Black Sun: Depression and Melancholia.* Leon Roudiez, Trans. New York: Columbia University Press, 1989.

———. "Women's Time." *Signs: Journal of Women in Culture and Society,* Vol. 7, 1981.

Leed, Eric. *The Mind of the Traveler: From Gilgamesh to Global Tourism.* New York: Basic Books, 1991.

Lyon, Thomas. *A Literary History of the American West.* Fort Wroth: TCU Press, 1987.

Malone, Michael P., and Richard W. Etulain. *The American West.* Lincoln: University of Nebraska, 1989.

Marshall, Paule. *Praisesong for the Widow.* New York: Plume/Penguin, 1983.

Marx, Leo. *The Machine in the Garden: Technology and the Pastoral Idea In America.* London: Oxford University Press, 1964.

McDowell, Linda. *Gender, Identity and Place: Understanding Feminist Geographies.* Minneapolis: University of Minnesota Press, 1999.

McHale, Brian. *Postmodernist Fiction.* New York: Routledge Press, 1987.

Minh-ha, Trinh. *Woman Native Other: Writing, Postcoloniality and Feminism.* Bloomington: Indiana University Press, 1989.

Modleski, Tania. *Loving With a Vengeance: Mass-produced Fantasies For Women.* New York: Routledge, 1990.

Morrison, Toni. *Song of Solomon.* New York: Plume Contemporary Fiction, 1987.

Moynihan, Ruth, Susan Armitage and Christine Fischer Dichamp. *So Much To Be Done: Women Settlers on the Mining and Ranching Frontier.* Lincoln: University of Nebraska Press, 1990.

Muir, John. *The Mountains of California.* Berkeley: Ten Speed Press, 1977.

———. *The Yosemite.* Garden City, NY: Natural History Press, 1976.

Nash, Roderick. *Wilderness and the American Mind.* New Haven: Yale University Press, 1967.

Nicholson, Linda, Ed. *Feminist Contentions: A Philosophical Exchange.* New York: Routledge, 1995.

Pease, Donald *Visionary Compacts: American Renaissance Writings in Cultural Context.* Madison: University of Wisconsin Press, 1987.

Perloff, Marjorie. *Postmodern Genres.* Norman: University of Oklahoma, 1988.

Primeau, Ronald. *Romance of the Road: The Literature of the American Highway.* Bowling Green, OH: Bowling Green State University Popular Press, 1996

Proulix, Annie. *Close Range: Wyoming Stories.* New York: Scribner, 1999.

Reynolds, Susan Salter. "Tangle of Repose; Three Decades After Publication of Wallace Stegner's *Angle of Repose,* Messy Questions About His Use of Mary Hallock Foote's Writings Are Haunting the Famed Novelist." *The Los Angeles Times.* March 23, 2003.

Robinson, Marilynne. *Housekeeping.* New York: Farrar, Straus & Giroux, 1980.

Rowlandson, Mary White. *The Sovereignty and Goodness of God, Together With the Faithfulness of His Promises, Displayed; Being a Narrative of the Captivity and Restoration of Mrs. Mary Rowlandson.* Richard Slotkin and James Folsom, Eds. Middleton: Wesleyan University Press, 1978.

Sacks, Peter. *The English Elegy: Studies in Genre.* Baltimore: John Hopkins University Press, 1985.

Schiesari, Juliana. *The Gendering of Melancholia.* Ithaca: Cornell University Press, 1992.

Schlissel, Lilian. *Women's Diaries of the Westward Journey.* New York, Schoken Books 1982.

Sedgwick, Eve Kosofsky. *Between Men: English Literature and Male Homosocial Desire.* New York: Columbia University Press, 1993.

————. *Epistemology of the Closet*. Berkely: University of California Press, 1991

Sharp, Paula. *Crows Over a Wheatfield*. New York: Simon and Schuster, 1996.

Shute, Jennifer. *Life Size*. New York: Houghton, Mifflin and Co., 1992.

Siegel, Kristi (Ed). *Issues in Travel Writing: Empire, Spectacle and Displacement*. New York: Peter Lang Publishing, 2003.

Simpson, Mona. *Anywhere But Here*. New York: Alfred A. Knopf, 1986.

Slotkin, Richard. *Gunfighter Nation: The Myth of the Frontier in the Twentieth Century*. New York: Harper Perennial, 1992.

————. *Regeneration Through Violence: The Mythology of the American Frontier*. Middlebury: Wesleyan University Press, 1973.

Smith, Carlton. *Coyote Kills John Wayne: Postmodernism and Fiction of the Transcultural Frontier*. Dartmouth: New England University Press, 2000.

Smith, Christine Hill. *Reading a Victorian Gentlewoman in the Far West: The Reminiscences of Mary Hallock Foote*. Boise State University Western Writers Series, No. 154. Boise: Boise State University Press, 2002.

Smith, Diane. *Letters From Yellowstone*. New York: Penguin Books, 1999.

Smith, Henry Nash. *Virgin Land: The American West as Symbol and Myth*. Cambridge: Harvard University Press, 1978.

Smith, Sidonie. *Moving Lives: Twentieth Century Women's Travel Writing*. Minneapolis: University of Minnesota Press, 2001.

Spivak, Gayatri. *The Post-Colonial Critic: Interviews, Strategies, Dialogues*. New York: Routledge, 1990.

Stegner, Wallace. *The Angle of Repose*. Garden City: Doubleday, 1971.

————. *Selected American Prose*. New York: Holt, Rinehart and Winston, 1958.

Steinbeck, John. *The Grapes of Wrath*. New York: Viking Press, 1939.

Stowe, Harriet Beecher. *Uncle Tom's Cabin*. New York: Modern Library, 1996.

Stuckey, Sterling. *Slave Culture: Nationalist Theory and the Foundation of Black America*. New York: Oxford University Press, 1987.

Tompkins, Jane. *Sensational Designs: The Cultural Work of American Fiction, 1790–1860*. New York: Oxford University Press, 1986.

————. *West of Everything: The Inner Life of Westerns*. New York: Oxford University Press, 1992.

Twain, Mark. *The Adventures of Huckleberry Finn*. New York: Penguin Classics, 2003.

Walsh, Mary Ellen Williams. "*Angle of Repose* and the Writings of Mary Hallock Foote: A Source Study," *Critical Essays on Wallace Stegner*. Boston: G.K. Hall and Co., 1982.

Wesley, Marilyn C. *Secret Journeys: The Trope of Women's Travel in American Literature*. Albany: State University of New York Press, 1999.

Wilson, Rob. *American Sublime: The Genealogy of a Poetic Genre*. Madison: University of Wisconsin Press, 1992.

Winnicott, D.W. *The Maturational Process and the Facilitating Environment*. New York: International Universities Press, 1965.

Wister, Owen. *The Virginian: A Horseman of the Plains.* Grosset and Dunlap, 1911.

Wolff, Janet. "On the Road Again: Metaphors of Travel in Cultural Criticism." *Cultural Studies* 7.2 (1987): 224–239.

Wyatt, David. *The Fall Into Eden: Landscape and Imagination in California.* London: Cambridge University Press, 1986.

INDEX

TRAVEL
WRITING
ACROSS
THE
DISCIPLINES

THEORY AND PEDAGOGY
Kristi Siegel, General Editor

The recent critical attention devoted to travel writing enacts a logical transition from the ongoing focus on autobiography, subjectivity, and multiculturalism. Travel extends the inward direction of autobiography to consider the journey outward and intersects provocatively with studies of multiculturalism, gender, and subjectivity. Whatever the journey's motive—tourism, study, flight, emigration, or domination—journey changes both the country visited and the self that travels. *Travel Writing Across the Disciplines* welcomes studies from all periods of literature on the theory and/or pedagogy of travel writing from various disciplines, such as social history, cultural theory, multicultural studies, anthropology, sociology, religious studies, literary analysis, and feminist criticism. The volumes in this series explore journey literature from critical and pedagogical perspectives and focus on travel as metaphor in cultural practice.

For additional information about this series or for the submission of manuscripts, please contact:

Peter Lang Publishing. Inc.
Acquisitions Department
P.O. Box 1246
Bel Air, MD 21014-1246

To order other books in this series, please contact our Customer Service Department:

(800) 770-LANG (within the U.S.)
(212) 647-7706 (outside the U.S.)
(212) 647-7707 FAX

Or browse online by series:

www.peterlangusa.com

9 780820 470870